WHISPERING THUNDER

Doing life with a God who speaks

Kristian Reschke

Whispering Thunder
Doing life with a God who speaks

by Kristian Reschke

Cover & Artwork: Daniel Wood (danielwood.de)

Photo: Joy Kröger (joykroeger.de)

Editing: Silke Ranisch-Lilienthal

Technical editors: Ralf Miro (NT), Matze Miro (AT)

Consultation: Anne Schultz-Brummer, Caroline Trautwein, Mathias Bosch

Translation: Michael Rogers, Bright Translation (brighttranslation.com)

Lector: Ed Einsiedler

Aside from those stated above, almost all names used in the book have been changed.

Directions

This book is equally well suited for group study or personal reading. Questions and points for consideration under the headings "Mull it over" (personal reflection) and/or "Team Talk" (group discussion) can be found after most sections of the book. These are intended to help you press deeper into the topics discussed, whether individually or within the context of group study with family, friends or in a home group setting.

For Liv and Leif.

In remembrance of Storch. († 26.06.2015)

In recent years there have been many people
who have provided us with spiritual, physical and emotional support.

Thank you – this is your book, too.

WHAT OTHER PEOPLE ARE SAYING ABOUT THIS BOOK

Kristian Reschke is a dear and valued friend of mine. He is a man who is willing to do what it takes to put his faith into practice, and to find credible and powerful ways to convey biblical truth in a contemporary, understandable way. He writes from the heart, and also out of a deep love for the Word of God. When he writes about putting biblical truth into practice, it is clear that he is not merely conveying facts learned from books. What he writes is evidently the fruit of his daily experience of the Father's love and his continual endeavour to convey to others the love and will of God, and the boundless opportunities that are to be found in life with Him. At the same time, this book also expresses a great love for those around him. He believes in people's potential and knows that hearing God's voice and responding appropriately can help these people to live out of the fullness of God's promises. As such, he is equipped to help the reader realise his or her own potential and to live a more powerful life.

In this book, Kristian provides an honest and insightful account of his own personal story. This, in turn, enables the reader to identify with and apply the topics discussed on a personal level. The book then takes a thorough and accessible look at how various biblical characters hear God's voice and respond. Stories are brought to life and the reader really experiences what it is to hear God's voice.

I particularly like the practical examples and suggestions as to how the information provided can be applied as part of daily life. It is also clear that the author has a wealth of experience from which to draw, demonstrating an ability to learn from both successes and failures. As a result, what were once barriers – potentially insurmountable obstacles to faith – are transformed into opportunities to overcome.

A significant portion of his book is dedicated to the topic of the paternal love of God, contrasting the image of God with the image of man. Achieving a sense of harmony between these two 'images' is something that is worth striving after, as it opens us up to hearing the voice of God and removes any false apprehension that we are focussing on our own performance rather than clinging to His love. The combination of experienced love and a willingness to listen and respond in obedience is simply a wonderful thing.

Last, but by no means least, I sincerely wish that not only all those within the Vineyard Movement but as many followers of Jesus as possible truly take this book to heart and dare to take courageous steps of faith.

Martin Bühlmann (Berlin, Germany)
National Director of Vineyard Churches in Germany, Austria and Switzerland

Following the path of great spiritual leaders like Brother Lawrence and Therese of Lisieux, Kristian Reschke compellingly argues from his own experience and from a thoughtful reading of key scriptures that the great message of the Bible boils down to one word: listen! And what a richly relational world he invites us into — one with a God who communicates to us both when we're listening and when we're not, who never leaves us on our own with our problems but always, as the Psalmist promises, counsels us with his loving eye on us. This God who speaks has been central to my own experience of faith from the first moment I was jolted out of atheism to today when I lead a network of churches that has discovered that the transformation Jesus offers us is, more than anything else, all about connection. May the ever-communicating God that Whispering Thunder describes speak to you in fresh and lasting ways as Kristian exhorts you, teaches you, and models how you can walk further into this world where you're never alone.

Dave Schmelzer (LA, US)
Executive director of Blue Ocean Faith, Co-host of Blue Ocean World podcast, Author of Not the Religious Type: Confessions of a Turncoat Atheist

In this important book, Kristian Reschke provides the reader with a biblical framework and practical tools for hearing the voice of God. "Whispering Thunder" is more than a "users manual" or a theological study. It has the authentic feel of a seasoned discipler sharing lessons learned from decades of following Christ. For as long as I have known Kristian, he is a disciple of Christ, intent on making other disciples. He takes the lessons learned from those who discipled him, works them out in his own life, learns new lessons and then passes what he has gained to us. Lessons learned from one generation don't have to be lost to the next. This book is a must for those who want to grow in their ability to hear and know God.

Charles Bello (OKC, US)
Churchplanter, Spiritual Director, Senior Pastor of Crestwood Vineyard

One of our mentors, Steve Nicholson, used to always challenge us to 'believe in the importance of our mission.' In Kristian I see someone who believes in the importance of his mission. And that is to be commended! It is a joy and a privilege to be around people like Kristian and Kim, who are courageously living out the calling on their lives.

I find 'Whispering Thunder' compelling because of the vulnerability with which Kristian writes. I am grateful for the personal stories and reflections, as well as the honesty with which he relates them. It is this transparency, which draws the reader in and begins to deconstruct the idea that hearing God's voice is only for the 'super spiritual'.

I meet many Jesus-followers who are 'stuck' in their journey and in hearing God. My sense is that this book will help many get 'unstuck'. This book is versatile and will lend itself to personal study, small groups or even as a training manual for a class or larger group. I intend to recommend and give this book to many people.

Harmony Smith (Northern Ireland)
Senior Leader of Belfast City Vineyard

From the first time I met Kristian as a young Jesus Freak worship leader in Hamburg back in 1992, I've known that he has an infectious passion for Jesus with a creative gift of communicating it to others, whether in story, musically or in a casual conversation. But now in his book, Whispering Thunder he adds to this passion a skillful and theologically nimble presentation of the essential yet rather ticklish issue of hearing the voice of God for ourselves. I enthusiastically recommend it to anyone — believer or seeker alike — who may be wrestling with this issue.

Mike Turrigiano (NYC, US)
Director and Senior Missional Coach for the Main & Plain

Many years ago I was reading in Genesis 18 the story of how Abraham interceded for Sodom. Abraham begged for mercy if only there were 50, 45, 40, 30, 20 or 10 righteous in the city. As I read this passage I was overwhelmed with God's love and mercy for his people. I exclaimed in wonder: "How you loved them!" It only took a fragment of a second before I heard God say: "I love YOU!" The rest of that day was like walking on a cloud. All I could do was laugh to myself with joy and tell everyone I met that God had spoken those words to me. I drew from that moment for a long time after that.

But hearing God or even understanding that God speaks was not always so easy. In my very first months as a believer I sat in church one Sunday, squinting at the pulpit where the priest would preach. As I was a little vain I had left my glasses at home, and I was trying to figure out what it was that was placed on top of it. After a while I realized it was a tray of bread. That particular priest often used props in his sermons and I waited eagerly to see how he would use the bread. However, he never once mentioned it and when the service ended I walked up towards the front to ask him about it. Then I saw that it wasn't bread at all, but one of those giant Bibles.

At the time I just laughed at myself for not bringing my glasses, and it actually took a few years before I realized it had been one of the first times God had spoken to me, and on a very profound subject! How I would have cherished a book like Kristian's back then, so that I could have learned not only that God speaks, but how I could grow in listening and interpreting.

Kristian has written a book that is grounded in the word, with excellent personal stories and practical examples. And as a „good rabbi" he gives helpful study questions, that will make the readers think for themselves and help them discover their own language with God, so very unique for each person.

I warmly recommend this book to all who desire to grow in their ability to hear God's voice, whether a new believer or a seasoned disciple, whether you are comfortable or struggling with the notion of God speaking to you.

It's time for us to walk as sons and daughters, who hear God for ourselves, and follow him where ever he leads.

Annika Hanefors (Sweden)
Senior Leader of Gothenburg Vineyard

CONTENTS

TUNING UP – HEARING FROM GOD IS A GAME THAT EVERYONE CAN PLAY

*"Everyone on the side of truth, **listens** to me."* [1]

What was.

In the 1990s the subject of "hearing God's voice" experienced a major awakening. This took place under the heading of "prophecy and prophetic ministry". The positive was that followers of Jesus received fresh inspiration to listen to God and to be open to what He has to say today. There were a host of conferences, books and workshops on the subject, however, to a large extent these aimed to identify and build up those with a specific prophetic gifting. And this is where development began to slow. Rather than the prophetically gifted sharing their experiences in the manner described in Ephesians 4 [2] – that is, with a view to teaching others to hear God *for themselves* – people with these giftings were often encouraged to assume the role of oracle. A "You can do it, so please listen to God for me" mentality emerged. The intellectual separation of the gifted and the non-gifted resulted in the creation of a specialisation, which was not in reality aligned with God's heart. Under the false pretext: "I do not have the prophetic gift," many diverted their attention away from the subject once again, rather than accepting Jesus' invitation to a lifestyle of listening, which should mark the lives of those who follow him. [3]

---

1   John 18:37 NIV, Emphasis KR.

2   "So Christ himself gave the apostles, the prophets, the evangelists, the pastors and teachers *to equip* his people for works of service (...)" (Eph 4:11–12 NIV, emphasis KR).

3   "My sheep listen to my voice, I know them and they follow me;" (John 10:27 NIV).

What is.

Within the context of the development of postmodern society, the Christian Church faces major challenges, but is also enjoying fantastic opportunities.

One thing that many churches find **challenging** in modern times is that people can no longer be won over by the mere presentation of a moral framework or the citation of Christian slogans. Christian communities that cling too tightly to their cherished traditions, rigid concepts or pre-formulated responses run the risk of manoeuvring themselves into a position of social irrelevance.

People today have a desire to hear God "in their own language"[4]. Within church monocultures they often struggle to find a safe environment for this. When we sense their intuitive defences, we conclude that these people are rejecting Jesus. However, is it possible that they are not rejecting our message, but rather that they are merely objecting to our outdated notion of what it is to be human?

On the other hand, one thing that **works in our favour** is the fact that the postmodern human being is a seeker. As such, he is essentially on the right path, as "(...) everyone who asks, *receives*; the one who *seeks*, finds; and to the one who *knocks*, the door will be opened." (Mat 7:8 NIV, emphasis KR).

This poses the question as to what seekers will find when they encounter us. Our responsibility to deliver a culturally relevant message becomes very much apparent!

People are looking for authenticity – they are looking for followers of Jesus who – like themselves – are *looking* for Jesus, but are also *encountering* and *living life with Jesus*. They want to grasp, sense and experience God in us, and not merely be told about Him[5]. If we live out our discipleship with this in mind, our everyday life will become an expression of the love of God.

---

4   "When they heard this sound the crowd came together in bewilderment, because each one heard *their own language* being spoken." (Acts 2:6 NIV, emphasis KR).

5   "That which was from the beginning, which we have heard, which we have seen with our eyes, which we have looked at and our hands have touched – this we proclaim concerning the Word of life." (1 John 1:1 NIV).

This book is an invitation to follow God unconditionally. Only when we are ready to *live a life marked by hearing from God* and to *adjust our behaviour accordingly*, does God emerge as an active participant in our lives and really start to make things happen. This is just what the world is waiting for[6].

And what is to come.

In 2011 I sensed God saying these words:

> *This is a generation of my presence, not of my book.*
>
> *The previous generation wanted to accumulate knowledge of me, this generation wants to experience me.*
>
> *I will no longer allow myself to be confined within the pages of a book. The past generation read my book to see what they could experience with me. This generation will first experience me, and then turn to my book to verify that it was indeed I.*
>
> *I have left the book; I am on the streets and am seeking friendship with those who want to continue to write my book with their lives. Those who desire knowledge of me can have my book – those who want me, will continue to write it.*

I long for our church communities to be places where we teach people to hear God better for themselves, rather than just telling them what He says. I am convinced that we find ourselves in a time when the subject of "hearing God's voice" is experiencing another resurgence. This time it is not about releasing the gifted, but rather promoting listening to God as a "game that everyone can play" - a sport where the Holy Spirit holds the playbook!

I hope that my book emboldens you to continue to write God's book with your life.

---

6   "For the creation waits in eager expectation for the children of God to be revealed." (Romans 8:19 NIV).

PRELUDE – HOW I WAS FOUND

"The Word became flesh and made his dwelling among us."[7]

*"Jesus, be the Word in my life – above all, through everything and
at all times."*

It is 1990 – a Monday, I am 17 years old, and it is shortly before eight o'clock. I am sitting at my desk, trying to wake up for the first period at school. My thoughts are running wild – the weekend had been unlike any other before it. On Friday evening, following a weeklong course on the basics of Christianity, I had *prayed the prayer* and "given my life to Jesus".

I remember that the previous evenings of the course were nothing spectacular, simply passing me by with nothing to report – in terms of content, I had barely understood anything. However, on the Friday evening, when the offer to "give your life to Jesus" was issued, I thought to myself: "My life can't get much worse than it is now – if Jesus can do something good with it, then he should have it."

As these memories flew through my head, I suddenly realised something astonishing: my back became pleasantly warm and felt as though someone has placed a fleecy fur coat over me. I barely noticed it at first, but as the heat increased, my upper body began to shake, and I abruptly snapped out of my drowsy state. What was happening? I glanced over at my classmate, in the seat next to me. From his bored expression I could deduce that he didn't appear to notice the power that I was experiencing. My mind was somersaulting: 'Have I

---

7   John 1:14 NIV.

gone mad? Do I have a fever? Am I dying?' Fear began to rise up within me, but in precisely this moment something happened that would change my life forever. I heard His voice[8]!

> *"Kristian, it's just me – you invited me into your life – from this point forward we will always be together."*

I was completely astounded: 'That's insane, God can speak!' No-one at the basic Christianity course had clued me in on this vital detail.

This was the first time that I heard and understood Jesus. It also marked the beginning of *my relationship with Him*. Only many years later would I understand that *His relationship with me* had already begun a long time before. I was on His mind before He created the world[9]. God had spoken to me throughout my entire life, drawing me to Himself and pursuing me – I had finally noticed Him[10].

I began regularly attending church events, in an attempt to hear more of "the voice". After a few months this led to a two-fold realisation on my part.

Firstly, it became clear to me that I had actually encountered the Creator of the universe. What's more, He was worth focussing my life on – I wanted to give Him everything, absolutely everything!

Secondly, I realised that I had absolutely nothing in common with the other people who knew Him! Their language, their lifestyle, their dress sense, their taste in music etc. weren't from the same planet. They were certainly nice people, but as far as I was concerned at the time, they represented everything that I would have considered to be square and uncool. I still remember my sense of astonishment as I stepped into church – bleached white walls, light brown chairs in neat rows, grey carpet and a huge wooden cross behind a Perspex lectern. This room was like a combination of a trade fair stand and a dental practice. I experienced a real culture shock and felt extremely ill at ease in this group. I was plagued with the thought that God would require me to become like these people. In spite of the

---

8   I heard Him inwardly, but loud enough that I couldn't have missed it or mistaken it for my own thoughts.

9   No wonder, seeing as He created the world for me!

10   "No, the wisdom we speak of is the mystery of God—his plan that was previously hidden, even though he made it for our ultimate glory before the world began." (1 Cor 2:7 NLT)

fact that this was a very large church indeed, I couldn't find anyone who was like me. The experience was disconcerting – but I couldn't be on my own, right?

After a few months I was advised to join a home group – a *youth home group* – although the mere word alone made me tense up! The experience was abysmal – in a small apartment setting everything seemed even more uptight than in the church service. The evening culminated in an argument about how much you have to strive to be accepted by God. In the end a consensus was reached that "there is no condemnation if you believe in Christ" – that is to say: even if you don't make enough of an effort, God accepts you nonetheless. I couldn't follow the exchange of blows between these long-term Christians – I clearly wasn't part of their world, and they weren't part of mine.

Back at home I felt extremely frustrated, and in tears I cried out: "God, I know that I really have encountered you! I want to follow you my whole life, without compromise, but you have to send me just ONE person that is in some way like me and understands me, otherwise I just can't do it!" Somehow I felt that this had been the right prayer. I sensed an internal YES and felt satisfied. At this point I was as yet unaware that it would take another twelve months of prayer and wrestling, before God's YES would manifest itself.

Finally, this is how it happened: I sat in the church service somewhat bored and considered simply going back home, when I caught sight of a rather striking guy two rows in front of me. He was quite tall and was wearing ripped jeans, a really baggy t-shirt and a Chicago Bulls cap. I thought to myself: 'What is he doing here? He must have got lost – he certainly can't be a Christian!'[11] My thoughts were interrupted by an announcement by the pastor: "Today Martin and Conny Dreyer have returned to us from Amsterdam. They worked there for a year with Steiger Ministries and will now report back to us."

The guy with the cap casually rose to his feet and sauntered up to the front, arm in arm with a woman who looked every bit as interesting as he did. His jeans were torn across the back, revealing his underwear for all to see. I put two and two together and swiftly made five, thinking to myself: 'This homeboy wants to disrupt the service!' However, on reaching the front, the pastor warmly embraced him and handed him the microphone. As Martin and Conny recounted their experiences in Amsterdam, my heart began to burn

---

11   No-one in this church had holes in their trousers or wore a cap to church – except me!

in such a way that I had to get a grip of myself to avoid crying out. They spoke of services held in bars, actors who had come to know Jesus, artists who prayed to Jesus – Martin seemed to have met all of the people for whom I had been looking for the last 18 months. After his report I grabbed him and announced: "I've been praying for a whole year that I would meet someone like you. We have to talk!" He laughed and said: "I've been praying the exact same thing!" It was love at first sight!

Over the coming weeks we began to meet every Friday evening to pray to Jesus together, to read the Bible and dream of a move of Jesus in our generation. After a few months, an increasing number of hungry souls joined our ranks. Before I even really noticed it, "Jesus Freaks Hamburg" was born, and a breath-taking period in my life began.

Childhood in chains

Allow me to wind the clock back a little further: I grew up in Hamburg, as the youngest of five siblings in a pretty normal family. My first memories begin at around the age of six. For reasons that, to this day, I do not completely understand, even back then I was continually asking existential questions. I was driven by a deep desire to figure out where I came from and where I was headed. Such an attitude is healthy, in principle, but perhaps not for a six-year-old! No one could provide me with answers to my questions, or even help me to formulate these questions in a meaningful manner. Time and again I was plagued by the thought that without someone who had a plan for my life, my existence was meaningless. I lost the will to live, and felt isolated, miserable and as though I did not belong.

As I entered my teens, depression and suicidal thoughts increasingly became part of my identity. I began to hate my life, I stopped communicating with my parents and often chose to isolate myself – in other words: I was at a real low! If I met people who were happy, I considered them part of a conspiracy of people who had reached an agreement to cover up the unmistakable 'sadness of life'. As I write about it now, even I can't help but laugh, but at the time I was totally serious.

I cannot remember any major encounters with God during my childhood. That said, I did pray a number of childlike prayers, which were certainly heard. For instance, one evening, with an ardent longing for a BMX bike, I "asked God for one". How it came about I have no idea, but by the next day I had the bike!

One of my sisters was spiritually open and told all sorts of stories about her spiritual encounters. This piqued my interest: Could it be that the answer to my existence could be found within the spiritual realm? I began making attempts to establish contact with the invisible world, but without a great deal of success.

As a teenager I began reading Hermann Hesse and other 'melancholics' – some of my friends had found answers there. These authors did indeed provide fitting descriptions of the pain I was experiencing, expressed with plenty of flowery language – however, they could not offer solutions that I understood. Their fundamental argument went something like this: there are people who are capable of more profound feeling than others. They are to be considered *special* and must learn how to live with deep pain – and ultimately they will also be capable of experiencing a more profound sense of joy. Most helpful – now it was at least clear to me that I was something *special*! Mind you, my own particular brand of special meant that I *only* experienced the deeper pain and never the more profound joy[12].

I began experimenting with drugs and alcohol. Under their influence, the dark shroud over me became penetrable, and everything felt a little lighter. However, I never really managed to find reliable dealers, and so thankfully my experiences with drugs were rather limited.

Relationships were another way that I compensated for the pain. Unfortunately all of these relationships ended quickly and unhappily. Not really a great surprise – who would want to be with someone who continually wants to die?

At 17 years old, and at the height of my existential crisis, my parents suddenly announced, beaming with joy: "We have found Jesus!" At first their declaration was meaningless to me, until over the following months I noticed that they were changing. They became more cheerful and were continually inviting guests around. My father, who could occasionally be rather aggressive, became gentle like a lamb – it was amazing.

---

12   I concluded: 'I'm probably extra special!'

One day my mother unexpectedly invited me to attend a course on basic Christianity – "Maybe Jesus can help you?" It truly is a miracle that I went along with her proposal, especially when you consider the fact that I hadn't talked to my parents for two years – despite living under the same roof.

All of these events ultimately led to me hearing God's voice for the first time – that Monday morning in school.

Jesus breaks the chains

It is 1999, I can't remember the exact day. It is morning on Penang Island, Malaysia. In front of me on the table are Indian Roti[13] and a cup of Teh Tarik[14]. After around eight years in church leadership, I have decided it is time for a break and am attending a discipleship training school in Southeast Asia. As I am eating my breakfast, I remember how I heard God for the first time and marvel at the events that have unfolded as I have followed His voice.

The past ten years have transformed my life immensely: in 1990 I had asked God for just one other person like me. With the Jesus Freaks God has answered this prayer one thousand-fold. He has also allowed me to experience the planting of a church and even the establishment of a movement in which I am now serving as a leader, without any preparation or training whatsoever.

The memories flash before my eyes like a film, as Jesus, completely unexpectedly, draws near, preparing to pour out His freedom on me.

As I am considering whether or not to treat myself to a second cup of tea, without any prior warning God talks to me, almost audibly[15]: "Kristian, in this moment, would you say that you want to live?"

---

13   Flat breads that you dip in extremely hot sauces.

14   Very strong, very sweet, milky, shaken tea.

15   It was one of those moments when that voice inside your head is so loud that you aren't entirely sure whether it is coming from inside or from outside.

Shocked, I freeze still – even for my taste His voice is a little too clear in this moment! Although I have been in church leadership for years, depression and suicidal thoughts have from time to time still been part of my everyday life. At the same time as hearing the voice, I see a picture in my mind's eye of a fork in the road ahead of me. My answer will determine the future path that I am to take. I understand what God wants: He is asking me to give up the right to want to die. I feel an immense struggle taking place inside me. I can still see the fork in the road in front of my eyes. Finally I manage to speak out the words: "Yes, God, I want to live." As I speak this out, His presence surrounds me, and I relax – I know I have taken the correct route. I sit there in silence, enjoying His presence, and take a large sip of tea. I feel proud and satisfied. That was simpler than I had first assumed.

Then, suddenly, God speaks to me again: "Kristian, right in this moment would you thank me that I created you?" This is too much for me! God has put His finger right on the point where I feel most pain. Countless times I have reproached Him for having created me. I begin to weep and pull my hat over my face, so that no one around me notices. Sobbing, I say to God, as quietly as possible: "You can't ask that of me, You have no right – I've gone through all this terrible stuff because of you!" I pause and listen to myself. I sense Jesus looking at me lovingly, but with a sense of unyielding resolution, as if to say: 'There will be no negotiation on this point'.

God has me cornered – it is time to turn things around and lay down the years of reproach. I weep without any concern for my surroundings, and pray everything that comes to mind. I repent, thank Him for creating me and give myself over to Him. In the months that follow I do this time and again, and begin to live free of the desire for death.

1ST MOVEMENT – OVERTURES

GOD IS A GOD WHO SPEAKS, AND PEOPLE CAN HEAR HIM

Chapter 1

The Creator speaks up

"In the beginning God created the heavens and the earth; Now the earth was formless and empty, darkness was over the surface of the deep, and the Spirit of God was hovering over the waters. ***And God said***, *"Let there be light," and there was light."*[16]

If asked to name the most well known character traits of God, many people would lead with love, grace, omnipotence or perhaps holiness. These attributes are described right throughout the Bible, and are brought to life in the person of Jesus. However, long before addressing God's love, holiness, omnipotence or grace, the scriptures reveal a rather different and extremely relevant characteristic: God speaks!

If we look closer it becomes evident that this is not merely a description of His ability, but is rather a fundamental aspect of His being. God is a God who speaks, communicates and thereby seeks relationship with us.

Creation and the voice

It is worth noting that God *speaks* our world into existence. In this process we see a first glimpse of God's desire for a relationship with His creation: God first speaks *to* it and then *with* it.

So, too, in the subsequent steps of creation do we experience the creative power of His words. "And *God said*, "Let there be a vault between the waters to separate water from water. (...) And *God said*: Let the water under the sky be gathered to one place, and let dry ground appear. (...) Then *God said*: Let the land produce vegetation: seed-bearing plants and trees on the land that bear fruit with seed in it. (...) And *God said*: Let there be lights in the vault of the sky to separate the day from the night. (...) And *God said*: Let the water teem with living creatures, and let birds fly above the earth across the vault of the sky. (...) And *God said*: Let the land produce living creatures that move along the ground, and the wild animals, each according to its kind." (Gen 1: 6-24 NIV, emphasis KR).

We can only recognise God through his revealed deeds. Thus, *what* God does and *how* He does it, *speaks* of who He is. God communicates His being in the method of His creation. Rather than creating silently, He speaks. Rather than concealing His act of creation from us, He has the events recorded and made public. He thus reveals His desire to be heard by a counterpart. In human beings He creates this counterpart – in Adam and Eve, creation can respond to God.

God gifts the two humans with a capacity for communication that only He himself possesses. The ability to hear, understand and respond – a combination that is not found anywhere else in the rest of all creation. Here the special honour reserved for man becomes evident for the first time. For a rock created by God cannot, as we understand it, hear, understand or respond. It lacks the capacity to actively communicate. The same applies to plants. A dog can certainly hear, however its capacity to understand and communicate is limited. In the specific combination of giftings that enables human beings to hear, understand and respond creatively, we find an initial indication of what it means to be created in "His image" and in "His likeness". "Then God said, "Let us make mankind in our image, *in our likeness.*" (Gen 1:26 NIV, emphasis KR).

When I read the Bible for the first time, I was very touched by the story of Adam and Eve. What I found astonishing wasn't so much the events surrounding the forbidden fruit, but rather the relaxed nature of the communication between God and man.

At this point I did not yet know very many followers of Jesus, but the majority of those I did know seemed to tense up as soon as it came to talking to God (they called it "praying"). They altered their voices, word selection or posture and tried to come across either as particularly expressive or particularly humble. Adam and Eve didn't really appear at all familiar with the concept of "praying" – they just chatted with God. When I look at them I do not see any trace of spiritual jargon, embarrassing silence, tense clasping of hands or compulsion to kneel. It seemed to be the most normal thing in the world for them to be in direct relationship with the Creator of the universe. What I saw in them really encouraged me to approach God in a more relaxed fashion.

As I continued reading the Bible, a number of people stood out to me who really experienced God's voice. These people who heard God, believed what He said and then responded accordingly; appeared to live successful and fulfilled lives. Their positive response to His voice enhanced His presence, increased His blessing and directed them in living out their calling. In contrast, people who refused to listen to God generally came to an unhappy end. They experienced distance rather than the close relationship God promises, and they tended to miss out on His blessing.

In the Old Testament I was inspired to read about Noah, Abraham, Moses and the prophets, who on some occasions even had lengthy conversations with God. They even dared to contradict Him and wrestle with Him. Even for David, who was a man after God's heart[17], the recipe for success did not appear to be faultlessness, but rather a willingness to respond positively to God's voice. The psalms that he penned struck me as being like a diary of his communication with God and testified of the high and low points in their relationship.

Moving on to the New Testament, Jesus was introduced as the new Adam. He personified the prototype of a new humanity, to which I now belonged. The instinctive nature of his relationship with God ought to be fundamental for me as a disciple.

---

17   Acts 13:22.

Following on from his baptism, hearing from God was not a special occurrence for Jesus, it was the norm[18]. Everything he did was birthed in his perception of his father[19]. He heard God through the Holy Spirit, nature, angels, the Old Testament scriptures and many other sources.

Likewise in Acts, hearing from God was the rule for believers, rather than the exception. They invested time waiting on His voice and allowed themselves to be guided by the Holy Spirit. They heard God speak through the texts of the Old Testament and through angels, but also through God's actions.

It seemed to me that the Bible was a huge inventory of examples of instances when God spoke to people. The narrative repeatedly focussed on the perception of God's voice in the lives of individuals, groups of people or entire nations, and the consequences of their choice to listen to Him. Regardless of which story I looked at, the invitation always seemed to be the same: live a life of listening to God!

Viewed in this light, I found the Bible to be a monumental source of encouragement to live a life of listening. Now, if I were to sum up the entire message of the Bible in one word, it would be this: listen!

Summing up – Creation and the Voice

We can deduce that God reveals Himself to us as a God who speaks, and that His words have creative potential. In just the same way as His voice speaking into the "void" created our world, so too does his dialogue create relationship with us. God reveals Himself through His works and His word. The primary and most important exercise for us as His children, disciples and friends is to learn to hear and understand Him. The quality of our relationship with God will depend on whether or not we have learned to hear Him and to respond to His voice in complete faith.

---

18   Jesus did, on a few occasions, have to wait on his father's voice, however, only upon his death on the cross is it reported that he did not hear his father's voice (Mark 15:34).

19   John 5:19.

The relational universe

Quantum physics would now assert that we live in a relational universe. In contemplating both the micro- and the macro-cosmos, we can discover a host of different relational systems, dependencies and interactions. All parts influence one another, co-depending on and interacting with one another. This means that the universe unfolds in relationship. There is nothing in the universe that does not influence its surrounding environment, and with this, the system as a whole. In a nutshell: everything that exists either directly or indirectly influences everything else!

When considering the structure of our own planet, these interconnections become all the more apparent. For example, whether plants are growing or are dormant depends on the season. The phenomenon of the ebb and flow of the tides occurs in relation to the gravitational pull of the moon. Ecosystems flourish due to the diverse interactions and relationships within the communities of organisms. Our bodies also consist of a highly complex network of relationships between the parts. Paul writes about these interactions: "If one part of the body suffers, all the other parts suffer with it, and if one part is praised, all the other parts share its happiness." (1 Cor 12:26 GNT).

All of the component parts of are body are in relationship with one another: if our heart is functioning well, all of the organs benefit; if our foot is in poor condition, all of the other parts of the body suffer as well. A minor irregularity in our hormone balance can have a negative impact on the entire system.

God also reveals Himself as a triune God, i.e. a relational God. We can see evidence of the Trinity's desire for contact and togetherness in the life of Jesus. We see how the persons of the Godhead act in perfect harmony and interdependency with one another. The Father sends his son Jesus, to bear witness to His love for human beings[20]. Jesus, on the other hand, declares that he came to do the will of the Father[21] and the Holy Spirit comes to continue the work of Jesus[22].

---

20   John 3:16.
21   John 5:30.
22   John 14:26.

Interestingly, in our Western mindset, which emphasises individualism, the described dependencies and interactions are often perceived as negative[23].

We praise people who "manage on their own", are "independent" and "realise *their personal dreams*". Our "sovereignty" as a nation and as individuals is upheld and defended. Personal protection by means of insurance policies and financial nest eggs are believed to guarantee a high level of independence.

However, for us as followers of Jesus, the concept of independence holds the danger that we might create controlled distance between God and ourselves. If we incorporate this yearning for autonomy into our religious practice, the result will be a misplaced attempt to realise God's will based on human potential. Even church leaders often only learn how little God values independence the hard way, as the result of burn-out and major disappointment.

His design

When God gifted us with creation, He used the best design template available to Him – Himself. In his letter to the Romans, Paul describes that the design of the material world is modelled on God's being. "For since the creation of the world God's invisible qualities – his eternal power and divine nature – have been clearly seen, being understood from what he has made." (Rom 1:20 NIV).

The fact that God uses His own being as His model when constructing the relational universe, and through this also reveals Himself to us as the triune God, sends a clear message: God "is" relationship and wants relationship with His creation. An existence detached from Him completely contradicts the make-up of the cosmos and God's being.

In this respect, the fact that man still strives for autonomy is astonishing, particularly given that he is assigned a special role in God's plan. God elects man to be His direct counterpart! The design of man clearly expresses God's desire: He creates him in "His

---

23   When I told of my longing to hear God's voice at all times at a workshop, one irritated participant commented: "That almost sounds as if you are dependent on God!" I didn't quite know how to respond to her without turning her way of life upside down.

image", "His likeness"[24]. God gifts him with special relational capacity, namely the ability to actively communicate, to love of one's own free will and to express creativity.

We see these abilities put to full use in Jesus. During his time on earth they enable him to live as a beloved son – a love relationship between himself and his father would not have been possible without his God-given relational capacity.

Summing up – The relational universe

We can recognise God's nature in His works. God has created a relational universe for us, as a means of expressing that He is a relational God and wants a relationship with us. Although the person who is estranged from God prioritises independence, God's plan for him is that he exist as His counterpart. By creating us with the ability to communicate with Him, He reveals His desire for relationship and instantly makes this possible.

---

24   Gen 1:26.

Communication and Relationship

Hearing God – do you mean with your ears?

This book deals with communication between God and man, and in particular with the question of how we can learn to hear God's voice. What do we mean, technically speaking, when we refer to "hearing God's voice"? Do we expect to hear His audible voice in our ear?

I am often asked: So how do you hear God's voice, how does He talk to you? My answer is tricky, yet simple at the same time: through everything!

It is simple because we do not need to satisfy any (!) conditions in order to be able to hear Him. And it's tricky because we never know when and how He will speak. This shows that mindfulness and an expectancy that one will succeed in hearing His voice are of major significance.

God's communication is not dissimilar to communication between humans. For instance, in inter-human communication we have many different ways of interacting. We generally select the means of communication that is best suited for the particular occasion, i.e. one that will be understood by our counterpart and that we have at our disposal. At different points in time this may be a flower, a hand gesture, a phone call or direct conversation, an email or even a glance. In the same way, God selects the form of communication that best gets through to us. Depending on the situation this can be a colour, a thought, a Bible verse, a sunrise, a song or really anything at all.

When I talk about God's voice in this book, by "voice" I mean any form of communication that He uses.

Worth noting: although God's channels of communication vary, His message doesn't change. The hand that God reached out to us, in the form of Jesus, will always remain the core message in His communication with us. The form of expression used in conveying this message is as diverse as creation itself.

Communication as the basis for relationship

God's primary end when it comes to mankind is relationship. In the previous section I described how God created His children with the ability to hear him and to talk to Him. We also saw that God has talked with His children since creation, with a view to establishing relationship. Within the context of a relational universe, His communication provides the basis for closeness with Him. Had God not desired closeness, but rather distance, He would not have created human beings with the ability to communicate with Him. Instead God places within us the ability to respond to Him creatively. At the same time, He doesn't oblige us to actually do so.

It becomes clear: God wants closeness with man – but on a voluntary basis. This free will is made possible in that God affords mankind the space to exist "independently of God" – in the material world. Voluntary relationship is only possible if there is a place to which those involved in the relationship can withdraw from one another. When, after eating the forbidden fruit in the Garden of Eden, mankind chooses to withdraw, God seeks him out, through both active and passive points of contact. Active in that He calls out: "Where are you?"[25] And passively in that God reveals Himself in His creation – for His works speak

---

25   Gen 3:9.

of Him[26]. We describe these active and passive points of contact as His communication. God's continual communication enables and sustains relationship with man.

What is communication, when and where does it take place?

The starting point and the basis for every human relationship is likewise communication. This can be verbal or non-verbal. Paul Watzlawick puts it this way:

"You cannot *not* communicate."[27] This means that even when you do *not* wish to make contact with your surroundings, in the fact that you remain silent or withdraw, you are still sending a message (e.g. "leave me in peace"). Relationship is the product of communication, and communication is the product of intentional closeness. As such, you communicate with those around you, and thereby enter into relationship with them, whether you want to or not.

We enter into a host of relationships on a daily basis, which often only last for a moment or a few minutes. Here our communication either affects closeness or distance. If I decide to give way to another driver at a junction, I might indicate this by nodding my head or by performing a hand gesture. He then indicates to me, perhaps with a smile, that he accepts my proposal. Through communication we have entered into a brief relationship with one another, which has established closeness. We both then drive on and the relationship ends with the end of our communication.

However, in just the same way, communication can encourage distance. If I behave aggressively towards another driver, for instance by cutting him off, I am still communicating, but this time I am creating distance, not closeness. Instead of a smile I am rewarded with an angry look, or worse. Thus, defensive communication within a relationship doesn't result in the relationship "ending", but instead generates distance. If we view the way God acts through the lens of Watzlawick's understanding of communication,

---

26   "Ever since God created the world, his invisible qualities, both his eternal power and his divine nature, have been clearly seen; they are perceived in the things that God has made." (Rom 1:20 GNT).

27   Watzlawick, Paul / Beavin, Janet H. / Jackson, Don D. (2007)[1969]: Menschliche Kommunikation. Formen, Störungen, Paradoxien. 11. unveränd. Auflage, Bern: Huber, P.53. [Original German: "Man kann nicht *nicht* kommunizieren"].

based on the hypothesis that "**You** cannot *not* communicate", we can deduce that "**God** cannot *not* communicate." And so everything that we know about God begins to speak to us.

The fact that God created the world speaks, and *how* God created the world speaks.
The fact that God created us and *how* God created us speaks.
The fact that God has revealed Himself and *how* God has revealed Himself, speaks.

Everything that God has revealed of Himself to us, thus speaks of Him. "*His purpose in all of this is that they should seek after God*; and perhaps feel their way toward him and find him." (Acts 17:27 TLB, emphasis KR).

Our "life" also speaks

If we turn Watzlawick's idea around, it becomes clear that our entire life speaks to God in just the same way. Because nothing in us is hidden from Him, our thoughts, our posture, our acts, wishes and ideas speak just as loudly to Him as our words. Just as we cannot *not* communicate with other humans, neither can we *not* communicate with God.

Our communication with God thus turns out to be more comprehensive and multifaceted than we previously thought. In the same way that everything we know of Him ought to speak to us, everything He knows about us – that is everything about us – speaks to Him.

However, unlike God we have to *learn* to hear and understand His "voice", i.e. the manner in which He speaks!

"There are many different languages in the world, yet none of them is without meaning. But if I do not know the language being spoken, those who use it will be foreigners to me and I will be a foreigner to them." (1 Cor 14:10–11 GNT).

The quality of our relationship with God

If we work on the basis that we exist within a relational universe, then, in effect, we humans, as part of creation, are in a relationship with God. However, this relationship can vary in terms of quality. Here the transitions between the various quality levels are fluid.

A low-level relationship is the purely "passive" relationship that we have as creations of the Creator. This "one-sided relationship" takes place without us even acknowledging that God exists. In spite of the fact that by creating us God expresses that He wants us, we do not enter into direct, wilful communication with Him, considering that as far as we are concerned, He does not exist. This one-sided communication structure is similar to a one-way street that runs from Him to us. However, we are blind to its existence. While to other people it can be crystal clear that we are His creation and that He wants relationship – they can see the street – we ourselves remain completely unaware.

A mid-level relationship would require acknowledgement that God exists and that we are His creation. We would then see that there is indeed a one-way street that leads to us. In the moment that we recognise His communication with us, *we* enter into relationship with God. We are now faced with the question as to whether we can foster closeness with Him. Although the revelation of our counterpart leads us into an active relationship, the quality of this relationship nonetheless depends on our subsequent response. Many followers of Jesus remain at precisely this point in their relationship with God, as they fail to find a way in which they can engage in communication with Him. Our level of revelation then remains limited to a knowledge that God *exists*, but lacks an awareness of the fact that God *loves*. Although we now believe that He created us, we find it difficult to understand that in so doing He was communicating His desire for relationship. We fail to grasp that His self-revelation should not be the destination, but rather the starting point of our journey.

A high-level relationship begins with the recognition that God loves us. We discover that the "one-way street" actually runs both ways and becomes wider with increasing levels of traffic. We begin to believe in God's desire for a connection with us and then actively reciprocate. We desire increased closeness and conclude that targeted exchange with Him cultivates this. In the realisation that our response to His voice determines our level of nearness to Him, we actively seek Him and His will. Because our relationship with Him cannot go any deeper than our mutual communication, we experience our communication as a means of monitoring the quality of our mutual relationship. We want our relationship with Him to grow and achieve this by seeking to continually mature in our understanding of Him.

Learning to hear and learning how to actively turn a deaf ear

After the Fall, man begins to hide from God, and learns to "ignore". Thus, Adam hides when he hears God's voice[28]. A little later, his son Cain lowers his gaze in an attempt to conceal his anger from God, and ignores God's direct instruction to take control over the sin that is welling up in him[29].

We discover how God speaks to Adam and Cain, *after* they have sinned. This shows us that He continues to talk to us, regardless of whether or not we come to Him. By giving man the ability to hide when He calls, or to "ignore" him, He blesses man with the dignity of free will. However, at the same time He also allows man to choose a painful path and to continually lose his way in a world of seemingly unending alternative options. Reading on, we see that a general alienation from God quickly develops: not long later Noah is the only person left who is walking with God[30].

> When our son Leif was four years old, he realised that you can "miss" what your parents are saying, and that on occasion it is even useful not to hear things. Initially we were somewhat confused when he failed to react to phrases such as, "It's time to brush your teeth!" or "Tidy up your toys back into your room!" Had he suddenly developed hearing difficulties? We tested his hearing by very quietly asking a specific question: "Would you like a piece of chocolate?" His prompt reaction revealed that there was nothing wrong with his ears whatsoever. He had simply learned to act as though he didn't hear us when he saw an advantage in it. It was highly evident that he was indeed descended from Adam!

We are all aware of this phenomenon of selective hearing from our own lives. Phrases such as, "Oh, I didn't see that!" or "Ah, I didn't know that!" can rescue us from many a dicey situation. We have learned to intentionally use such assurances as a means of ignoring or overlooking things, whether consciously or sub-consciously, when this appears to benefit us.

---

28   Gen 3:8f.
29   Gen 4:5ff.
30   Gen 6:8-9.

We have the same tendency when it comes to God's voice. Adam's behaviour serves as a prototype for the rest of humanity that followed after him.

In actual fact, in a world in which we are bombarded by excessive quantities of information, our ability to blank out and ignore voices can also be a blessing. However, at the same time this gift cheats us, as we generally only hear "what we want to hear". So in the end, we actually ask God to speak to us through barriers – such as fear or mistrust – yet all the while there is still a hidden, internal "No!" objecting to what He is saying. In cases such as this we require the experience of His love in order to rebuild trust and open ourselves up to hearing His voice.

> At the age of six, a friend of mine called Jane experienced an extreme betrayal of trust on the part of her father. This resulted in an internal decision never to listen to a father figure again. Even after she came to know God, it was several years before she could really open herself up to hear the voice of her Heavenly Father.

Fear regarding hearing God speak can be reinforced by wrongdoings on the part of authority figures, major disappointments or lies about God, to name but a few examples. If we want to enter into a mature relationship with Him, we have to expose these barriers and give God permission to say *anything, whenever* and *wherever*. Even if we do not identify any barriers within ourselves, regular introspection is worthwhile: am I ready to hear *everything* that God has to say to me? Are there areas in my life in which I am not "interested" in hearing His opinion? God is only too happy to provide us with information when we approach Him with questions such as this.

Even people who do not know God personally are prevented from opening themselves up to hearing His voice as a result of fear. Within our society the image of a gracious God, who created the world as an expression of His love, is mistaken for that of a grouchy, dissatisfied, vengeful, moody and disinterested old man. If we are not familiar with Jesus' message, the idea that God can talk to us often draws our focus to a long list of mistakes and offences, which He will hold against us wherever possible. On the other hand, the notion that God would want to communicate His love, acceptance and forgiveness seems almost "alien" to us.

41

Guided by the spirit of this world[31], people have become masters at ignoring God's voice or explaining away what He has to say. If God speaks through internal impressions or dreams, psychological explanations are soon found. If He speaks through external events or natural phenomena, which are particularly fitting given our situation, we call it a "great coincidence". Although, deep down, lies a longing that these blessed encounters or life-giving impulses might be the loving words of a good God, we lack the guidance or courage to actually follow them. If a person feels incapable of fulfilling what he assumes to be requests issued by God, then he would rather not hear them at all, let alone draw close within His presence. Nonetheless, God doesn't stop asking us to trust Him. And thus, for all people, the process of learning to trust God begins with sensing God's call and embracing His guidance.

Intergalactic police officer or loving doctor?

When I began my journey of relationship with Jesus, Jesus rang in a host of changes in my life. A number of things happened, almost incidentally, without me having done very much to bring them about. However, in some areas I was required to act directly and cooperate. Although I learned that my obedience had positive effects, I was not always willing to change my life in accordance with what He said. In particular, it was when his gentle nudges were uncomfortable that I would discreetly ignore them or attempt to explain them away. I found this new manner of being led by the Holy Spirit to be unnerving. A lot of what I "heard" from God simply didn't make any sense to me. Were these internal impressions, illuminating Bible verses and thoughts really His voice, or was I just imagining it all?

> After a few months with Jesus I had the sudden "internal impulse" to register my television with the German television licensing agency. I had previously been of the conviction that it was not right to continue paying money for poor programming. "If they improve the programming, I will be happy to pay!" As the feeling kept on

---

31   "At that time you followed the world's evil way; you obeyed the ruler of the spiritual powers in space, the spirit who now controls the people who disobey God." (Eph 2:2 GNT).

coming back over a period of months, I began to wonder – why was I hearing two different internal voices on the same subject?[32]

In a conversation with my wife Kim the penny dropped. As we were talking about God's provision, Jesus butted in, bringing to mind a thought that I just couldn't ignore: "Kristian, could it be that your disobedience is blocking my provision?" I was completely bowled over and stammered: "I think God wants me to pay the television licence – that impulse I feel inside is His voice!" I still remember how Kim simply smiled, as if she had known the entire time[33].

The reason I was hesitating to follow His prompting was because I did not trust Him! When God spoke to me as He did in the matter regarding the television licensing, I got annoyed and began to view Him as an "intergalactic police officer" who wanted to prevent me from having any fun. Only some time later, when I had experienced more of his presence and love, did my image of Him change. I understood: God wasn't looking for *His* best, but rather *my* best! He wanted to love me, not rule over me. He didn't sense any kind of moral gratification when I obeyed Him – He hadn't come into my life as a police officer, rather more like a doctor. Strictly speaking, God was more on my side than I was myself.

Communication with God is personal

Different relationships require different forms of communication. It is the life-long pursuit of any follower of Jesus to find out and learn what *their own* personal communication with God can look like.

In any relationship we have to learn to listen to and understand our counterpart. At the same time we must also learn to communicate in such a way that people can hear and understand us.

---

32   I later read how Paul describes this precise occurrence in Romans: Human conduct "...shows that what the Law commands is written in their hearts. Their consciences also show that this is true, since their thoughts sometimes accuse them and sometimes defend them." (Romans 2:15 GNT).

33   Whether this was the case I will leave to the prudent judgment of any ladies that happen to be reading!

Different relationships have different patterns of communication. I communicate differently with my wife Kim to how I communicate with my son Leif, my friend Daniel or with God. If I want to tell Kim that I love her, I give her a back rub. If I were to do that to Leif, he would assume that I want to tickle him and would begin tussling with me. As for Daniel a loving back massage would put him a little ill at ease, and I cannot simply reach out and grab God by the shoulders. In contrast, I often express my love to Him by sitting in silence, closing my eyes and giving him that moment. Neither Kim, nor Daniel or Leif could draw a great deal of love from this form of expression.

So every relationship has a personal pattern of communication. God is also seeking a love relationship with each of His children; one that is true and personal. And this is also something that is absolutely imperative, as he has made each child to be unique, with special giftings!

An expression of this might be the development of a personal love language between myself and God. Couples who have been together for a long time also have a shared love language. Certain expressions, signs or movements may appear insignificant to external onlookers, yet for the partner they carry a clear message. The more advanced the relationship, the more defined the level of non-verbal communication generally is.

Similarly with God: the deeper my relationship with Him is, and the more secure I feel with Him, the more richly my personal love language with Him can develop.

Learning how to relate means learning how to listen

Ever since I got to know Kim I have been learning to listen to and understand her. During the first few years of our marriage in particular, this was a major challenge.

After we got married, without noticing it I very quickly fell into "done-and-dusted" mode: I had conquered Kim and no longer made such an effort with her. After all, by saying "I do" I had clearly expressed my love for her "once and for all"! As a result, after 24 months of marriage, in tears Kim broke the news to me that she was in love – and it wasn't with me! I was completely taken aback. Friends of ours from the USA heard of our crisis and immediately invited us to come and live with them for a while. They also booked us in for two weeks of pastoral care and marriage counselling, which we thankfully took them up on. During our conversations with the marriage coach, it became clear to us what had happened: Kim had no longer felt affirmed by me and therefore no longer felt loved. She had within her a deep longing for recognition, which I had previously had no idea about (the small print)! My switching into relaxation mode had created within her an affirmation vacuum, into which another man had stepped.

As we recovered from this crisis, we decided to completely transform our culture of communication. We wanted to learn how *to listen* to the needs of the other person and to regularly make room for genuine *discussion*. On discovering that Kim did not find it quite so simple to openly express her needs as I did, I was faced with the challenge of paying particular attention to her non-verbal communication.

I learned that her posture, her silence or a fleeting glance could mean "the whole world". In order to give myself to her, as Christ did for the church[34], I had to learn to understand the woman who had been entrusted to me – I had to learn her own unique language! This language really did have its pitfalls, as often what Kim *didn't* say was of greater significance than what she did say. I also had to realise that a "yes" from her could also mean "I don't know, you decide" or even "no". In the same way, her "no" could mean "yes" if delivered in a certain way[35].

I was repeatedly asking her: "Why can you not just clearly state what you want?" After a few years I realised that she viewed my willingness to understand her world as a sign that I loved her. By expending a great deal of energy attempting to access her world; her internal thought-life, I was attributing great value to her and to our relationship.

Didn't Jesus do precisely this for me? He demonstrated the value I hold in his eyes through what he went through for me.

---

34   "Husbands, love your wives, just as Christ loved the church and gave himself up for her." (Eph 5:25 NIV).

35   Me: "Let's go out for dinner this evening." Her: "No darling, it's really not necessary." (Translation: I'd love to, but show me more clearly that you really want to also!).

Learning to listen means engaging

God is God and He alone decides how He will communicate with us. However, due to our proclivity to view ourselves as being positioned at the centre of our lives, we expect God to initiate communication on the frequency that we ourselves favour. If we truly want to go deeper in our relationship with Him, we must learn to understand how He speaks to us and engage with His form of communication. Listening thus requires humility and a constant willingness to tune our receiver to Him. This is the only way that we will become familiar with every nuance of His voice. Actively engaging with His communication is an important part of the loving relationship that he invites us into.

Tuning your receiver

In 2010 my friend Daniel and I encountered a classic communication crisis. 24 months previously we had planted a church together in Hamburg and were trying to perform our leadership tasks to the best of our collective ability. One of the main challenges we encountered was when we shared our dreams for the church with one another. Daniel is rather introverted, pensive and quiet. In contrast, most people find that I am expressive, willing to take risks and talkative. I often sensed that our conversations ended in a stalemate, feeling as though Daniel didn't really ever just say what he wanted. It must have been a similar experience for him, but the other way around: Kristian always just says what he wants!

In a conversation between friends, with the aim of clearing things up, he explained to me: "Kristian, I don't transmit at the same frequency as you. *If you want to understand me, you'll have to tune in your receiver!*" I immediately understood what he meant: I had expected him to communicate as directly, openly and assertively as I did, but he was a very different person to me. That day our communication and our friendship took a giant leap forward!

How our receivers are tuned is determined by a variety of different factors. These can include: our gender, personal preferences, past experiences or cultural background. While on his travels, Paul experiences how this prescribed framework can become a barrier to hearing God. He writes about the different receivers that exist in various cultures and outlines the problems that this presented when proclaiming the gospel. "Jews demand signs and Greeks look for wisdom, but we preach Christ crucified: a stumbling block to Jews and foolishness to gentiles." (1 Cor 1:22–23 NIV).

Paul proclaims Jesus as God, who, in order to rescue humanity, became vulnerable and weak – even allowing Himself to be murdered. On the cross, rather than speaking through miracles and logic, God speaks through suffering and sacrifice – something that seems unworthy and paradoxical for a god! In order to accept this message, the Jews and Greeks had to set aside their previous way of thinking and submit to an entirely different perspective.

Our own expectation as to how God should speak can thus present a major obstacle to us hearing Him. If we really want to get to know God, we must refrain from attempting to control the relationship by placing demands on Him. We must open ourselves up to engaging with His voice and His means of communication. If we fall into pre-conceived ideas as to how God should speak, our experience can be akin to that which Paul describes of the Jews and Greeks – we reject the voice that we so long to hear. We try to direct God, rather than following Him[36].

Communication as an expression of relationship

"It is the glory of God to conceal a matter, to search out a matter is the glory of kings."[37]

"The path down to the depths is steeped in mystery!"

God does not communicate merely as a means of conveying knowledge to us. The often blurry nature of His communication makes this much clear. Have you ever asked yourself why God often communicates so mysteriously? Why doesn't He just speak plainly and

---

36   Our chances of directing God are pretty close to zero, however, our chances of following Him are pretty good!

37   Proverbs 25:2 NIV.

clearly to us? By using signs, internal impressions, dreams, visions and texts that are thousands of years old, His communication leaves room for interpretation. Why would He so desire that it is only through faith that we may fully comprehend His words?

In all that He does, God desires to draw us deeper into relationship with Him. His communication always issues an invitation to get to know Him more, to explore Him and to understand His character. Every word He speaks holds the potential to bring us closer to being the person He sees within us.

If we follow the trail of breadcrumbs that is His voice, by asking Him questions, meditating on His words, allowing them to impact us and believing in them, we no longer encounter mere information, but rather His heart. *We* have been granted permission to get to know Him, to explore Him   this is the special honour that he has bestowed upon us!

What can we talk about?

*"I have thanked God and interceded for others – now what should
I talk to Him about?"*

For many people, the notion that God invites us into a true, loving relationship is difficult to grasp. The fact that God actually longs for deep and personal communication with us is something that many people, even followers of Jesus, fail to get to grips with. The reason for this is that a perspective such as His appears far removed from our reality.

We find that dialogue with God can be quickly pushed to the bottom of our increasingly unmanageable daily to-do list. It is often something that it is merely squeezed in, in the form of a short prayer before tucking into a meal, before going to sleep or at a home group or church service. In terms of content, this communication is generally composed of our requests, intercession and thanks. We are driven less by a longing for God, and more by routine or the admonitory memory verses still rolling around at the back of our minds. Our conversations with Him are hence often result-oriented or topically driven; lacking in depth, passion and joy.

My good friend Charles Bello was in an intense season of intercession for his church when God spoke to him directly: "Charles, do we always have to talk solely about church?" My friend responded in bewilderment: "But Jesus, what should we speak about then?" In the months that followed, God answered this question through a number of deep encounters. God began to speak about very personal topics, which previously Charles had successfully managed to keep out of his relationship with God. As a result, my friend's faith increased enormously in substance and joy.

In 2007 I went through a long season of intense intercession. During this period of time I developed such a passion that my conversations with God consisted almost exclusively of requests for those around me. One day, almost as if from nowhere, God spoke up with a clear message: "Kristian, I want you to stop asking me for things for one month." I was perplexed and answered: "But God, that's not biblical!" Before the words had even left my mouth I realised how absurd it is to reproach God for being "unbiblical". Rationally, I continued to press Him: "God, what should we talk about then?" I realised that this question also sounded rather odd. It revealed the extent to which I had distanced myself from a loving relationship with God. "God, please help me with this!" I finally said. "Only if you *don't* ask me to!" I heard Him answer. I heard this reprimand repeated a few times over the weeks that followed. At the same time, my relationship with God began to flourish once again as I gave Him space to direct our conversation.

Let us once again consider what we can talk about when talking to God (aside from our requests). My suggestion is this: anything that fosters a loving relationship with Him.

The primary end of communication with God is to express our relationship with one another. Our goal is the deepening of a love relationship and not a working relationship.

This intimate connection can by all means birth times of intense prayer and intercession – Jesus himself experienced moments such as this. However, as was the case for Jesus, this happens as the result of an encounter with God, and should not be the focus of the encounter itself.

At some point, every follower of Jesus is faced with the question as to whether his or her communication with God should produce a result, or whether it should be viewed as a goal unto itself. Does God want to realise His agenda through us, or are we His agenda?

The manner in which we approach God is determined by our answer to this question. Do we tend to view ourselves as God's workers? Is our communication defined by what we have on our spiritual to-do list and what we can achieve for Him. If so, then our dealings with God will be result-oriented and factually defined. If we consider ourselves to be His children, who get to spend time with daddy without any obligation whatsoever, then communication becomes an encounter.

With the help of a simple exercise, we can discover what the focus of our relationship with God is: encountering Him, or receiving blessing and doing ministry. *Try and go for 14 days without talking to God about your needs, your wishes or those of others (the church)*[38].

Does a conversation still take place when these topics are taken off the table, or have we created a topical vacuum? Finding oneself in a vacuum at this point is by no means negative – it can in fact open up new horizons between us and God.

The resulting silence can actually be one of these new horizons. If we learn to be silent with God, we are allowing Him space to determine the topics to be addressed during our time together. More and more often we become a part of what He is doing, rather than merely talking about it. In periods of silence and inner emptiness we can also express our devotion, humility and willingness to listen to Him in a more focused manner. It thus becomes our prayer that we might approach him with a clear agenda.

When a friend of mine noted in disappointment how superficial her faith was, she decided to wait on God in silence for ten minutes each day. After a short period of time she reported back to me in astonishment at how her silence had given rise to an encounter, without her having had to "do anything" to initiate it. It is this encounter that is God's will for us, as we will see in the next section.

---

38   If the mere thought of this exercise triggers feelings of guilt within you, then your focus has already been revealed.

Created to be like Him

"Then God said, "Let us make mankind in our image, in our likeness, so that they may rule over the fish in the sea and the birds in the sky, over the livestock and all the wild animals, and over all the creatures that move along the ground." (Gen 1:26 NIV).

"And God blessed them and told them, "Multiply and fill the earth and subdue it." (Gen 1:28 TLB).

> My mother always wanted to keep a vegetable garden. She fulfilled this wish in her old age when my parents retired to southern Germany. For a long time she delighted in the garden as a gift from God. After a few years I noticed that she was no longer capable of tending to it. She began to really labour over it. I asked her: "Why do you still bother growing your own potatoes in your seventies?" Her answer blew my mind: "God gave me this garden – therefore it is my responsibility to care for it." I was taken aback. I lovingly drew her attention to the fact that God had not given her the garden in order to benefit from her service as a gardener. In fact, the garden was intended to bring her joy – not to be a burden. Without realising it, my mum had stepped out of the role of a blessed child and into that of a labourer. God's gift to her had become an arduous obligation.

In the account of creation we read how God created mankind in His "image" and according to His "likeness". This refers not only to man's ability, but also to his position within the cosmos. While the rest of creation serves a purpose or fulfils a task, mankind is allowed to exist as an aim unto itself. In just the same way as God is at rest within His existence and doesn't have some higher task to fulfil, man can also rest in who he is.

However, if we read how man was appointed within his living environment, we can get the false impression that God created him to carry out two tasks: (1) to increase in number and (2) to rule over the Earth. Looking at things from this perspective, we view man merely as a divine instrument for the cultivation of the Earth. This kind of mindset distorts the facts – it assumes that man has been created for the Earth, rather than the Earth being created for man.

"And God *blessed* them..."[39]. The twofold challenge issued to man, to multiply and to rule, begins with a blessing. This blessing makes it clear that God was not issuing a demand, but was rather enabling man to rule and create alongside Him. God declares mankind not as the housekeepers of creation, but instead as its rulers. What God created ought to serve Him, to facilitate and enhance His existence. The world is the setting in which man can get to know and learn to love his Creator. The creation is God's birthday present to mankind, and not his work assignment.

In empowering him to multiply and rule, the special standing that God affords man is evident. In all of creation it is only man that God created in "*His image*" and "*His likeness*". He is assigned the task of ruling over creation as a result of this unique privilege.

So too is the command to multiply empowering. God shares His creative capacity with man, enabling him to produce children, out of his own free will and at his own initiative. God wants a genuine counterpart; human beings who are creative and rule, and who can bear responsibility for both of these tasks – humans who are like Him.

Result-oriented living, inside and outside of Eden

Because, in the Garden of Eden, Adam and Eve have everything at their disposal that they need to live (material, social and spiritual), it is not necessary for them to live with a result-oriented mindset.

Only as the story unfolds do we see how this need developed as a result of man establishing distance between himself and God. All of a sudden man is required to provide for himself, separate from God. At the same time, as a result of his insecurity with regard to God's unconditional acceptance, he develops a propensity to interpret God's gifts as work orders, as a means of "making amends". The gift of the Sabbath is an example of this: the Pharisees exploited the Sabbath in order to serve God, and ignored the fact that the "day of rest" was intended to serve them[40].

---

39   Gen 1:28.

40   "Then he said to them, "The Sabbath was made for man, not man for the Sabbath." (Mark 2:27 NIV).

Following expulsion from Eden, man is no longer capable of receiving value and honour through God's affirmation. Where he comes from is now less important than how he can perform.

If we take a closer look at the protagonists of the creation account in the Hebrew, the account's original language, we can also trace this development in their naming practices. To this end we must take a small detour into the Hebrew (way of thinking).

"Then the Lord God formed a man from the dust of the ground and breathed into his nostrils the breath of life, and the man became a living being." (Gen 2:7 NIV).

In Genesis 2:7, "the LORD God formed a man from the dust of the ground". The Hebrew word for "ground" is "adama" and amazingly it is related to the name of the first man, Adam. If we were to recreate this very much intentional play on words in English, we could say: "God created the 'earthling' (Adam) from the dust of the earth (adama)." The name of the first man thus describes his origin – that is "from the earth", i.e. out of God's creation – and not his function.

"So the Lord God caused man to fall into a deep sleep; and while he was sleeping, he took one of the man's ribs and then closed up the place with flesh. Then the Lord God made a woman from the rib he had taken out of the man, and he brought her to the man. The man said: "This is now bone of my bones and flesh of my flesh; she shall be called 'woman', for she was taken out of man." (Gen 2:21–23 NIV).

We also see the same principle applied in the creation of the woman. The man (Hebrew: "isch") gives the being that God formed out of his rib the name "ischah". "Ischah" literally means "from isch" – that is, "from man"[41]. Thus, when choosing a name Adam applies the same principle as God did for him – he names his wife based on her origin – so after himself. This works nicely in the English translation, with the words "man" and "woman".

---

41   A little background information for the theologically discerning reader: Ischah can be derived from isch in two ways. 1. AH is the female ending, like IN in German or E in French (Friend = FreundIN / amiE). 2. When used as the ending of a noun, as a so-called "he locale", AH can function as a local directional marker, i.e. meaning "from" or "toward". Thus "from the man" or "toward the man". Here the direction is not necessarily specified, although there do exist terms such as "mizafonah" -> from the north (Jer 1:13) and "haschamajmah" -> towards heaven (Gen 15:5).

Similarly to the case of the creation of Adam, her name – and (based on associations that exist within the Hebrew mindset) her identity as well – is derived from her origin and not her function.

The woman thus inherits her status through her descent. In naming her based on the fact that she was taken from him, Adam ascribes to her the same worth that he himself previously received from God. "Adam named his wife Eve, because she would become the mother of all the living." (Gen 3:20 NIV). However, after the Fall a serious change unfolds. The man gives his wife a new name – He names her "chawa" (Eng: Eve, the living one), for she is an "em-kol-chaj", a "mother of all living things".

This is Adam's first act *after* the Fall. He names Eve (and simultaneously assigns her a role), without having first received a commission or authority from God to do so. (She clearly wasn't an animal that he should have taken it upon himself to name her! (Gen 2:19)). Here the man's lordship over the woman, triggered as a result of separation from God, becomes evident for the first time. However, with the new name (bear in mind: in the Hebrew mindset one's name is an indication of one's identity) the woman depreciates in worth – she is now worth what she can produce[42].

Her origin is now less important than her performance, than the output that she generates. A new, result-oriented relationship has begun between Adam and Eve, which will be propagated throughout all generations to come.

Nowadays the tendency to view people with a higher output as more valuable than people who produce fewer tangible results is prevalent in western cultures. It is not without reason that we talk about living in a performance society.

---

42   According to the common Jewish school of thought in biblical times, it is a severe stigma if a woman cannot bear children (1 Sam 1:10; Gen 30:22; Luke 1:25). In contrast, a woman who has given birth to many children is held in high esteem. In the reports of the Old Testament it is men who dominate proceedings. As a general rule, all that is mentioned of women is how many children they have provided to their husbands (Gen 4:17; Gen 25:2; Gen 29:34; and many more).

Nakedness and grace

"Then the man and his wife heard the sound of the Lord God as he was walking in the garden in the cool of the day, and they hid from the Lord God among the trees of the garden. But the Lord God called to the man, "Where are you?" He answered, "I heard you in the garden, and I was afraid because I was naked; so I hid." And he said, "Who told you that you were naked? Have you eaten from the tree that I commanded you not to eat from?" (Gen 3:8–11 NIV).

Just stop …

In 2008, in Hamburg, as we set out on our church planting adventure, I was full of zeal for God. However, my desire to expand His kingdom was not driven solely by the Holy Spirit, but also by my longing for His love and acceptance. Unwittingly, I had deduced the following: those who achieve a lot for God will receive a great deal of recognition and love from Him. Unfortunately I only saw this hidden mechanism for what it was much later.

I really began striving, and continually sought out strategies that would bring me greater success. As I was complaining to God about my exhaustion and the lack of breakthrough, I heard His voice internally (His voice sounded as loving as ever, but also slightly irritated): "Kristian, just stop doing things by yourself!" This certainly gave me something to think about.

A long process began, during which God laid the topic of grace on the table. At the same time, within the context of a coaching process that I had embarked on, I began to grasp my deep need to partner with what God was doing. I increasingly set my own ideas and my own agenda to the side, quietened myself, and waited for Him to act.

Months later God spoke to me once more about how He wanted His grace to be the foundation of my life. I wanted to press into this and for a whole week I repeatedly asked Him what I could do to facilitate my gaining a deeper understanding of His grace. On a flight from Hamburg to Basle I suddenly heard the answer, spoken by His quiet voice inside my head: "Kristian, only by my grace can you gain a greater understanding of my grace" – oops, it was, without a doubt, time that I stopped trying to do things by myself!

Adam's nakedness before God symbolises his sudden feeling of imperfection and this marks the beginning of his attempt to help himself. This also becomes clear in his vain attempt to hide. Just as the snake deviously predicted, "good" and "evil" have now been revealed to him – God is good and he is evil!

By concealing the sin, Adam's awareness of his own failure suddenly becomes greater than his understanding of God's grace. This imbalance can quickly shift us into the role of a labourer or servant, and can rob us of our identity as a child. As a result we set about practising religious activism and attempt to become worthy recipients of God's grace through works, even though this very approach turns its back on God's grace(!)[43].

Many followers of Jesus are blind to how strongly the modern-day urge to busy ourselves has infiltrated our relationship with God. Indicators of this influence can be found in the inner conflicts that come as the result of the continual prompting by our conscience to be "active" for God. If we do not follow Him, we feel that we are rejected and of lesser value. In contrast, we only then feel of value to God if we manage to produce a good result. We want to be useful to Him, and to assist Him in fulfilling His agenda. The motto on which we base our discipleship is this: there is a lot to do – let's get going! We allow ourselves to be encouraged by Bible verses that talk about the fact that workers are required to gather the harvest (Mat 9:37-38) or quote the parable of the talents (Mat 25:15ff). We tirelessly push ourselves and others to "get involved" and "fully commit". If pressure to produce results is what drives our relationship and our communication with God, then the concept of discussing the personal or intimate details of our lives with God becomes somewhat far-fetched.

The slightly exaggerated, result-oriented relationship with God that I have presented here can appear highly spiritual to those looking in from the outside. However, because it is built on an image of God that does not allow for Jesus, it will ultimately destroy our love

---

43   "You who were trying to be justified by the law (i.e. by your own performance) have been alienated from Christ; you have fallen away from grace." (Gal 5:4 NIV, explanatory note KR).

relationship with Him. If we allow more space for our activity for God than we allow for God himself, we live entirely for Him, but only live with Him to a limited extent. In extreme cases this can even mean that our commitment becomes idolatry.

Life with God cannot be successful if it is driven by the guiding principles of this world. The biblical picture of relationship between God and man – which Jesus models for us – must serve as our basis.

Child rather than labourer – Jesus' relationship with his Father

Of all the people to have ever existed on the Earth, Jesus had the most important agenda to fulfil. At the same time, we observe him practising continual, deep and intimate communication with God. When he speaks with his Father, he does so as a child and not a labourer.

We must grasp the fact that Jesus' behaviour serves as the model for his followers. On Jesus' lifestyle, Bill Johnson repeatedly notes: "Jesus is the most normal Christian in the Bible."[44] In order to better understand Jesus' example, we shall now look more closely at his life, with regard to his sonship and his communication with the Father.

"The moment Jesus came up out of the water, he saw the heavens open and the Holy Spirit in the form of a dove descending on him, and a voice from heaven said, "You are my *beloved son*; you are my *delight*." (Mark 1:10–11 TLB, emphasis KR).

During his baptism, the Father addresses Jesus as a "beloved son". The Father "delights" in him and confirms Jesus as his son, before (!) he begins his ministry. With this statement, the Father voices His acceptance of Jesus, on account of his *descent*. Here Jesus is not presented to the world as the Son on account of his great deeds, but rather because he comes from God and *is* His son. This status is not the result of Jesus' works, but is instead the starting point for these works.

For the remainder of his life, Jesus has nothing to prove to his Father. At no point is he required to struggle for His love and acceptance. Everything he does, he does because he is accepted, not in order to be accepted. Jesus operates without any pressure to produce results. Instead of having to produce results, he views himself and his life as being the

---

44   Source: Twitter, @billjohnsonBJM, 16.05.2010, 15:11h.

fruits of his Father's labour. "But Jesus said to them, "My Father never stops working, and so I keep working too." (John 5:17 NCV).

Just as the Father removes any potential pressure to be successful from Jesus through His unconditional acceptance at the moment of his baptism, so too does He want to lift this pressure off of us. We can live as Jesus lived – released from the awkward position of having to be successful or produce results, and thus free to enjoy a love relationship with God. "For the Father loves the Son and shows him all he does." (John 5:20 NIV).

Pressure: no - Objectives: yes

Although Jesus lives without pressure, he has clear objectives set out before him[45]. To do the works of the Father is his response to His love and acceptance. It is this practice of operating from a place of intimacy with his Father that has his most vocal opponents, the success-dependent Pharisees, up in arms. The Pharisees are not striving for an intimate relationship with God, but rather seek to deliver an exceptional performance for him.

In order that they do not accidentally act in a manner contrary to His will, they live within a complex system of traditions and rules, which leaves very little room for interaction. Jesus ignores their rules, calls God 'daddy' and lives as His beloved child.

He invites his followers to live the same way, and even speaks a word of warning: "Truly I tell you, unless you change and become like *little children*, you will never enter the kingdom of heaven." (Matt 18:3 NIV, emphasis KR).

If we begin to live within the role that God originally intended for us as His children, our communication will be defined by this worldview. We ourselves, those around us and the whole of creation will thus experience the life-changing effects of the knowledge that we are God's beloved children. Our world is crying out for role models, whose actions are not born out of pressure to succeed, but are instead inspired by the love and acceptance of God. Paul sums up as follows: "For creation waits in eager expectation for the *children of God* to be revealed." (Rom 8:19 NIV, emphasis KR).

---

45   For example, to call people to repentance (Luke 5:32), to destroy the works of the devil (1 John 3:8) and to give his life as a ransom (Mark 10:45).

Summing up – Communication as the basis for relationship

An awareness of his acceptance as a child of God was the foundation for Jesus' ministry. What would happen in our communication with God if we were to assume that, as a loving Father, He desires deep friendship with us? Is it reasonable to talk to God about the tricks you saw in the last football match you watched, fashion trends, the latest gossip adorning the tabloids, or perhaps future inventions? What does He think about fast cars, good recipes or the laws of physics? Does He have something to say about globalisation, or maybe your argument with your neighbours? What sort of topics move Him, which He would perhaps like to share with His children?

"God, how are You, what are You thinking about, what do You want to do today?"[46]

---

46   Lyrics translated from the song "wie geht es dir?" (How are you?), released on VineyardNeuDeutsch03, 2011.

Chapter 3

Does God really want me? – undergoing a change in perspective

Nowadays many of the significant ideas that define my relationship with God come as the result of everyday conversations, as an aside to a chat between Father and son. However, this wasn't always the case. For a long time the question as to whether God *really* wanted me held me back from a trusting relationship with Him. My insecurity defined my communication with Him and torpedoed my desire to live like Jesus.

Through His continual conversation with me, God watered my trust and provided me with the security I lacked. I would now like to share with you the process I went through in order to change my perspective.

The unknown God wants to become known.

While visiting Athens, Paul speaks of an altar that had been erected for an "unknown god"[47]. Admittedly, his account seems very much ironic – in order to erect an altar to a god

---

47   Acts 17:23.

that wasn't known to them, the builders must have been extremely religious indeed! Paul uses the image of the "unknown god" as a bridge to sharing about Jesus, who at this point was actually unknown to the Athenians.

As I read this story, the question sprung to mind as to why this "unknown god" in Athens was unknown to his followers. There could only be one reason: this god was unknown because he wanted to be unknown. No-one can keep a 'god' secret against his will. Every 'god' decides for himself whether or not he is revealed.

It suddenly dawned on me that we only know God because He wants to be known by us. Had he not wanted to be found, then there is no way we would ever have set eyes on Him. God's self-revelation in creation[48] and in Christ[49] serves as a continual reminder that He longs for relationship.

From the very beginning, my journey of faith was accompanied by fundamental questions of trust. *Does God really exist? Does God have a plan for my life? Will God provide for me? Does He love me?* In all of these questions I managed – after considerable time spent wrestling – to come to a positive conclusion.

During these battles of the mind, I also experienced doubt as to whether God *really wants* me. At this point I was confident that He loved me, but: did He love me "voluntarily" or did he "have to" because God "is love"[50]? Was I perhaps an unplanned child that he was now simply obligated to love?[51] My mistrust in God had in fact reached an all-time low[52].

I considered myself so worthless that I couldn't believe that He wanted me. In this mental crisis, as doubts rose up in front of me like skyscrapers, I heard God's calming

---

48   "For since the creation of the world Gods invisible qualities – his eternal power and divine nature – have been clearly seen (...)." (Rom 1:20 NIV).

49   Heb 1:2-3.

50   1 John 4:16.

51   Many years later God spoke to me as I was writing in my spiritual journal: "Kristian, you weren't planned by your parents, but you were planned by me!"

52   Luckily He also steps in at our lowest point: "I was on my way to the depths below, but you restored my life." (Ps 30:2 GNT).

voice from within: *"Kristian, if I hadn't wanted you, I wouldn't have made you. Had I wanted you to be different, I would have made you different."*

That sounded convincing! In the days that followed, God continued to speak, this time through sections of Paul's letter to the Ephesians: "I want all people (otherwise I wouldn't have made them), but not all people want me. In grace, I have elected all people, but not all accept my election[53]." God explained to me that while He was certainly capable of concealing Himself, He had instead been seeking me out my entire life. He reminded me of moments during my childhood in which He had drawn close to me, even though I didn't recognise Him at the time. God had always been there for me and had patiently waited for me to acknowledge Him. Since this encounter I have become convinced that every human being – myself included – is wanted by God.

Jesus revealed God to us as a loving, attentive and caring Father. This image of God is by no means unproblematic, not least on account of the fact that, for many of us, our experience is that fathers shirk their responsibility, leaving mothers to raise their children on their own. When on top of this faced with a list of ongoing catastrophes in the news, one might begin to wonder whether our heavenly Father has likewise shirked His responsibility and broken off all communication with His children. In fact, the exact opposite is true! It is humanity that has abandoned God, setting itself the goal of pursuing its own interests and focusing its love back towards itself. We see God's heart in this regard in His reaction to the sin of Adam and Eve. Rather than God angrily punishing them, He calls out searchingly: "Adam, where are you?"[54] In immediately directing His attention towards the guilty pair, God's desire to repair the broken relationship is revealed. His constant call and his mindfulness towards continue to this day. This applies for all people, regardless of their background, and regardless of whether they are living out a just or unjust lifestyle.

---

53   In Ephesians 1 Paul speaks of how, in Christ, God elected mankind to become his children (v. 5). He also speaks of the offer of grace, forgiveness and our appointment as heirs in Christ (v. 7-11). He then speaks of the belonging to Christ experienced by those who have actively accepted God's offer in faith (V.13). The sonship of God in Christ is revealed as an offer of grace, which we as humans can either accept or reject.

54   Gen 3:8.

Summing up – Does God really want me?

"We want Him because He wanted us first."[55]

Through Bible passages that have come to life, dreams and His internal voice, over a period of around two years God repeatedly spoke to me about how much He wants me. At the end of this season, I really began to believe Him and noted the following in my spiritual journal:

> "God wants me. He reaches out to me, communicating His love and His compassion in countless ways.
>
> Had He not wanted me, He wouldn't have created me or revealed Himself to me. On this basis, my call to Him is actually a response to His call to me.
>
> Were He not looking for me, then I wouldn't be able to find Him. As such, my search for Him is my 'yes' in response to His search for me.
>
> His call[56] to humanity will not stop for as long as this world exists, even when we actively choose to hide from Him."

---

55   cf. 1 John 4:19 NIV.

56   Adam, where are you? (Gen 3:8).

Chapter 4

Hold on a minute, does God speak to everybody?

"The first word from God to any person lies hidden within that person's being: every person is a YES from God."

God directs his attention towards people with the same degree of love, as it is His desire that all get to know Him[57]. His devotion is expressed on many communicative levels. A person can live in relationship with God to the extent that he or she receives His call.

Strangely, I meet many followers of Jesus with the false understanding that only "Christians" hear God speak. This notion is neither biblically anchored nor logical. Right through the Bible God speaks to people who do *not* know Him personally. Examples include the Pharaoh[58] (through dreams), King Belschazzar[59] (through the writing on the wall), Pilate's wife[60] (through a dream) and the astrologers from the East[61] (through a spectacle of nature and a dream).

---

57   Acts 17:30; 1 Tim 2:4-6.

58   Gen 41:8ff.

59   Dan 5:1ff.

60   Matt 27:19.

61   Matt 2:11ff.

During his life on Earth, thousands heard the Father speak through Jesus without them knowing God personally. Indeed, every person heard God before he or she knew Him. Only by hearing the voice of God can we receive the revelation required to be able to begin a relationship with Him.

This is also made clear in the story of Adam and Eve. God created in them "an image" that is "in His likeness"[62]. He begins speaking with them and they respond. Did Adam and Eve already know God before they heard Him? No, only through His communication was He revealed to them.

The fact also that God makes demands of people shows that we humans must be capable of hearing Him. How could God expect us to live in accordance with His will if it were not possible for us to hear Him?

God spoke to each of us many times before we first noticed Him and believed in Him. His voice in the story of our lives can be traced back to our very first memories. It is worthwhile asking the Holy Spirit to reveal to us moments in which He spoke to us *before* we knew Him. This strengthens our belief in His eternal plan for us and our empathy towards the experiences of people who appear detached from Jesus. If we invite such people to get to know God, without appreciating that God is already active in their lives, we are behaving like the spiritually clueless, and in some cases even close doors that are already open.

To be human means to be capable of hearing God

When I had only known Jesus for a few months, I was so excited to have found the *only true God* that I took evangelising my friends to the extreme. When my friend Herbert wanted to tell me about his own spiritual journey, I argued, full of zeal, that Jesus was the only way and that everything else was invalid. He started on me, really annoyed: "Do you believe that I have never experienced God? Are you telling me that everything supernatural that I have ever experienced was just an illusion?" I had hurt him and had communicated "the God of Love" without expressing love. Our relationship was only rescued on account of my immediate apology.

---

62   Gen 1:26.

At the time I reflected long and hard on this encounter. How could it be that my friend claimed to have experienced God, without knowing Jesus? Jesus was, after all, "the only way"[63]. Were my friend's spiritual experiences all demonic encounters or was there a third option? It was not until years later that I stumbled upon an answer that I found astonishing: People can hear God and even follow Him without knowing Him personally!

Although all people can hear God, not all people realise they are hearing Him. If people who do not (yet) know God personally affirm individual aspects of His being and His will, they are thus living in the truth[64], without knowing its name. This can happen within the microcosm of our everyday lives, when a faithful spouse, a loving father or a compassionate person lives out God's nature. On the other hand it can also be found in major social developments or innovations that express God's will. As such, the abolition of slavery in the USA, the discovery of Penicillin or the invention of the aeroplane[65] were first and foremost divine ideas, long before man began to strive after them. Many things that in truth began as the voice of God, are later sold as an accomplishment for humanism or the great idea of one individual thinker.

So if God's ideas become evident in the lives of people or societies, this means that He has been heard, for the understanding of His nature comes solely through His revelation.

That said, we cannot equate hearing God to knowing or understanding Him. Our knowledge of God is a process that begins with our recognising Him as God. Our understanding of God increases with the quality of our relationship with Him and our comprehension of His nature. We see these connections in the lives of Jesus' twelve disciples. Although they walked with God, side by side, for three years and listened to Him "in persona", there were misunderstandings. Even having been filled with the Holy Spirit, discussions, questions

---

63   John 14:6.

64   Jesus answered, "I am the way and the *truth* and the life. No-one comes to the Father except through me." (John 14:6 NIV, emphasis KR).

65   During a flight God spoke to me about the invention of the aeroplane. He explained that it was "not easy" to find a person who wanted to believe that man could fly, and who was ready to accept the vision of building an aeroplane. When I asked God why He wanted to teach people to fly He said: "So that the message of Jesus can be spread throughout the world more quickly." The concept was fairly obvious – especially seeing as that very moment I was sitting on a plane to Warsaw with a view to teaching about Jesus there. This fascinating dialogue was later confirmed to me in the letter to the Colossians. Speaking of Christ, the letter states: "(...) *all things* have been created through him and for him" (Col 1:16 NIV, emphasis KR). "All things", which naturally includes aeroplanes.

and diversions were part of their journey of discipleship. We increasingly see the apostles growing into their hearing, knowing and understanding of God, akin to growing into a pair of shoes that will always be too big.

Our interpreter

Our relationship with the Holy Spirit is the key, not only to hearing God's voice, but also to being able to understand Him. "But the Advocate, the Holy Spirit, whom the Father will send in my name, will teach you all things and will remind you of everything I have said to you." (John 14:26 NIV).

One of His tasks is to explain to us what it is that we are hearing from God. "But when he, the Spirit of truth, comes, he will *guide you into all the truth.* (...)." (John 16:13 NIV, emphasis KR).

Jesus prophesied to his disciples that they would be guided to "all the truth"[66] by the Holy Spirit. While partial aspects of the truth were clear to the disciples, they would gain a full understanding of what God was saying through the Spirit. This revelation of the truth occurs as the fruit of the relational process. So although all people can hear God, only those in relationship with the Holy Spirit have access to the ability to understand God's prompting and fathom His character. The apostle Paul also describes this relationship to the church in Corinth.

"But it was to us that God made known his secret by means of his Spirit. The Spirit searches everything, even the hidden depths of God's purposes. It is only our own spirit within us that knows all about us; in the same way, only God's Spirit knows all about God. We have not received this world's spirit; instead, we have received the Spirit sent by God, so that we may know all that God has given us." (1 Cor 2:10–12 NIV).

Back to Herbert for a moment. He too had heard God within the context of his spiritual experiences, however, he could only comprehend His voice within the framework that he had at his disposal at that particular moment in time. Herbert did not have the interpretation of the Holy Spirit and therefore had no box in which to place God who

66   John 16:13.

wants to have a loving relationship with each of His children. He saw God as a "cosmic force" or a "force of fate". Accordingly, he classified God's voice speaking to him within this rather impersonal framework.

As followers of Jesus our task is to make people aware that God speaks to them. We have the opportunity to expand their understanding and to point them towards what is obvious. Jesus continually did this with the twelve, and with all those he encountered.

Kisses from heaven

I started chatting with Sarah, a neighbour, outside our house. She was going through a really dramatic time. Her brother had recently died following a long period of illness, and because her family was estranged she was bearing the burden of grief alone. I just listened, barely knowing what I should say. I simply thought: she needs God's comfort. At the end of our chat I offered her the chance to ask God to bring her comfort. I recounted to her how I myself had experienced comfort through "kisses from heaven[67]". She took me up on my offer, slightly bewildered, but thankful. Over the following days I asked God to comfort Sarah.

A short time later she spoke to me, beaming, outside our front doors: "I experienced it!" At first I didn't know what she meant, and with a friendly smile tried to encourage her to provide me with a more detailed explanation. "The kisses from heaven – I experienced it," she continued. She told me about how she was sitting in her room thinking about her deceased brother. She had pulled the curtains leaving only a small gap, even though the sky was overcast. Suddenly the clouds parted in just one spot and a ray of light shone through the gap, directly onto her face. In that very moment she felt as though she was seen, supported and comforted. God had kissed Sarah, and she recognised it because I had provided her with a context for it in advance – namely that there was a God who wanted to comfort her personally.

---

67   By this I mean a spontaneous demonstration of God's love in our everyday life. These only become visible if we open our eyes to see them. I have noticed that God often gives me gifts in the form of encounters, touches or other little things, in order to bless me. These are the moments upon which we later reflect, saying: "It's funny – that's exactly what I needed!"

After this gratifying encounter, the story continued a few days later, when another neighbour called and asked whether we could make use of a few chairs that she "wanted to get rid of". I must explain that Kim had wanted new chairs for around our dining table for ages (ideally in a 1950s style – what else!). After a closer look Kim exclaimed in excitement that these were the exact chairs *we* had wanted. On the way to collect the chairs I met Sarah, who asked me why I was carrying the chairs. I told her about the spontaneous offer of the new chairs and how Kim had been wanting them. She laughed and simply said: kisses from heaven!" Looking back, I have to laugh – she was right, I had actually overlooked God's kiss to Kim!

TEAM TALK: HOLD ON A MOMENT, DOES GOD SPEAK TO EVERYONE?

1. Was it already clear to you that God speaks to all people, in a host of different ways? What does this say about His attitude towards people?

2. Can you think of instances when you heard Jesus before you knew him personally? What happened? Did you interpret his voice correctly or indeed listen to him at all, or was there misunderstanding?

3. To what extent does the fact that everyone hears God impact how you approach people who are far from Jesus?

Chapter 5

Why doesn't God speak more clearly?

Lie back, close your eyes and ask God to show you instances when He 'kissed' you without you knowing it over the last 24 hours.

Do not attempt to listen in your own strength, but rather wait on his revelation – God is required in order for you to notice God.

Take a few minutes, enjoy His attention on you, fully take it in and delight in the fact that He has seen you.

Did you hear something? Isn't it crazy that God encounters us without us noticing Him? Why does He behave so secretively, why does He speak so quietly? Why doesn't He simply bypass the limits of our understanding and speak to us in a way that is clear and unambiguous?

Human dignity

The reason why God tends to talk to us quietly lies within His desire to preserve our dignity. God created us with the ability to decide for Him or against Him – that is to say, with the dignity of free will. If God were to speak to us with power, at full volume, He would run the risk of restricting our free will. Here is an illustration of this notion: if I *ask* my son to tidy his room, he can freely decide whether or not he wishes to do so. However, if I yell at him to tidy up, expressing my full authority, he no longer acts out of free will, but rather out of a place of fear.

God's clear voice can be extremely frightening. Isaiah[68] and Ezekiel[69] can tell us a thing or two about this. The speech of the risen Jesus leaves Paul blinded for a period of time[70] and causes John to fall down "as though dead"[71]. It is evident that God could force all people to submit to His will with just a single word. However, this is profoundly contradictory to His plan of creation and His loving nature. Christ reveals to us a Father who wants to be loved by us, and not feared. Consequently, as a general rule[72], He woos us rather than coercing us. Our God-given free will gives us dignity – something that God also seeks to safeguard in His communication with us.

The responsibility to believe

Jesus' demeanour towards his contemporaries is neither loud nor spectacular. He doesn't boast or attempt to convince them. He issues an invitation, but doesn't force himself on them; speaking indirectly in parables and stories. He doesn't try to generate hype, often performing his miracles behind closed doors and instructing the healed to remain discreet. Only on a select few occasions does he personally reveal himself as the Messiah. It is evident

---

68   Isaiah 6:1ff.

69   Ezekiel 1:28ff.

70   Acts 9:3ff.

71   Revelation 1:17 NIV.

72   The New Testament offers a few exceptions.

that Jesus always leaves room for those listening to accept his words, or to reject them. In other words: he doesn't take away anyone's personal responsibility to believe.

Couldn't God have just come down here Himself?

As I was getting to know Jesus, I discussed this premise with a friend. He said: "I do not believe that there is a God, and if there is, He has no interest in human beings. If God wanted us to know Him, He could simply come down and speak to us all personally – then it would be clear to everyone; God could do that, right?"

I had only known Jesus for a short period of time and didn't know what I should reply to such an argument. When later reflecting on the conversation, I noticed how God spoke to my heart. "Kristian, the problem is not that I am not revealing myself, but rather that people don't want to believe me." It was immediately clear to me what He meant: God had done precisely this in Jesus: He came down and revealed himself publically – many people heard him, but only a few chose to believe in him. It is not down to God, but to us!

Willingness to be obedient

"With great power comes great responsibility"[73].

"The servant who knows the master's will and does not get ready or does not do what the master wants will be beaten with many blows. [48] But the one who does not know and does things deserving punishment will be beaten with few blows. From everyone who *has been given much, much will be demanded*; and from the one who *has been entrusted with much, much more will be asked.*" (Luke 12:47–48 NIV, emphasis KR).

Reasons why God speaks softly can thus be found in the preservation of our dignity and the upholding of our responsibility to believe. Another aspect is the demand that we

---

73   Quote: Peter Parker, also known as Spider Man. If you wish to gain a deeper understanding of this concept, you should definitely watch the films Spider Man (2002), Spider Man 2 (2004) and Spider Man 3 (2007). It is not strictly necessary that you also watch The Amazing Spider Man (2012).

respond obediently, which increases for us the more He reveals Himself to us. One reason why we do not hear God clearly is that we are not ready to obey.

With great revelation comes great responsibility to act accordingly. If He were to speak unmistakeably clearly to us and we failed to obey, we could expect severe consequences.

For instance, when he doubted the message of the powerful angel Gabriel, Zachariah became mute for a period of time[74]. Jesus prophesies a harsher judgement over the towns that did not repent, even though it was there that he performed the majority of his miracles[75] – and even though it was here that the call to repentance had been loudest. So the fact that God speaks quietly to us can, in a manner of speaking, be viewed as an expression of His grace. In grace, God only reveals Himself to us to the extent that we are prepared to obey Him. Anything else could result in harm to us. If we want more revelation, we receive it to the extent to which we obey what we have heard.

Obedience to God is something that we can practice – an obedient heart is the key to greater revelation from God. "Because you were loyal with small things, I will let you care for much greater things." (Matt 25:21 NCV).

---

74   Luke 1:18ff.
75   Matt 11:20ff.

TEAM TALK: WHY DOESN'T GOD SPEAK MORE CLEARLY?

1. What do you think about the notion that in His communication with us God is concerned with preserving your dignity and respecting your free will? What advantages and disadvantages do you see in this? Have you ever experienced an exception to the rule and experienced God speaking extremely forcibly and clearly? What happened?

2. God's desire is that we believe what He says. If this is not the case it means that we are choosing to believe in another voice. In which areas of life do you have the tendency to believe other voices more than His? Write some down and share with the group. Now describe what your life would look like if you were to achieve a break-through and believe. Bless one another by praying for break-through in the identified areas.

3. "Obedience to God is something that we can practise." "An obedient heart is the key to a deeper relationship with God." In your mind, do these two statements make sense? Why/why not?

4. Where would you place yourself on an obedience scale from 0-10?[76] What prevents you from being obedient to God's voice? What enables you to be obedient to God's voice?

---

76   0 = I am practically never obedient to God when I recognise His will, 10 = I am obedient to God every time I recognise His will.

Chapter 6

God's longing for us to listen

"Those who are in love have learned to listen to one another –
even when no-one is speaking."

We previously discussed the fact that God is a god who speaks and who created us with the ability and the desire to hear Him. His desire for relationship is evident in His continual communication with us, which continues regardless of our response. We have seen that His communication with us is not result-oriented, but instead aims to foster relationship. His desire to go deeper into relationship with us can be seen in the manner in which the content addressed becomes more profound as he communicates with us. He continually leads us deeper into the truth[77], by revealing Himself to us more. Our responsibility is to be accessible to His voice and to respond positively to His word.

So what would an appropriate response on our part look like if we are to understand that God continually communicates with us? In the story of the two dissimilar sisters, Mary and Martha, we can find a helpful tip as to what God wants from us in terms of a response:

---

77   John 16:13.

Jesus and his friends were invited into the home of a woman called Martha. We are told the following of her sister Mary: "Mary [...] sat at the Lord's feet listening to what he said[78]". Martha, on the other hand, gets going with her pots and pans in order to look after the guests.

From a modern-day perspective, Mary's actions are not particularly remarkable – Jesus is a renowned teacher and miracle-worker and it is perfectly normal that she doesn't want to miss anything. However, if we understand the story within the cultural framework that existed at the time, Mary's behaviour is unusual, even revolutionary.

I shall now provide a brief explanation of Mary's situation as a woman living at the time of Jesus. Jesus not only lived at the time of the Mosaic covenant, but also during the time of rabbinic Judaism. This gradually came to be following the return from Babylonian exile (under Ezra, described in the book of the Bible of the same name, approx. 430 B.C.).

Rabbinic Judaism was, to a certain extent, the human continuation of the Mosaic covenant and differed in many respects. God had not only given Moses the Ten Commandments, but we can also count a total of 613 instructions (248 commands and 365 prohibitions). In order that none of these instructions could be broken, so-called "fences" were erected around the commands and prohibitions. If the command were "Don't cross the street when the light is red", the "fences" would be: "Do not get too close to a traffic light" or "Avoid everything that is red". It goes without saying that the additional rules repressed the actual purpose of the command (in this case to protect people from getting into accidents) and made life somewhat laborious.

Many of these refinements resulted in, or at least indirectly promoted the incapacitation of women. Rabbinic Judaism restricted women instead of protecting them – as was the intention of the decrees of Mosaic Law. This was one of the reasons why there was barely any other group of people that was as oppressed among the Jews at the time of Jesus as women. They were considered second-class citizens, received no respect and had no voice in public settings. They were considered the property of their husbands or fathers. Girls and women were given no access to education whatsoever. Similar to women in some Arabic states nowadays, they were prohibited from speaking with men in public.

---

78   Luke 10:39.

The Pharisees and Sadducees considered it beneath themselves to even acknowledge a woman's presence in the same room as them. If a man visited a home, the woman of the house was required to eat in another room. Women did not have a political voice either and could not testify as witnesses before the court. If a husband no longer wanted his wife, he could divorce her for the slightest of reasons. During church services, women were required to remain in the outer courtyard of the temple and were not permitted to read the Torah. A rabbinic interpretation of the law at the time stated the following: "It is better to burn the Torah than to entrust it to a woman. (...) If a man teaches his daughter the Torah, he is teaching her obscenity."[79]

In a nutshell: a woman should and could not be taught by a man in public!

So how should Mary's behaviour be interpreted in light of this historical context? In acting the way she does, Mary breaks several taboos at once:

1. She remains in the same room as a Rabbi and by sitting at his feet even intentionally attempts to get physically close to him.
2. She disregards the role assigned to her by her culture – this would have been to care for her guests.
3. She receives teaching in public.
4. She allows herself to be served, rather than serving.

Martha, on the other hand, does what rabbinic Judaism had been teaching women to do for 400 years: she withdraws and serves behind the scenes. However, when Martha notices that Mary is not helping her in the kitchen, but is instead sitting with Jesus, she speaks out in complaint. She asks Jesus to reprimand Mary. Jesus, however, takes it upon himself to protect Mary and at the same time reveals **the key** to a successful relationship with God – listening. "Martha, Martha," the Lord answered, "you are worried and upset about many things, [42] *but few things are needed—or indeed only one. Mary has chosen what is better, and it will not be taken away from her.*" (Luke 10:41–42 NIV; emphasis KR).

This story really got me thinking. How would I have behaved if Jesus had popped in to visit? Or better still: How do I act when Jesus shows up in my everyday life? Do I use these

---

79   Alvin J. Schmidt, Veiled and Silenced: How Culture Shaped Sexist Theology, P. 83, Mercer University Press, Macon, Georgia, 1989.

moments to submit to him and just listen, or to try to earn his attention and affection? I recently discovered another real-life Martha story:

> While in a coffeeplace, I suddenly noticed God's presence. My first thought was: God wants to do something here! I was excited and began scanning the room. I was the only customer there. Eventually my gaze settled on the waitress and I thought to myself: "Perhaps she has something wrong with her knee?" I built up the courage and asked her about her knee, offering to pray for her. We engaged in a pleasant conversation, but she did not need healing. BAM! – I felt like a clown, whose big act had fallen flat on its face. To no avail I asked God for an explanation, before returning to my coffee feeling somewhat frustrated.
>
> Days later I received his answer completely unexpectedly, like a letter dropping into the mailbox of my mind: "Kristian, do you remember when I drew close to you there in the coffeeplace? I simply wanted to sit down with you there and enjoy being close – like friends do. The knee was your idea."

So back to Martha. Although she doesn't come out so well in the story just described, we shouldn't view her in too negative a light. After all, it was she who invited Jesus into her home. At the time this was a very courageous and unusual thing for a woman to do. By opening up her home, she demonstrates faith and creates a space in which Jesus can teach. But then she oversteps the mark and begins preparing food, without asking whether Jesus is hungry. Jesus is actually feeling a very different need – he wants listeners. Martha wants to present herself and her abilities, to be a good host and servant – she wants to show what *she* can do for Jesus. In and of itself, there is nothing wrong with her behaviour – "it's no sin" – and yet in setting to work for Jesus she neglects his words, which, as Peter says, bring "eternal life"[80].

Jesus' response to Martha's accusation towards Mary is one of my favourite statements in the Bible: "Martha, Martha (…) *few things are needed — or indeed only one. Mary has chosen what is better.*"

---

80   John 6:68.

Jesus establishes a clear value and elevates listening far above business. Being busy for God isn't a bad thing (otherwise Jesus would not have spoken of 'what is better'), but here it stands in the way of the ONE THING THAT IS NECESSARY.

God longs for us to be transformed from faithful workers into loving listeners. It seems kind of crazy, but here Jesus makes it absolutely clear that only ONE thing is actually NECESSARY in our relationship with God. There are many things that are useful and good, but only ONE that is essential: *listening*.

Our response to His voice is simply to listen

In a loving relationship with God our first *response* to His revelation should not be to act, but rather to listen. God gives us everything we need, but listening is not something He can do for us. This decision lies with us. In each moment we alone are responsible for understanding the extent to which we must create space in which to listen.

In an interview for television broadcaster CBS, presenter Dan Rather asks Mother Teresa about her prayer life – however, her answer renders him speechless.

Dan Rather: "When you pray, what do you say to God?"

Mother Teresa: "I don't say anything, I listen."

Dan Rather: "Well, okay ..., when God speaks to you, then, what does He say?"

Mother Teresa: "He doesn't say anything, He listens."

It is reported that at this point in the interview Dan Rather takes a long pause, bewildered and clearly unaware as to how he should react to this answer.

Finally Mother Teresa ends the uncomfortable situation for him and says:

"And if you don't understand that, I can't explain it to you."[81]

---

81   Sam N. Kawesa, Praying with impact. P.131, B.I.G. International, Farmington Hills, MI 48336.

MULL IT OVER: GOD'S LONGING FOR US TO LISTEN.

1. What was the last thing God said to you? Can you remember? If yes, consider *why* you heard Him in this moment. What enabled you to distinguish His voice in this moment?

2. If you can't remember, close your eyes for a moment and ask Him to remind you what He last said to you. Then ask Him what prevented you from noticing His voice.

TEAM TALK: GOD'S LONGING FOR US TO LISTEN.

1. Where would you place yourself on a listening scale from 0-10?[82] Share your thoughts within one another: What are your greatest barriers to hearing Him? Which practical steps could be taken for each of you to move up a rung on the listening scale?

2. In which situations do you resort to busy 'Martha mode'? Make a list of these situations and consider this question: What exactly is it that triggers "the Martha" in you? Share your findings with one another and then consider the following together: What would have to happen for us to listen in these situations?

---

82   0 = There is no room in my everyday life to listen to God. 10 = There is always room in my everyday life to listen to God

2ND MOVEMENT – DIALOGUE

GOD'S VOICE FROM ADAM AND EVE TO ACTS

God's communication with people in the Bible

In this next section I want to examine instances when God speaks to people in the Bible. How did they hear God? What was unique about their communication with God?

Even if we have to read between the lines a little here and there, by taking a look back we can draw exciting conclusions about our own ability to communicate with God. The reason for this is that through these accounts we discover how God has been speaking to man since the beginning of time. If we hear Him today, we are joining the ranks of Adam and Eve, Abraham, Joseph, Ezekiel, Mary, Jesus, Paul and many others, and you can learn from them. Just like them, we are responsible for responding to His voice. As was the case for them, in our response to His revelation our discipleship and our obedience become evident.

God created human beings with the ability to hear Him and with the intention that they would live in relationship with Him. However, in the accounts of the Old Testament that follow on after Adam and Eve, we witness the continual alienation of man from God. The vast majority of people appear to exist removed from God, without direct relationship and lacking His blessed influence. Generally speaking, it is only the select few who are in a relationship with God that is marked by listening. It is to these individuals that God reveals His will, His plans and Himself. They serve as mouthpieces and mediators to the rest of humanity. God's original plan that every person would live out a personal and unique relationship with Him would only again be fulfilled thousands of years later in the arrival of Jesus and the outpouring of the Holy Spirit. "The virgin will conceive and give birth to a son, and they will call him Immanuel" (which means "God with us")." (Matt 1:23 NIV).

As we learn how Cain and his descendants move "out of closeness with God"[83], in Jesus God draws close to man. In Emmanuel, God once again draws right up alongside human beings. Those who accept Emmanuel themselves become a dwelling place of God. God lives in them through the Holy Spirit and the prophetic words of Moses that Paul refers to in Romans are fulfilled: "The message is very close at hand; it is on your lips and in your heart." (Rom 10:8 NLT).

---

83   See Gen 4ff.

Chapter 7

Characters of the Old Testament

Below we will begin by looking at characters from the Old Testament and will examine how they experienced God speaking to them. Many, but not all of these individuals are referred to as prophets[84]. However, this heavy title should not prevent us from making their experience our own. Prophets are given a special position in the Old Testament, as God's words of revelation were limited to people such as them. If we are to understand faith from the perspective of the priesthood of all believers[85] we can, with a clear conscience, view their experiences as inspiration for our own lives. Whereas prior to the arrival of Jesus the

---

84 The word "prophet" as used today originates from the Greek and consists of two parts: "pro", meaning "before" or "instead of, on behalf of" and "phemi" meaning "to speak, or announce". So a prophet is someone who predicts or speaks in place of or on behalf of another. As such we can understand prophecy as externally inspired communication, which is then passed on. This might be, for example, a prediction, a declaration, a warning or invitation. The message is not always conveyed in words. Biblical prophets communicated through songs, words, symbolic acts, texts etc. And God also spoke to them in just as diverse a range of ways. So by definition a prophet is first and foremost someone who, inspired by someone else, then communicates on their behalf. Therefore he does not share his own opinion, but rather that of someone else.

85 1 Pet 2:9.

task of passing on the word of God was reserved for "specifically called individuals", today it is the task assigned to every follower of Jesus[86].

Perhaps when reading the Bible we find the stories of some individuals to be overly dramatic and difficult to emulate. However, we must consider that the reports of their lives were written down specifically in order to lead us to a safe place in our relationship with God. They should inspire us to look for more and should serve as a springboard to a more profound experience of God.

All of the followers of God in the Bible wanted their contemporaries to live in the same or greater awareness of God than they themselves were living. Leading people into relationship with God was the actual goal behind their speaking out. For example, Moses longed for all Israelites to encounter the Holy Spirit and to be prophets like he was. "I wish that all the LORD's people were prophets and that the LORD would put his Spirit on them!" (Numbers 11:29 GNB).

Paul exhorts the Philippians to follow his example of spirituality. "Join together in following my example, brothers and sisters, and just as you have us as a model, keep your eyes on those who live as we do." (Phil 3:17 NIV).

James writes of the prophet Elijah, who was one of the stand-out figures of the Old Testament: "Elijah was a human being just like us (...)." (James 5:17 NCV), and he encourages us to imitate his faith.

The writer of the book of Hebrews encourages us quite specifically to emulate the faith of our role models. "Remember your leaders, who spoke the word of God to you. Consider the outcome of their way of life and imitate their faith. Jesus Christ is the same yesterday and today and forever." (Heb 13:7–8 NIV).

Jesus himself prophesied and desired that his disciples would experience more profound experiences of God than he himself did. "Very truly I tell you, whoever believes in me will do the works I have been doing, and they will do even greater things than these, because I am going to the Father." (John 14:12 NIV).

---

86   As the Father has sent me, so I am sending you. (John 20:21, NIV).

In light of this, as we now consider the relationships that individual heroes of the faith enjoyed with God, we do so with a view to encouraging you to listen to God yourself. We can and should expect to experience God's voice in the same way they did, and in fact even more distinctly.

Adam and Eve – how did they hear God?

The story of Adam and Eve holds a great fascination for me. On the one hand, on account of the fact that the pair find themselves on a completely untouched planet, whereby they even get to participate in its design – and, on the other hand, because their relationship with God can be viewed as prototypical for all subsequent generations.

Prior to the Fall, Adam and Eve experience a world in which separation from God has not yet caused any damage whatsoever within the ecosystem or the relational structure between man and woman. Likewise, the relationship between human beings and God still functions without limitation. They experience their relationship towards one another, the environment and God as was originally planned. It is an existence without shadows - life in "paradise". Adam and Eve are naked. They are not ashamed in front of one another, their physical difference is neither of advantage or disadvantage to either of them. Their nakedness also serves as an indication that the climatic conditions were what would be described as "perfect". Their living environment provides sufficient food – there is no need for the sweat-inducing cultivation[87] of the earth, as the conditions are ideal for plant growth.

They also live in harmony with the wildlife[88]. Adam is allowed to name the animals. This act of naming is an expression of his lordship over them and his responsibility towards them.

Life is protected by God; death is a stranger in the Garden of Eden. God Himself passes in and out of the garden and speaks openly with the pair, like a friend.

---

87   This is only required outside of the garden, once distanced from the presence of God (Gen 3:17ff).

88   Eve speaks with the snake without showing any sign of fear or astonishment – it appears that it is normal for her to speak with animals.

God's conversation with Adam and Eve

The first time God communicates with man is not through words, but through touch. "Then the LORD God *formed* a man from the dust of the ground and *breathed* into his nostrils the breath of life, and the man became a living being." (Gen 2:7 NIV, emphasis KR). While God verbally created the rest of creation, He pays particular attention to man and touches him. This unusual treatment serves as an early indication as to the special position to be assumed by man within the framework of creation. By establishing this difference, God also reveals His desire for intimacy with us – touch is the most intimate form of communication. Following this touch, God begins *speaking* to man.

"So God created mankind in his own image, in the image of God he created them; male and female he created them. God *blessed them* and *said to them*, "*Be fruitful* and *increase in number; fill the earth and subdue it. Rule* over the fish in the sea and the birds in the sky and over every living creature that moves on the ground. Then God said, "I give you every seed-bearing plant on the face of the whole earth and every tree that has fruit with seed in it. They will be yours for food. Then God said, "I give you every seed-bearing plant on the face of the whole earth and every tree that has fruit with seed in it. They will be yours for food. God saw all that he had made, and it was very good." (Gen 1:27–31 NIV, emphasis KR).

> This reminds me of the birth of our son Leif, for I had precisely the same impulse. Leif came into the world in very dramatic fashion, by way of an emergency Caesarean section. Kim was still out cold from the anaesthetic when the midwife handed this little person over to me. As he lay on my chest blubbering to himself, I couldn't stop hugging him and talking to him – that is, communicating. I talked about things that I would teach him, blessed him and prophesied of God's good plans for him. In this moment it would have been impossible for me to have kept silent.

Perhaps it was the same for God when He saw man? In any case we read how He blessed Adam and Eve and talked about their purpose. His communication with the "new-borns" shows His interest and active mindfulness.

What does God say, specifically?

"Be fruitful (...) increase in number, fill the earth..."

First of all God blesses human beings with the ability to increase in number. The fact that God wants there to be more humans indicates how much humans please Him. To this end, He passes on a portion of his creative potential – from this point forwards, man will be able to participate in deciding whether or not other people exist.

"Subdue it (the earth) and rule (over the animals ...)"

God then issues man the call to take on the task of creation, and grants him the authority to rule over the animals. God has a plan for mankind and has prepared jobs and an adventure for them. Paul later describes this as follows: "For we are God's handiwork, created in Christ Jesus to do good works, which God prepared in advance for us to do" (Eph 2:10 NIV). God confirms man's special place within the framework of creation by giving human beings authority and responsibility to rule over the animals.

"I give you every seed-bearing plant. (...) They will be yours for food."

God also promises to provide for man. He knows that, as physical beings, they are reliant on food, and He provides this accordingly.

To summarise, God's communication with human beings results in the following affirmations being issued:

- You are my handiwork.
- You are wanted.
- You are called.
- You have special worth.
- You are provided for.

These are affirmations that every child requires of his/her parents in order to start life on a sound footing. God's communication with Adam and Eve provides them with significance and security. Without his words they would have had no sense of orientation.

What is special about Adam and Eve's communication with God?

It is striking that we find two accounts of creation in Genesis, which do not contradict one another, but do differ in terms of the details. The first account of creation[89] paints a rough and broad picture of the events, and flows into the topic of Sabbath rest, to which God Himself adheres. In the second account[90] we see the same events in much greater detail, as if viewed through a magnifying glass. It begins with the creation of man and provides answers to life's existential questions, which we are still wrestling with today. Here we also read that God issues man with a commandment.

"The LORD God took the man and put him in the Garden of Eden to work it and take care of it. [16] And the LORD God commanded the man, "You are free to eat from any tree in the garden; [17] but *you must not eat from the tree of the knowledge of good and evil*, for when you eat from it you will certainly die." (Gen 2:15–17 NIV, emphasis KR).

God gives the first human being just one command. In so doing He enables him to choose the level of relationship he wishes to have with God. The man can now – by either adhering to or ignoring the command – decide for or against God. He is on the path to responsibility.

I have often asked myself why it was that God issued but this single commandment in the idyll of paradise. Doesn't this make God Himself to some extent guilty with regard to man's poor decision-making and the chaos that reigns on *His* planet? But it is only through this commandment that man receives dignity and freedom. Had God not given Adam and Eve the option to decide against Him, they would not have truly been free and would never have fully matured as human beings[91]. Their similarity to God would not have been able to develop any further. At best they would have been beloved robots, whose programming ensured that they blindly follow every command.

---

89   Gen 1:1 – 2:4a.

90   Gen 2:4b – 2:25.

91   God decided out of His own free will to create man and to seek relationship with him. No-one compelled Him to do so, or acted as His advisor. Because He created man in His own image, He also gave man the freedom to decide for Him or against Him. Love can only unfold within the context of free will.

If we view God's desire for relationship as being a central facet, then us giving Him our "yes" in spite of having other options is of great value to Him. On the other hand, a "yes" to the one who "programmed" us would be worthless.

Adam, where are you?

God's communication with man reaches another level once Adam and Eve have decided to ignore the commandment and eat of the forbidden fruit. "Then the man and his wife heard the sound of the Lord God as he was walking in the garden in the cool of the day, and they hid from the Lord God among the trees of the garden? But the Lord God called to the man, "Where are you?" He answered, "I heard you in the garden and I was afraid because I was naked; so I hid." And he said, "Who told you that you were naked? Have you eaten from the tree that I commanded you not to eat from?" The man said, "The woman you put here with me – she gave me some fruit from the tree, and I ate it." Then the Lord God said to the woman, "What is this you have done?" The woman said, "The serpent deceived me, and I ate." " (Gen 3:8–13 NIV).

His communication with mankind does not cease following man's momentous act of disobedience[92]. Entirely to the contrary - as Adam and Eve hide, filled with fear of the consequences of their actions, God begins to call out to them. His proactive attempt to draw close to the guilty parties is a prophetic image for all coming generations, which would reach its climax in the person of Jesus[93]. It reveals His grace and His willingness to call the sinner to Himself, and to forgive him.

The questions God then asks testify of His longing and His faithfulness towards the two perpetrators. God does not ask these questions because He has lost sight of events, but rather to give Adam and Eve the chance to show remorse and admit their mistakes.

As Adam reveals himself, and identifies fear and nakedness as the reasons for his hiding, God comes to him once again, in the same way as He had done when He called out asking

---

92   God's silence would have been a harsh punishment.

93   See, among others, Matt 3:2; Mark 1:15.

where Adam was. He gives him the opportunity to admit his guilt, by means of the spoken word, as it were. "Have you eaten from the tree that I commanded you not to eat from?"

However, the impact of the sin is already showing its effect. Instead of surrendering to a gracious God, Adam points the finger at Eve. He also attempts to shift a portion of the guilt onto God – after all, He was the one who made this Eve! "The man said, "The woman you put here with me – she gave me some fruit from the tree, and I ate it." "

In a third attempt to win the man over, God now turns to Eve. "Then the Lord God said to the woman, "What is this you have done?" "

Likewise Eve, rather than turning back to God and accepting responsibility, she offloads the guilt onto the snake. "The woman said, "The serpent deceived me, and I ate." "

Once God has tried three times to stir the human beings to repentance to no avail, He outlines the consequences that a life outside of His presence would have for Adam and Eve. These include enmity between man and the snake, difficulties in childbirth, the man's lordship over the woman, work experienced as a burden, nature's rebellion against man and death[94].

Following expulsion from paradise we notice how communication between God and man becomes more fragile. In spite of God warning Him, having killed his brother Abel, Cain moves "out from the Lord's presence"[95]. Along with his descendants, he stands as a symbol for humanity that will go their own way, distancing themselves from God.

What can we learn from Adam and Eve?

God's direct spoken communication with Adam and Eve indicates their special standing within creation. His voice speaking to us is a form of contact and brings acceptance, calling, special worth and the promise of His provision – confirmations that every child desperately needs from their parents.

---

94   A good summary of the adverse effects described in verses 14-20 is Murphy's Law: "Whatever can go wrong, will go wrong".

95   Gen 4:16.

God not only speaks to them, but also with them. The fact that God turns to them in this special way reveals His longing to enter into a love relationship with man. The ability to communicate actively with God and with one another sets them apart from the rest of creation.

When God speaks with Adam and Eve it passes on abilities to them, and at the same times places them in a position of responsibility to accept the consequences of their actions. Without having heard the commandment in advance, it would have been difficult for them to accept responsibility for eating the fruit. It is only their communication with God that leads them to the fullness of their humanity, as they become aware of their ability to act independently or in dependency on God.

First and foremost, their story shows us that God wants relationship with man and that acting contrary to His revelation causes a break in the relationship.

Noah – how did he hear God?

Noah was a true rarity in his lifetime, as he was "the only good man of his time." What's more, we read that he "had no faults" and that "he lived in fellowship with God (...). (Gen 6:8-9 GNT)

In the first report of God speaking to him, He talks about the Flood and the construction of the ark. The text simply states: "God said to Noah, (...) build a boat (...)." (Gen 6:13f). At this point there is no further information as to the way that God spoke to Noah. We can assume that Noah heard God audibly. From his relaxed reaction (he doesn't fall on his face, he doesn't build God an altar and sacrifice animals or the like, as is often the case when people hear God's voice in the Old Testament) we can deduce that the communication between the two of them was nothing unusual – it was the rule rather than the exception. Noah does not answer with words, but instead through action: "Noah did everything that God commanded." (Gen 6:22 GNT).

In Genesis 7 God issues further instructions regarding the ark. It reads similarly to before: "The Lord said to Noah (...)." Once again, Noah's positive response is his answer to God: "Noah did everything the Lord commanded." (Gen 7:5 GNT).

95

In Genesis 8 we again read how God speaks directly to Noah, who then obeys God's words. Once the Flood had abated, God spoke to Noah and his sons once again, in a similar way, and through them restored His connection with humanity. He illustrates and emphasises His statement through the celestial symbol of the rainbow, which even today still represents a prophetic symbol of God's offer of peace to mankind.

What is special about Noah's communication with God?

The way in which God and Noah communicate appears simple and familiar. That said, God's message to him is by no means insignificant – it involves the obliteration of most of humanity! – God speaks to Noah without the appearance of angels, lightning, smoke or any trumpets whatsoever. We see that even a huge announcement from God can be delivered in an extremely objective fashion. Noah's unemotional response gives you the impression that he was used to hearing God and receiving direct and sophisticated instructions. This notion is reinforced, as we read that Noah "found grace". He was selected to build the ark because he was "good" and "without fault" and because he "lived in fellowship with God"[96]. These descriptions only make sense if Noah could already look back on a long history of obedience towards God's voice. He must have heard God speak clearly very often prior to being commissioned to build the ark.

What can we learn from Noah?

Our actions speak

Noah's communication with God is characterised less by long dialogue and negotiation, and more by simple obedience to God's voice. God speaks and Noah acts. This shows that our action towards God is just as much a form of expression as our words. If we consider Jesus' parable of the "disobedient" sons, we could even say: God hears our actions louder

---

96   See Gen 6.

than our words[97]. Noah's righteous faith, which is also mentioned in the New Testament, becomes powerfully evident in his action, and not so much in his words[98].

TEAM TALK: OUR ACTIONS SPEAK.

1. Are you aware that your actions speak louder to God than your words? Read the parable of the two workshy sons (Matt 21:28). Share with the group: which son would you tend to identify more with?

2. Are you aware that your actions can be an expression of prayer? Consider the areas of life in which you pray by acting righteously.

Deep secrets require a deep relationship

Noah was 600 years old when the Flood struck the Earth[99]. As the result of a long and faithful relationship with God, he was capable of hearing God on a very personal level. On account of his righteous and faultless existence, God entrusted His plans to him and allowed him to become a part of them. We can see how long-term obedience to God's revelation enables us to share deep secrets with God and to play a role in serious matters. The level of revelation from God that we are able to handle depends on the extent to which we are able to hear His voice and obey. Important revelations from God sometimes require a long period of preparation, involving both listening and acting.

TEAM TALK: DEEP SECRETS REQUIRE A DEEP RELATIONSHIP.

1. Do you want to partake in the deep revelations of God? Discuss this statement: The steadfastness of your faithfulness and devotion is a key factor in determining the level of revelation that God can entrust to you.

2. Discuss: Where would you place your faithfulness and devotion towards God on a scale from 0–10?[100]

---

97   Matt 21:28ff.

98   Heb 11:7.

99   Gen 7:6.

100   0 = non-existent, 10 = as was the case with Jesus.

3. Ask God to reveal the areas of your life in which He particularly wants to see reliability and faithfulness. Note down what you feel God is saying and share with the group. Pray together and ask God to complete this work in you[101].

4. Share your findings from this exercise with a friend and ask him or her to follow-up with you as to how things are going in 4 weeks time. You can repeat this exercise by yourself every few months.

Abraham – how did he hear God?

Abraham is known as the "Father of Faith"[102]. He earned this title on account of his ability to hear God and to respond to His voice in complete faith. Below we will only consider God's communication with Abraham in excerpts. His entire life story can be found recounted from Genesis 12 onwards.

In the first report of God talking to Abraham[103], God speaks directly to him and encourages him to take the radical step of leaving his homeland. "The LORD had said to Abram, "Go from your country, your people and your father's household to the land I will show you." (Gen 12:1 NIV).

God gives him these specific and momentous instructions, accompanied by huge promises. "I will make you into a great nation, and I will bless you. I will make your name great and you will be a blessing." (Gen 12:2 NIV). Abraham answers through action. "So Abram went, as the LORD had told him, (...)." (Gen 12:4 NIV).

We do not receive more detailed insight into how God speaks to Abraham during this initial encounter. However, his obedience marks the beginning of a life story that is characterised by versatile communication with God. The very next time they exchange words, Abraham's encounter with God shifts up a notch. The Lord "appeared to Abram

---

101   "(...) he who began a good work in you will carry it on to completion until the day of Christ Jesus (...)" (Phil 1:6 NIV).

102   See Romans 4.

103   At this point in time he was actually still called Abram.

and said (...).” (Gen 12:7). In this description we see how God is longing for a deeper relationship with Abraham, as this time he doesn't just get to hear, but also gets to see[104].

As a result of God's blessing, the herds belonging to Abraham and his brother Lot grow to such an extent that they decide to part ways. Then God speaks once again: “The LORD said to Abram after Lot had parted from him, “Look around from where you are, to the north and south, to the east and west. All the land that you see I will give to you and your offspring forever.” (Gen 13:14–15 NIV). Given the choice of words, here too we can assume that this is direct, verbal communication.

The next time God speaks to him we read: “... the word of the Lord came to Abram in a vision.” (Gen 15:1). Whether or not this refers to an internal vision or an outward vision (in front of his eyes) is not made clear. It may have been a vision in a dream, as in the following sentences it becomes clear that the events take place at night.

In the vision Abraham answers God and a lively discussion unfolds. God leads him out beneath the starry skies and uses the innumerability of the stars as an illustration to demonstrate the number of descendants He was promising. During this conversation with God, when Abraham asks for a sign to confirm God's promise he is instructed to cut some animals in two and to lay out the carcasses. Some time passes while Abraham obeys the instruction and awaits God's response – presumably an entire day. We read that he has to drive away birds of prey that want to steal the meat – the majority of birds of prey hunt throughout the day. As evening falls once again, God causes Abraham to fall into a “deep sleep”. Seemingly, what God wants to say now requires this peacefulness. As he sleeps, a “thick and dreadful darkness” comes over Abraham – this sensation is not part of a nightmare, but is rather God's voice. Abraham experiences an emotional preview of what God is saying to him in that moment regarding the future suffering of his descendants. “Then the LORD said to him, “Know for certain that for four hundred years your descendants will be strangers in a country not their own and that they will be enslaved and mistreated there.” (Gen 15:13 NIV).

Whether Abraham receives these premonitions while awake or as part of his deep sleep is not entirely clear. However, he does appear to be awake when God's message reaches its climax.

---

104   Although the extent remains unclear.

When it becomes dark, God speaks, in particular through a supernatural sign. A "smoking firepot" and a "blazing torch" pass between the cut apart animals. The meaning of all of this is the sealing of the covenant that God concludes with Abraham.

So here God speaks to Abraham in a dream (or a vision), in the form of emotions, by means of a personal appearance and through supernatural signs. God also later speaks to him by giving him a new name[105] [106], in person[107], by visiting him in physical form[108], through lengthy conversation[109], through an angel[110] and through massive blessing[111].

What is special about Abraham's communication with God?

If we read about the life of Abraham, it would appear that almost every important event in his life is accompanied by direct communication with God. At times his relationship with God feels like that seen between two peers; good friends. It is striking, for example, how boldly he negotiates with God regarding the sparing of Sodom and Gomorrah[112] or how he laughs in God's direct presence, when He predicts that Abraham will have a son in his old age[113]. James picks up on this special relationship, when he writes that, through his faith, Abraham was called a "friend of God"[114]. We can see this friendship being lived out in his colourful communication with God.

---

105   God changes his name from Abram (Exalted Father) to Abraham (Father of Many).
106   Gen 17:5.
107   Gen 17:22.
108   Gen 18:1.
109   Gen 18:20ff.
110   Gen 22:11.
111   Gen 23:6; 24:1.
112   Gen 18:20ff.
113   Gen 17:17.
114   "Abraham believed God, and it was credited to him as righteousness, and he was called God's friend." (James 2:23 NIV).

What can we learn from Abraham?

Hearing, believing, acting

As was the case with Noah, so too in Abraham do we see that it is not just hearing God's voice that strengthens Abraham's relationship with Him. The hearing must be accompanied by believing and acting. This triad permeates Abraham's relationship with God, right through to the end of his life. "By *faith* Abraham, *when called* to go to a place he would later receive as his inheritance, *obeyed and went*, even though he did not know where he was going." (Heb 11:8 NIV, emphasis KR).

TEAM TALK: HEARING, BELIEVING, ACTING.

Most followers of Jesus want to hear God more – however: To what extent are we prepared to back up the hearing with believing and acting?

1. Consider times in the past when you have been challenged to back up hearing with believing and acting.

2. Discuss your failures and successes when it comes to hearing, believing and acting. In each case, what made you successful or why did you fail? What did you learn from this?

Unconditional devotion to God

Abraham remains humble and obedient, in spite of the fact that God has made unbelievable promises to him and has spoken with him personally on several occasions. This becomes clear in his willingness to sacrifice his son Isaac. His unusual encounters with God don't go to his head, but instead take him deeper in his relationship with God.

TEAM TALK: UNCONDITIONAL DEVOTION TO GOD.

Can we handle the blessing that we are asking God for? Do encounters with God leave us feeling a sense of humility or pride?

1. Discuss among yourselves: In what instance has an encounter with God left you feeling proud? What happened? What did you learn?

2. Discuss among yourselves: In what instance has an encounter with God left you feeling humble? What happened? What did you learn?

3. Where would you place yourself on a devotion scale from 0–10?[115] What factors makes it difficult to submit yourself entirely to God's will?

A broad picture of God

Abraham believed in a great God and did not limit their mutual interaction through narrow-mindedness or by being stuck in his ways. For this reason God was able to talk to him in diverse and unusual ways.

TEAM TALK: A BROAD PICTURE OF GOD.

1. Discuss among yourselves: Do you tend to only expect God to speak in the ways with which you are already accustomed, or can He speak to you in creative ways that take you by surprise and are beyond your expectations?

2. Go through the story of Abraham together (Gen 12:1ff). Which of Abraham's encounters with God would have been too much for you to cope with? Explain why.

3. Which would you have liked to experience? Explain why.

Moses – How did he hear God?

Although in his later life Moses was able to speak "face to face" with God, he only came to know God personally relatively late on. Moses grew up in Egypt in the court of the Pharaoh, but was forced to flee from there after he murdered an Egyptian. It was while in exile that he heard God speak for the first time, as he was putting sheep belonging to his father-in-law - the priest of Midian - out to pasture at the foot of Mount Horeb. God speaks directly to him through a burning bush, right there in the middle of his working day.

---

115   0 = I generally do what *I* want. 10 = I obey everything God says without any conditions.

"Now Moses was tending the flock (...) and he led the flock to the far side of the wilderness and came to Horeb, the mountain of God. There the angel of the LORD appeared to him in flames of fire from within a bush. Moses saw that though the bush was on fire it did not burn up. So Moses thought, "I will go over and see this strange sight—why the bush does not burn up." (Ex 3:1ff NIV).

Moses marvelled[116] at the fact that the bush did not burn up, so he went closer and God spoke to him from the burning thorn bush. He introduces Himself as the God to whom Moses' forefathers had prayed. The fact that God had to introduce Himself in this way would suggest that Moses had not known Him personally prior to this. "(...) "I am the God of your father, the God of Abraham, the God of Isaac and the God of Jacob." At this, Moses hid his face, because he was afraid to look at God." (Ex 3:6 NIV).

Not only does God reveal Himself to Moses audibly here, but also visibly, and commands him to lead his people out of Egypt. On account of Moses' doubts, a long conversation unfolds between the pair. Extensive conversations with God, such as this one, will become more frequent during the course of Moses' life. God also speaks to him through a miraculous sign: upon being thrown to the ground, Moses' staff is transformed into a snake, returning to its original form when he picks it up again. This sign and others will later become part of God's message, which Moses passes on.

Once Moses decides to take up God's commission, God speaks to him in person twice more to confirm and explain his mission. Both times the text simply says this: the Lord "said" to Moses[117]. Throughout his life we see this direct form of communication with God as being commonplace for Moses[118]. Furthermore, God speaks to him through personal revelations[119], through people[120], through His tangible presence, through the sound of

---

116   God's objective in performing a miracle is that we are amazed and thus pay Him some attention. We allow many divine revelations to pass us by unnoticed as we have forgotten how to "marvel", and like to appear cool and unfazed. If something in our everyday life amazes us, it is likely that God might be trying to get our attention. Only when Moses stepped closer, to get a better look, did God begin to speak to him directly (Exodus 3:4).

117   Exodus 4:19; 21.

118   S. a. Exodus 6:1; 10; 7:1; 7:8.

119   Exodus 15:25.

120   Exodus 18:13ff.

wind instruments and a loud voice[121]. To this list we can also add personal encounter[122], the appearance of His glory[123] when He allows His glory to shine down on Moses' face[124], an internal awareness[125] and wondrous signs[126].

What is special about Moses' communication with God?

Throughout his life there is something wonderfully natural about the way Moses communicates with God. God's direct speech no longer amazes him, but is instead a mere expression of their friendship. "The LORD would speak to Moses face to face, as one speaks to a friend." (Ex 33:11 NIV).

The consistently high quality of communication between God and Moses really stands out. God Himself says of it: "(...) When there is a prophet among you, I, the Lord, reveal myself to them in visions, I speak to them in dreams. But this is not true of my servant Moses; he is faithful in all my house. With him I speak face to face, clearly and not in riddles; he sees the form of the Lord." (Num 12:6-8 NIV).

After his death, it is then said of Moses: "Since then, no prophet has risen in Israel like Moses, whom the Lord knew face to face." (Deut 34:10 NIV).

Whereas the people of Israel were *only* allowed to see God's deeds, he saw God Himself[127] and was granted insight into His secrets. "He made known his ways to Moses, his deeds to the people of Israel." (Ps 103:7 NIV).

Moses not only heard God directly, but he also served as a powerful mouthpiece to Pharaoh and the people of Israel. To this end, and like no other person in his day, he received highly detailed and lengthy instructions to accompany commandments, laws and

---

121   Exodus 19:18.

122   Exodus 24:18.

123   Exodus 20:6 among others.

124   Exodus 34:29.

125   Exodus 17:7.

126   Exodus 17:22f.

127   What do we want to see – God's deeds or God Himself? The answer can serve as a barometer for our spiritual maturity.

the specifications for the construction of the sanctuary. By passing on these instructions, he communicates God's will to all of the coming generations[128].

Although when first commissioned Moses claims that he cannot speak well, God uses him throughout his life to speak to countless people. It would appear that the continual communication with God not only defines who he truly is, but also his ability to speak with authority and clarity.

Unlike with Noah, God's communication with Moses is often accompanied by powerful signs and wonders. These speak not only to those around him, but are also a continual encouragement to Moses himself and a confirmation of his calling.

What can we learn from Moses?

The ability to learn from God

It is encouraging to see that even though he approaches God so hesitantly at first, Moses learns how to hear God and gets to know Him in a very intimate way. This is particularly worth noting in light of the fact that, in Pharaoh's court, he had grown up in an environment in which God was not known and was even considered hostile.

As far as we are aware, Moses had no mentors to assist him in hearing God's voice. Instead, he learned directly from God

MULL IT OVER: THE ABILITY TO LEARN FROM GOD.

1. Ask yourself: Do you blame a lack of support or your circumstances for weaknesses in your relationship with God? Are you aware that it is first and foremost your willingness to listen to God and to learn from him that determines the quality of your relationship with God and not what is happening around you?

2. Commit to accepting responsibility for your relationship with God and ask God for forgiveness for times when you have delegated responsibility for your life to other people or to institutions. Share your resolution and repentance with someone else.

128   Exodus 22:1ff; 25:1ff.

Development of character

The first time he encounters God, Moses conveys an insecure and reluctant impression[129]. However, he grows into his calling, showing courage in his battle with Pharaoh and trusting in God's voice more than Pharaoh's threats.

TEAM TALK: DEVELOPMENT OF CHARACTER.

It is not the situation we find ourselves in when God speaks to us that is vital, but whether we are prepared to believe what He says about us rather than focusing on how we view ourselves.

1. Share experiences of times when you have believed in what God says about you more than what you think about yourself. What happened? What did you learn?

2. Discuss situations when you find it difficult to believe in what God says about you more than what you think about yourself. What might it take to change your perspective?

Humility

Even though Moses was allowed to experience astonishing revelation and encounter with God, he is characterised by deep humility and devotion. The Bible even says of him: "Now Moses was a very humble man, more humble than anyone else on the face of the earth." (Num 12:3 NIV).

TEAM TALK: HUMILITY.

Those with a proud and arrogant heart quickly become deaf to God's voice and run the risk that God will oppose them[130].

1. Discuss among yourselves: Are humility and a willingness to live in dependence on God part of your lifestyle?

2. How is humility towards God expressed in your life?

3. How is the willingness to live in dependence on God expressed in your life?

---

129   Exodus 3:11; 4:10.

130   See also James 4:6.

Balance

Although God speaks to him personally, "face to face", Moses remains grounded. He is also willing to hear God through the advice of others and to place value in the opinions of others[131].

TEAM TALK: BALANCE.

1. Although each of us can hear God directly through the Holy Spirit, He also speaks to us through other people. How willing are we to hear God through others? Discuss within the group.

2. What prevents us from accepting God's word from others? What helps us to accept God's word from others?

3. Do we appreciate that following God is a team sport and not a one-man show[132]? Discuss among yourselves: Do you tend to go it alone or to play as a team? Where does this attitude come from? When does this attitude become clear?

Generosity

Moses does not hold on tight to his unique position, but instead wishes that his leadership skills and his ability to hear directly from God were multiplied within the nation of Israel. "(...) I wish that all the LORD's people were prophets and that the LORD would put his Spirit on them!" (Num 11:29 NIV).

TEAM TALK: GENEROSITY

God asks us to use the abilities and resources that He gives us for the good of others. This can mean teaching others to do what we can do, or to share our love, money, time, resources etc.

1. How willing are you to pass on God's blessings, on a scale from 0-10?[133]

2. In which areas to you find it difficult/easy to give something away?

3. Share a situation in which you have passed something on in spite of it being difficult. What happened? What did you learn?

---

131   Exodus 18:17; Leviticus 10:19f.

132   See also Genesis 2:18.

133   0 = I don't want to pass anything on, 10 = I am always willing to pass things on in generosity.

Joseph – How did he hear God?

The account of the life of Joseph begins when he is seventeen years old[134]. Whether or not he had previously heard from God in person remains unclear. Joseph is the youngest of his brothers and his father Jacob's favourite son. Jacob gives him special treatment, thus making Joseph's brother jealous[135]. Joseph, in turn, appears to enjoy this special standing, and informs his father of everything that his brothers are up to[136].

The first report of God speaking to him involves two, rather full-on dreams, which foresee his future position of authority over his family. Whether Joseph understands that God is speaking to him at this point remains unclear. Unwisely, and presumably arrogantly, he tells the family of his dreams and thus incurs the wrath of his brothers and the chastisement of his father. As the story continues, his brothers' anger and jealousy result in him being sold as a slave into Egypt, where he lands in Potiphar's house.

During his time in Potiphar's service, we receive no information as to God speaking directly to Joseph. Yet, it is clear even to Potiphar that God is with Joseph. We read that "(…) the LORD was with him and that the LORD gave him success in everything he did"[137]. Potiphar thus entrusted Joseph with all of his affairs. We can assume that, in the blessing he experiences, Joseph hears God speak and perhaps even sees initial signs of the fulfilment of his calling to leadership.

The fact that he now has a living relationship with God becomes clear in that he declines the sexual offer from Potiphar's wife with the words: "How then could I do such a wicked thing and sin against God?"[138]. As a result of her false accusation, Joseph ends up in prison, where he once again experiences God's exceptional favour. He is placed in control over the prisoners, and here, too, God blesses him with success in all he does[139].

---

134 Genesis 37:2.
135 Genesis 37:3.
136 Genesis 37:2.
137 Genesis 39:3.
138 Genesis 39:9.
139 Genesis 39:22.

In prison, when Joseph interprets the dreams of two of Pharaoh's officials who have fallen out of favour, he does so with the following comment: "Do not interpretations belong to God? Tell me your dreams"[140]. What Joseph is implying here is this: God is with me; I understand Him and can interpret what He says for you. We see that his relationship with God has not fallen by the wayside while in prison, but instead, his ability to hear and understand God is a direct part of his everyday life in prison.

Joseph interprets the two dreams successfully and – following a further two years of waiting – receives the honour of being able to interpret two of the Pharaoh's dreams in person, dreams that speak to the future of the entire nation. At this point Joseph has matured in terms of his character and his relationship with God, accepting no honour whatsoever for himself from the interpretation of the dreams, but instead directing the focus onto God.

"Pharaoh said to Joseph, "I had a dream, and no one can interpret it. But I have heard it said of you that when you hear a dream you can interpret it. "I cannot do it," Joseph replied to Pharaoh, "but God will give Pharaoh the answer he desires." " (Gen 41:15–16 NIV).

Following on from this series of events, Joseph goes on to fulfil his full calling. He becomes the second most powerful man in Egypt and rescues his family from starvation.

There is relatively little information regarding how God continues to speak to Joseph. Only as his father Jacob lies on his deathbed does God announce to Joseph through his father that his people will some day return to the land of his forefathers. Although Joseph does not live to see this departure from Egypt, he believes in God's word. He issues his children with the instruction to take his bones with them as they are leaving Egypt[141].

---

140   Genesis 40:8.
141   Hebrews 11:22.

What is special about Joseph's communication with God?

Joseph's story is interspersed with instances of God speaking in dreams. Joseph's ability to decipher God's communication in image form is vital to his success in life, to the survival of his family and the survival of the Egyptian people. Furthermore, God communicates with Joseph by blessing him and awarding him favour among men. His story, in which he rises up through the ranks from slave to the second most powerful man in the entire nation is a clear indication of Joseph's election, favour and promotion by God.

What can we learn from Joseph?

Eyes on the prize

It is fascinating to see how, right at the beginning of Joseph's story, God sketches out the course of his life in two dreams. This purpose, as marked out by God, is something that Joseph never loses sight of, holding firm to God's word in spite of the fact that his circumstances appear to be entirely contradictory to its truth.

TEAM TALK: EYES ON THE PRIZE.

When God makes promises to us, we are still nonetheless required to continually decide to move towards the promised destination.

1. How willing are you to overcome resistance in order to see God's promises fulfilled? Place yourself on a scale from 0–10.[142]

2. Have you ever received specific promises from God, which have only been fulfilled much later? What happened in the meantime?

3. Which promises are you still waiting to see fulfilled in your life?

4. Reflect together: What would be a good way to approach unfulfilled promises?

5. For what reasons might it be a good idea to let go of a promise that we have held onto for a long time? How could we provide someone with support during such a difficult process?

---

142   0 = No willingness to overcome resistance, 10 = Constant willingness to overcome resistance.

Recognising favour as God's voice

There are no reports of God speaking directly to Joseph. However, Joseph heard God on many occasions, speaking through his circumstances. The protection experienced, God's guidance and favour always carry a message. Joseph is capable of seeing God's favour in the events in his life and this encourages him to cling tightly to God.

TEAM TALK: RECOGNISING FAVOUR AS GOD'S VOICE.

1. Is it clear to us that special favour in our career, with friends or in everyday situations is actually the encouraging voice of God? Discuss among yourselves: What do you think about this?

2. Share about situations in which you have experienced an unusual level of favour. What impact did the favour have on you and those around you? What could you learn about yourself and God?

Staying the course and maturing

The significance of his calling does not spare Joseph from having to endure great suffering, defamation and imprisonment. On the contrary, you get the impression that this suffering ultimately did him good. They forge his personality and thus enable him to successfully step into his subsequent position of leadership over Egypt.

TEAM TALK: STAYING THE COURSE AND MATURING.

Even a word from God that does not appear particularly significant can, under certain circumstance, take on new meaning several years later, and can also bring with it testing or the forming/maturing of our character.

1. Discuss among yourselves: What do you do when God's word to you is tested? How willing are you to be formed into the person that God's revelation has mapped out?

2. Share instances when you have gone through special times of preparation and maturing. What happened during this process? What were you able to learn? What was the result?

A posture of servanthood in your everyday

Joseph takes advantage of the fact that those around him hear God but do not understand. Within his sphere of influence and applying his divine gifting, he serves as he goes about his everyday work and thus becomes God's mouthpiece and interpreter.

TEAM TALK: A POSTURE OF SERVANTHOOD IN YOUR EVERYDAY.

Each of us lives with people who hear God but find it difficult to understand Him. With our gift of being able to understand God, we also have the responsibility to act as an interpreter and serve others.

1. Are you aware of people and situations in your everyday life who rely on you as an "interpreter for God"? Where have you experienced this in the past? What exactly happened?

2. Are there people around you who consider you trustworthy on account of the fact that you live a Jesus-centred lifestyle, and consequently allow you to explain God's word to them?

David – how did he hear God?

David's story begins with God speaking to the prophet Samuel regarding David's calling. God sends Samuel to David's father Jesse, who has eight sons, with the task of anointing one of these sons as king over Israel. Samuel does not know in advance which of the sons God has chosen. To Samuel's astonishment, God selects David, the youngest son. As the prophet anoints him with oil, we read: "(…) and from that day on the Spirit of the LORD came powerfully upon David." (1 Sam 16:13 NIV). This anointing will frequently be put to the test over the coming years and will be confirmed by God in a wide variety of ways.

A first real test comes when David is still young and he decides to face Goliath in battle. David faces this challenge, in spite of the fact that at this point in time he has no experience of battle and is not even physically strong enough to wear King Saul's armour. Because God had previously stood by him when battling other superior opponents, he nonetheless steps up, full of faith. "But David said to Saul, "Your servant has been keeping his father's sheep.

When a lion or a bear came and carried off a sheep from the flock, [35] I went after it, struck it and rescued the sheep from its mouth. The LORD who rescued me from the paw of the lion and the paw of the bear will rescue me from the hand of this Philistine." (1 Sam 17:34,35,37).

In this crisis situation, David is able to interpret past victories as God's Word to him. God's intervention on previous occasions thus becomes a form of prophetic encouragement for the moment at hand. The ability to deduce God's will for the present based on His past intervention will continue to play a significant role in David's life.

1 and 2 Samuel provide us with helpful insights into the life of David and his relationship with God. Following on from his anointing as king, his biography develops into a fully-fledged adventure. Young and inexperienced, he is called to serve in the royal court as Saul's personal musician[143], he fights and defeats the giant Goliath and is loved and celebrated by the entire nation[144]. He develops a deep friendship with Saul's son Jonathan[145], marries Michal, Saul's daughter, and thus enters into the inner circle of the royal family.

All of these events confirm his anointing and lead him to the conceivably favourable situation whereby he is to become the next king. Presumably David himself views this development as a confirmation of the promise that he will become king. King Saul views things entirely differently. With God having turned away from him, all he is concerned with is retaining his position of power. He shows increasing aggression towards David and attempts to kill him on several occasions. David finally flees from Saul and is subsequently pursued by him. Men who have nothing to lose, join ranks with David[146]. He lives in caves or in the desert, sometimes under the patronage of hostile kings, but always on the run. It is now that he experiences the first major breakdown of his life. Although at no point does the Spirit of God leave him[147], he has become unsure what God's plans are for his life. His ability to hear and understand God has suffered during his persecution. He asks the king of Moab for asylum, using the following words: "Would you let my father and mother come and stay with you *until I learn what God will do for me.*" (1 Sam 22:3 NIV, emphasis KR).

---

143   1 Sam 16:23.

144   1 Sam 18:15ff.

145   1 Sam 18:13.

146   1 Sam 22:1.

147   See 1 Sam 16:13.

As is typical of David's life, God speaks words of encouragement in this dire situation through a spiritual advisor – in this case the prophet Gad. Gad advises him: "Do not stay in the stronghold. Go into the land of Judah." (1 Sam 22:5 NIV).

Shortly after this we read how David is informed that Philistines are plundering their way through the country. He is forced to decide whether to attack the Philistines and help his people. "He inquired of the LORD, saying, "Shall I go and attack these Philistines? The LORD answered him, "Go, attack the Philistines and save Keilah." (1 Sam 23:2 NIV).

However, his men are afraid to confront the Philistines. Thus, David asks God once again, who duly confirms his pending victory. It can be assumed that here, for the first time, David petitions God via the ephod. In 1 Sam 23:6 it is actually reported that Abiathar, the son of the priest Ahimelek who had recently fled to David, was carrying the ephod with him. The ephod served as a type of oracle-pouch, and was used by priests to inquire as to God's will. From here on in the oracle-pouch becomes a standard tool used by David for communication with God. This is specifically described in two separate reports[148], but we can assume it is used at other points in time based on the paraphrase used[149].

Throughout the subsequent course of his reign, David comes to know another way in which God speaks, namely through His judgements. David experiences four instances of judgement during his reign, in the form of the death of Bathsheba's child[150], in his being driven out by his son Absalom[151], a three-year famine[152] and the spread of the plague[153]. In each instance he recognises this as a call of God, responds positively, humbles himself before God and experiences restoration. David has learned to hear God's voice both in his successes[154] and in the reprimands described above.

---

148   See 1 Sam 23:9ff; 1 Sam 30:7.

149   See 2 Sam 2:1; 2 Sam 5:19/23; 2 Sam 21:1; 1 Chr 14:10/14.

150   2 Sam 12.

151   2 Sam 15.

152   2 Sam 21.

153   2 Sam 24.

154   1 Sam 30:23; 2 Sam 5:10-12; 2 Sam 8:6/14.

What is special about David's communication with God?

Although David is praised throughout the entire Bible for his devotion and for his relationship with God, we seldom read of his communication with God taking place without an intermediary. In this respect he differs from Moses and Abraham, who conduct long, personal conversations with God. David, on the other hand, repeatedly hears God "indirectly" through events, spiritual advisors and meditation on the law[155]. Just like Joseph, David is able to hear God's good will in his favour and guidance. What's more, he hears God through prophetic, symbolic acts, supernatural victories, the oracle-pouch, people, God's judgements and reflection on his own life. The composition of songs and texts is also a strong communicative anchor for him. In the same way as we hear God by reading the psalms, so too did David hear God while writing them. The psalms and songs of David may have been written by him, but they are inspired by God[156]. For this reason they impacted David just as much as they impact us today[157]. In David's ability to formulate God's voice in the psalms, he not only hears God, but, like Moses, also becomes God's voice for all coming generations.

What can we learn from David?

Hearing God in events

When the rich landowner Nabal refuses to help David and his men and insults them, David sets out to kill him and all of the male members of his household. Nabal's intelligent wife Abigail hears of the incident and swiftly comes out to meet David. She apologises for her husband's behaviour and implores him to cancel his plans. David recognises God speaking to him in this encounter, telling him not to take revenge by himself.

---

155   Meditation on the law is a recurrent theme in his psalms.

156   In Psalm 40 David writes of a song that God "put in his mouth". Whether this refers to Psalm 40 itself or to another song is unclear. In the New Testament there are various descriptions as to how David speaks in the Holy Spirit or how the Holy Spirit speaks through him (Mark 12:35; Acts 1:16; Acts 4:25).

157   Anyone who has ever jotted down some prayerful thoughts will be familiar with the feeling of having a "ghost-writer".

"Praise be to the Lord, the God of Israel, who has sent you today to meet me." (...) May you be blessed for your good judgement and for keeping me from bloodshed this day and from avenging myself with my own hands." (1 Sam 25,32f).

David is forced to flee Jerusalem from his son Absalom, who has instigated a coup against him. Absalom wants to become king in his place. During David's protracted escape, a relative of the former king, Saul, rides alongside David, curses him and throws stones and dirt at him[158]. When David's soldiers want to kill him, David forbids it with these words:

"What does this have to do with you, you sons of Zeruiah? If he is cursing because the Lord said to him, 'Curse David,' who can ask, 'Why do you do this?'" (2 Sam 16:10 NIV). David recognises God's voice and judgement in Shimei's curse against him, and is therefore willing to endure the curse. He hears God's call in these events and responds in humility.

When David wants to bring the Ark of the Covenant with him into the City of David, he does not adhere to the transport regulations passed down by Moses. Uzzah, one of his men, dies on account of touching the Ark without thinking. David is frightened, distances himself from the plan and instead has the Ark brought to the home of Obed-Edom. After three months it becomes clear that God is blessing Obed-Edom and his entire household. In this blessing David recognises God's blessing for the further transportation of the Ark to the City of David and has the Ark brought to him[159].

TEAM TALK: HEARING GOD IN EVENTS.

1. Have you ever heard God speak to you through events in your life? Discuss among yourselves: Through which events did He speak to you? How did you notice He was speaking through these events? What did He say?

2. What can we learn from the three reports (1 Sam 25; 2 Sam 16; 1 Chr 15) in which God speaks to David through events? Read the stories and discuss: How does David come to recognise God's voice in the events?

3. What helps David to hear God speaking through events in these situations? What makes it difficult for David to hear God speaking through events in these situations?

---

158   2 Sam 16:5ff.
159   1 Chr 15:1 – 16:3.

God speaking through spiritual advisors

David allows God to speak to him through friends, prophets, seers and other advisors[160]. He doesn't close himself off to them, but instead seeks out their advice and even accepts their reprimands. His willingness and humility to submit to God's guidance issued through people is clearly evident.

MULL IT OVER: GOD SPEAKING THROUGH SPIRITUAL ADVISORS

1. Can you remember moments in which God warned, reprimanded or guided you through other people? Are there links between these events, i.e. does God speak to you more often through people in certain situations? If yes: what might be the reason for this?

2. Which people has God placed in your life, who you can regularly ask for advice? Do these people know that you value them as advisors?

TEAM TALK: GOD SPEAKING THROUGH SPIRITUAL ADVISORS.

1. Share instances in which God warned, reprimanded or guided you through other people.

2. Did you find it challenging that God spoke to you through another person? Why was it challenging? Why not?

3. Did you notice at the time that God was speaking to you through another person? How long did it last? How did you react? What was the result?

Fear of God rather than fear of man

When his men wanted to mutiny against his decision to attack the Philistines, David consulted God a second time. He receives a positive answer and does not allow himself to be affected by the concerns of his army. Unlike Saul he pays more attention to the word of God than to the pressure imposed by people. David allows fear of God to conquer over fear of man, which would become the final stumbling block for Saul[161].

---

160   See, among others, 2 Sam 12:1; 2 Sam 12:24; 1 Chr 21:7; 2 Sam 7:1.

161   1 Sam 15:24ff.

TEAM TALK: FEAR OF GOD RATHER THAN FEAR OF MAN.

God regularly challenges us to make decisions that go "against the flow".

1. Discuss among yourselves: Do we want to hear God's voice even if this means making unpopular decisions and being misunderstood by people?

2. Have you ever experienced this? What happened? What were you able to learn?

David doesn't seek success, but rather justice

Although God confirms David through favour and success, he also offers him "non-sacred" opportunities. These are opportunities that are not intended as a means of ensuring David's progress, but rather testing his faithfulness and character.

Situations whereby God creates opportunities for people without Him actually wanting them to avail of these opportunities can be found described throughout the entire Bible. For instance, there is the opportunity to eat from the forbidden fruit in the Garden of Eden[162] or Jesus' ability to call on angels, who would have protected him from capture in Gethsemane[163]. In the same way God twice delivers King Saul, whom He had abandoned, into David's hands. David thus has the opportunity to bring about his calling to become king by force. As his men demand that Saul be murdered, David allows room for God's sovereign action and doesn't seize the promised kingship for himself[164]. Exceptional opportunities that God gives us can thus be a means of communicating His favour, but can just as easily be a test.

TEAM TALK: DAVID DOESN'T SEEK SUCCESS, BUT RATHER JUSTICE.

1. What can we learn about God and ourselves through the "non-sacred opportunities" that God creates?

2. Have you ever been on the receiving end of a divine character test? Did you pass? What happened? How would you respond today if facing the same test?

---

162 Genesis 2:9/16ff.

163 Matt 26:52ff.

164 1 Sam 24:4ff; 1 Sam 26:8ff.

Samuel – How did he hear God?

Samuel's life story is extremely exciting and is used by many preachers when speaking on the topic of "hearing God's voice". It begins back before his birth, with the infertility of his mother Hannah, who pleaded with God for a child. Hannah promised that her child would be consecrated to God[165]. When later naming her child, Hannah makes it clear that Samuel had to a certain extent been conceived as a result of her intercession[166] – in the Hebrew the name Samuel sounds similar to "God has heard". The circumstances surrounding his conception define Samuel's later life. You almost get the impression that God has written the topic of prayer into his DNA – later, one of his main tasks is to stand as an intercessor on behalf of the people of Israel[167].

Once Hannah has weaned Samuel, she fulfils her vow and hands him over to the priest Eli[168]. Samuel grows up in the temple of Shiloh, under Eli's supervision[169], growing into a young man "in favour with the LORD and with people"[170]. Eli himself has two sons, who behave extremely disreputably and provoke God's judgement towards themselves[171]. The same is suffered by Eli, as he neglects to hold his sons to account.

Under Eli's priesthood, Israel does not experience a time of spiritual prosperity. As such, we read of the time when Samuel heard God for the first time: "(...) In those days the word of the LORD was rare; there were not many visions." (1 Sam 3,1 NIV). Samuel thus finds it difficult to recognise God's voice. At night, God calls him three times by name. Each time Samuel thinks it was Eli calling him, for "the LORD had not spoken directly to him yet" (1 Sam 3:7 NCV).

---

165   1 Sam 1:10ff.

166   1 Sam 1:20.

167   1 Sam 7:4; 7:8; 7:9; 12:18; 12:23; 15:10f; Ps 99:6; Jer 15:1.

168   1 Sam 1:24.

169   1 Sam 2:11.

170   1 Sam 2:26.

171   1 Sam 2:12ff.

The statement that Samuel had not yet heard God's voice is particularly astonishing, as we first read of how Samuel would help Eli with his priestly duties[172]. Samuel thus served as a priest, without knowing God personally. Eli had entrusted him with the practical duties of a priest, but had neglected to guide him into relationship with God. The text comments: "Eli's eyes were so weak he was almost blind." (1 Sam 3:2 NCV). This comment can also be viewed as symbolic of Eli's relationship with God.

Only when God calls Samuel for the third time does Eli understand what is happening: "Then Eli realized that the LORD was calling the boy. ⁹ So Eli told Samuel, "Go and lie down. If someone calls out to you again, say, 'Speak, LORD. I'm listening." (1 Sam 3:8–9 NIV). When Samuel responds accordingly to another call from God, God reveals to him the already announced judgement over Eli and his family.

Samuel's calling as a prophet and leader progresses quickly once he has come to know God, and the full extent of his ability soon becomes evident. "The LORD was with Samuel as he grew up, and he let none of Samuel's words fall to the ground. (...) And Samuel's word came to all Israel." (1 Sam 3:19 – 4:1 NIV).

His life after this is extremely eventful and is recounted in 1 Sam 4 – 28. The following events are of particular note: In a period of time in which the whole of Israel "had fallen away from the Lord"[173] Samuel initiates a spiritual revival and calls the people to repentance[174].

To this end, he mediates between the people, who want a king, and God, and, following initial resistance[175] with regard to the installation of the first King of Israel, Saul. From this point on, Samuel endeavours to support the king in carrying out his duty. However, at a later point in time, with Saul having repeatedly acted against God's will, he is commissioned with the task of anointing David, Jesse's son, as his successor.

In terms of his calling as a prophet, Samuel falls between two different periods during which God took action in the story of Israel. His actions thus mark the transition into the Era of the Kings. Prior to his arrival, Judges ruled over the people – he himself is the first in

---

172   "The boy Samuel ministered before the LORD under Eli" (1 Sam 3:1).

173   1 Sam 7:2.

174   1 Sam 7:3ff.

175   1 Sam 8:6.

a series of prophetic leaders, who stand alongside the subsequent kings. At the end of his life he can look back on extraordinary faith and (almost) life-long service as a prophet[176], seer[177], priest[178] and judge[179] [180].

What is special about Samuel's communication with God?

Learning to listen means getting to know someone

Samuel is a fantastic example of how hearing and getting to know God happen simultaneously. Although Samuel grows up in the temple under a mentor who knows God and even serves as a priest, he does not know God personally. The stories of the God of Israel and their historical details regarding the priesthood are well known to him, yet he shows no sense of expectation that he will meet with God personally. He only knows God as a result of his ears having "heard of Him", as Job expresses it[181]. Irrespective of the apparent spirituality of his surroundings, he can only really begin his relationship with God once he has heard Him personally.

Small person – huge revelations

Very early on, Samuel's life is marked by hearing God's voice. Even as a child he hears groundbreaking revelations from God and passes them on[182]. This process continues throughout his youth. "The LORD was with Samuel as he grew up, and he let none of Samuel's words fall to the ground." (1 Sam 3:19 NIV). It is not his religious endeavours or long-term efforts, but rather obedience and mindfulness to God's voice that open up this favour to him. These are the attributes that he later accuses Saul of lacking: "What pleases

---

176   Acts 13:19.
177   1 Chr 29:29.
178   1 Sam 7:9ff.
179   1 Sam 7:15.
180   "As for me, I am old and grey, and my sons are here with you. I have been your leader from my youth until this day." (1 Sam 12:2 NIV).
181   Job 42:5.
182   1 Sam 3:10-18.

the LORD more: burnt offerings and sacrifices or *obedience to his voice*? It is better to *obey* than to sacrifice. It is better to *listen* to God than to offer the fat of sheep." (1 Sam 15:22 NCV, emphasis KR).

Awareness of his prophetic gifting

Samuel receives many direct orders from God and serves as His mouthpiece. He hears God when withdrawing to pray[183], but also spontaneously in his everyday life[184]. In so doing he develops an understanding of the fact that God speaks through him and that his word is God's word - in that God makes his words come to be true[185]. When Saul fails to adhere to *his* instructions, he confronts him with these words: "You have not kept the command the LORD your God gave you." (1 Sam 13:13 NIV). A statement such as this makes it clear how important he – quite rightly – considers his own work to be.

What can we learn from Samuel?

Are there any Samuels around me?

On reading the report of Samuel's first encounter with God, I see two groups of people described, who are represented by Samuel and Eli.

Samuel represents people who do not yet know Jesus personally. They are conscious of a longing for "more", but without being able to put a name to this "more", or their calling. Like Samuel, who, without knowing God personally, intuitively opts to sleep in close proximity to the Ark of the Covenant[186], they are searching and are fundamentally open to an encounter with God.

These people hear God's call, but they lack a meaningful framework for interpretation. They classify vivid dreams, blessed thoughts and encounters or other calls from God as

---

183 1 Sam 8:6; 8:22ff; 15:10; 15:16.

184 1 Sam 9:17; 15:27f;1 Sam 13:14.

185 1 Sam 3:19 – 4:1 NIV.

186 1 Sam 3:3.

being esoteric, emotional or coincidental occurrences. We can often even find people such as this in our church communities or on the fringes of these communities.

Eli represents people who have come to know Jesus and have a fundamental desire to serve him. However, as the result of the stagnation of their spirituality, they have resigned themselves to the notion that God only speaks to them personally on "rare"[187] occasions, or only talks to those around them. For them, following Jesus has by and large been reduced to following a set of rules, which they love to share with others who are interested in actually growing in faith. They don't mean any harm in this – it is simply difficult to lead people beyond our own spiritual experience. Because they are relatively satisfied with where they are, this group barely has any internal longing for 'more' of their own left at all.

MULL IT OVER: ARE THERE ANY SAMUELS AROUND ME?

God is in the practice of drawing the people around us to Himself and waits for Eli to realize what He is up to. Consider the following questions as you go about your everyday life and answer them there and then.

1. Do you think it is possible that there are "Samuels" among your colleagues, friends or acquaintances, who are living with a longing for "more", without being able to name what this "more" is? Who might these people be in your life?

2. Do you think it is possible that God repeatedly speaks to them, but they are lacking an interpretation for his call on account of your spiritual blindness? How can you become more aware of your responsibility towards these people?

3. Do you think it is possible that the "Samuels" around you have more significant callings than you and that your life is actually meant to serve as a springboard for them[188]? Are you willing to make other people successful?

---

187   1 Sam 3:1.

188   Barnabas is one of the many examples the Bible offers in this regard. On several occasions he assists Paul in fulfilling his calling, while himself remaining in the background (Acts 9:27f; 11:22ff; among others). For the purpose of answering our questions, it is worthwhile studying the effects of his ministry on Acts. It is not for nothing that the name Barnabas translates as: son of encouragement.

TEAM TALK: ARE THERE ANY SAMUELS AROUND ME?

1. Do you feel more like an Eli or a Samuel, or are you a mix of the two? Explain.

2. Questions for Samuels: What events in your life do you expect God to be speaking through? Attempt to describe the hidden longing you are experiencing.

3. Questions for Elis: Which people around you do you expect God is drawing towards Himself? Have you ever been able to "interpret" God's call for people? What happened? What tips can you give other "Elis" with regard to dealing with "Samuels"?

Unjustified grief as a trap

On account of his disobedience, God soon turns away from King Saul. Samuel prophesies to him: "But now your kingdom will not endure; the Lord has sought out a man after his own heart and appointed him ruler of his people, because you have not kept the Lord's command (...)." (1 Sam 13:14 NIV).

When Saul falls short once again, God confides in Samuel: "I regret that I have made Saul king, because he has turned away from me and has not carried out my instructions." (1 Sam 15:10 NIV).

Samuel is deeply saddened by this and spends the entire night interceding on behalf of Saul, asking God to change His mind, although this is ultimately in vain. It remains unclear whether it is concern for his people, personal sympathy for Saul or his own limited knowledge of God that is the reasoning behind this prayer – in any case Samuel falls into a grief regarding Saul's progression that is not desired by God[189]. This continues on to the extent that God rebukes him: "The Lord said to Samuel, "How long will *you* mourn for Saul, since *I* have rejected him as king over Israel?" (1 Sam 16:1 NIV, emphasis KR).

His mourning, which was contrary to God's will, has two nasty consequences. Firstly, Samuel falls victim to the same bondage as Saul – fear of man[190]. He begins to fear Saul more than God and responds to Gods instruction to anoint a new king as follows:

---

189   1 Sam 15:35.

190   1 Sam 10:27; 1 Sam 13:7ff; 1 Sam 15:24; among others.

"(...) If Saul hears about it he will kill me." (1 Sam 16:2 NIV). Secondly, he places limitations on his prophetic vision. This is evident when the new king is being called, and he makes a very human snap judgement. "When they arrived, Samuel saw Eliab and thought, "Surely the LORD's anointed stands here before the LORD." But the LORD said to Samuel, "Do not consider his appearance or his height, for I have rejected him. The LORD does not look at the things people look at. *People look at the outward appearance, but the LORD looks at the heart."* (1 Sam 16:6 - 7 NIV, emphasis KR).

Fear of man and unclear prophetic vision have up until this point been completely unheard of in the life of the prophet. We can see how the human tendency to hold onto circumstances or people that God has "let go of" can distance us from God. This is a vital lesson, in particular for those of us whose main calling lies in the area of intercession, and is something that we must come to understand. If, in exercising our God-given gift, we pray outside of the will of God, we are engaging in manipulation – or to be precise, witchcraft.

MULL IT OVER: UNJUSTIFIED GRIEF AS A TRAP.

Are there "kings that have been rejected by God" (these can be people or situations) in your life that you are holding onto? Ask the Holy Spirit to bring revelation. Give yourself to God and ask Him to show you which new kings (new blessings) He wants to give you in their place.

Here is a prayer that may help you: *Dad, today I am letting go of .... Please forgive me for holding on. Show me what You want to give me in its place. Whenever you close a window to me, you open up a door – thank you for your faithfulness!*

Share what has happened with someone you trust and ask them to check in on how things are going in 2-4 weeks.

TEAM TALK: UNJUSTIFIED GRIEF AS A TRAP.

Discuss among yourselves: Have you ever had intensive contact with someone who willingly lives removed from God and been infected by their behaviour? What happened? How did you get free? What were you able to learn?

Chapter 8

Characters of the New Testament

Jesus and his Father's voice

*"In the past God **spoke** to our ancestors through the prophets at many times and **in various ways**, [2] but in these last days **he has spoken to us by his Son**. (…)The Son is the radiance of God's glory and the exact representation of his being."*[191]

*"**The Word** became flesh and made his dwelling among us. We have seen his glory, the glory of the one and only Son, who came from the Father, full of grace and truth."*[192]

Although God has always spoken in "various ways" to his children, in Jesus we experience an entirely new quality to His voice: Jesus not only brings God's word, but he is God's word

---

191   Heb 1:1–3 NIV, emphasis KR.

192   John 1:14 NIV emphasis KR.

become flesh. Everything that God ever wanted to say to us is apparent in his person. Jesus' life, action and ministry are the Father's voice talking to the world. Jesus is the perfect expression of the invisible God. Jesus is his Father's voice. He and the Father are one.

If we wish to examine the person of Jesus and his life in relation to God's voice, we are setting off on a multi-faceted journey through time.

We can see that since the beginning of time, God has been speaking to man in anticipation of the arrival of Jesus, thus preparing the way for him.

It also becomes clear that during his life on Earth, Jesus heard his Father on a daily basis and lived by following the direction of His voice.

Even following Christ's ascension, God continues to talk about Jesus, announcing through His *Word*, His *Spirit* and His *church*, that Jesus will come again[193].

Jesus is the central event in the cosmos[194] – he is God revealed! Jesus hears God perfectly and at the same time is God's perfect voice. As a consequence, John calls Jesus THE WORD of the Father spoken to us[195]. He is, as it were, the "God-hearing Word of God".

God talking about Jesus' coming

God prepared for the arrival of Jesus through prophetic clues, which permeate the Old Testament like a hidden map. The 300 or so verses, if viewed individually, seem like hints in a large puzzle. For this reason it is as yet unclear how complete the individual writers' understanding of the life of Jesus was. However, if you piece these references together, like tiles in a mosaic, they produce a wonderful, prophetic image of the coming and the mission of Jesus.

---

193   "The Spirit and the Bride say: Come." (Rev 22:17 NIV).
194   See Col 1:16.
195   John 1:1ff.

Examples

David prophesied the death of Jesus in astonishing detail around 1,000 B.C. "My mouth is dried up like a potsherd; (…) and my tongue sticks to the roof of my mouth; (…) a pack of villains encircles me. They pierce my hands and my feet. All my bones are on display; people stare and gloat over me. They divide my clothes among them and cast lots for my garment." (Ps 22:15 – 19).

In around the year 700 B.C. Isaiah writes of Jesus' mission and life. He speaks of the crucifixion and provides an advance summary of the entire gospel. "He was despised and rejected by mankind, a man of suffering, and familiar with pain. Like one from whom people hide their faces he was despised, and we held him in low esteem. Surely he took up our pain and bore our suffering, yet we considered him punished by God, stricken by him, and afflicted. But he was pierced for our transgressions, he was crushed for our iniquities, the punishment that brought us peace was on him, and by his wounds we are healed." (Is 53:3–5 NIV).

In the New Testament two writers refer back to the Isaiah quotation and declare it to have been fulfilled. "When evening came, many who were demon-possessed were brought to him, and he drove out the spirits with a word and healed all the sick. This was to fulfil what was spoken through the prophet Isaiah: "He took up our infirmities and bore our diseases." " (Matt 8:16–17 NIV).

" "He himself bore our sins" in his body on the cross, so that we might die to sins and live for righteousness; "by his wounds you have been healed." " (1 Pet 2:24 NIV).

Below, I consider God speaking about and to Jesus in detail. Wherever we can recognise God's voice speaking directly or indirectly, I have marked it in *italics* in the text.

God's voice speaking during Jesus' conception and birth

Jesus' conception is prepared for, accompanied and confirmed by God's voice. The angel Gabriel appears to Mary with the *message* that she will fall pregnant as a result of the work of the Holy Spirit and will give birth to God's son. The fact that her relative Elisabeth had recently fallen pregnant is remarked on by the angel as a means of *confirmation*[196] from God. During a visit, Elisabeth gives Mary a personal, *prophetic confirmation* regarding her role and the lawfulness of her pregnancy. However, it is not just to Mary and Elizabeth that God speaks concerning Jesus. When Joseph, her fiancé, notices that Mary has fallen pregnant without his involvement, he decides to break off the engagement – however, he intends to do so in secret, so as not to endanger Mary[197]. As a result, God *speaks* to him *in a dream, through an angel.* The angel explains that God himself is the father of the child and instructs Joseph not to leave Mary.

Jesus' birth is symbolically *foreseen in foreign lands* and is *announced by angels.* God *speaks* through a "rising star", which is interpreted by "astrologers" as a sign of the birth of a king. They come to Jerusalem, ask around as to where the recently born "King of the Jews" can be found, and as such bring the town into a state of excitement[198]. Luke also reports of how an *angel* appears to a group of shepherds and *informs*[199] them of the birth of the Messiah. An entire *host of angels* then appears to the shepherds, worshipping God and *prophesying* of Jesus' calling. When Joseph and Mary want to dedicate Jesus to God in the temple, Simeon *prophesies* openly about him, referring to him as the "Salvation of the People" and "Light of the Nations". Hannah, *a prophetess, agrees with Simeon's statement*[200].

---

196   Luke 1:36.

197   Adultery could result in stoning or at least public condemnation.

198   Matt 2:1-7.

199   Luke 2:8ff.

200   Luke 2:25ff.

God's voice speaking at the baptism of Jesus

When he is baptised, Jesus not only begins his public ministry, but also begins hearing his Father on a new level. This is initiated by the *audible voice of God*, heard by all those in attendance during his baptism, and by the *permanent touch* of the Holy Spirit. "(…) and the Holy Spirit descended on him in bodily form like a dove. And a voice came from heaven: "You are my Son, whom I love; with you I am well pleased." (Luke 3:22 NIV).

Through these interactions, Jesus receives the fundamental building blocks for his identity as the Son of God. His entire ministry, mindset and being flow from the powerful *affirmation* of his Father. These building blocks can be understood as follows: The continuing presence of the Holy Spirit *speaks* significant calling over Jesus[201]. The Father invests himself in Jesus, indicating that He wants to be with Jesus and believes in him. The act of publicly *addressing him as son* contains another assurance. It establishes his worth and points to his future – as son, he will be his Father's heir! The confirmation of the Father's love comes before Jesus begins his ministry, and is thus issued regardless of his subsequent life decisions and without condition.

God's voice and Jesus' temptation

We find out how dramatically important hearing God's voice is for Jesus when he is being tempted by the devil. The devil's aim is to call *God's word* into question. His three temptations attempt to call into question who Jesus should listen to, and consequently follow. To Jesus himself, this is clear. He understands that submission to the voice of God forms the basis for his sonship and his coming rule[202]. Jesus is followed by this voice immediately after his baptism, as the Spirit leads him into the desert[203]. Even though, after forty days of fasting, Jesus is hungry, his longing is not for food, but rather for God's voice. His response to the first temptation makes this clear. "The tempter came to him and said, "If you are the Son of God, tell these stones to become bread." Jesus answered, "It is

---

201   In Luke 4:18 the presence of the Holy Spirit falls on Jesus as a sign of his calling.

202   For those who are led by the Spirit of God are the children of God (Rom 8:14).

203   Matt 4:1.

written: 'Man shall not live on bread alone, *but on every word that comes from the mouth of God.*'" " (Matt 4:3–4 NIV, emphasis KR).

The devil is not preoccupied with getting Jesus to eat, but instead sets about trying to cast doubt over the words of the Father spoken to Jesus at his baptism. This is the same tactic that he successfully used to entice Eve to follow his voice instead of God's[204]. So, too, for Eve, it was not the eating of the fruit that fractured her relationship with God, but rather the decision to follow another voice. The fruit in itself was not holy or sacrosanct, but God's command was[205].

In contrast to Adam and Eve's disobedience towards God's voice in the garden, in the desert Jesus is obedient. His Father's promise guides him on. He waits on this guidance and is not willing to accept the guidance of another. However, this also means that he must learn to wait on God's voice and to trust in His guidance. This is the true test in the wilderness.

God's voice speaking to Jesus in the everyday

After this, we again see how Jesus lived in full dependency on communication with his Father. Jesus himself states this as the reason why he is able to do the work of his Father and to remain in a loving relationship with Him. "(...) Very truly I tell you, the Son can do nothing by himself; he can do only what he sees his Father doing, because whatever the Father does the Son also does. For the Father loves the Son and shows him all he does." (John 5:19–20 NIV).

What sets Jesus apart and makes him different from all other spiritual leaders of his day is not his knowledge of the Holy Scriptures or his ability to draw a crowd or perform miracles. It is the fact that he is guided directly by the Spirit of God. This enables him to act exactly as God Himself acts. God's guiding word is always within him. His action is identical to that of the Father – and therefore God gives him everything he asks for. Jesus also identifies this "connected life of hearing" for us as a basic premise for discipleship.

---

204   "Did God really say...?" (Gen 3:1).

205   God *is* His word – if I decide to go against His word, I am deciding to go against Him.

"If you remain in me and *my words* remain in you, ask whatever you wish, and it will be done for you." (John 15:7 NIV, emphasis KR).

In addition to continually listening to the Father on an everyday basis, there are one or two instances in Jesus' life that stand out in particular when it comes to hearing God's voice. Similarly to his baptism, when on the mount of the transfiguration, he and his friends together hear the audible voice of the Father. "While he was still speaking, a bright cloud covered them, and a voice from the cloud said, "This is my Son, whom I love; with him I am well pleased. Listen to him!" (Matt 17:5 NIV).

On top of this, the long-since deceased Moses and Elijah appear and *speak* with Jesus about his death and confirm his commission[206]. On another occasion the Father *speaks* to Jesus in the midst of a large crowd, and is audible to all present[207]. Another incisive instance of God speaking takes place in the Garden of Gethsemane *through an angel*, who bestows strength upon Jesus. Here, in his darkest hour, Jesus asks God directly as to His will for what lies ahead. Jesus' being fill with strength by the angel appears necessary and constitutes affirmation from the Father with regard to his mission. God's empowerment is his means of communication. " "Father, if you are willing, take this cup from me; yet not my will, but yours be done." An angel from heaven appeared to him and strengthened him." (Luke 22:42–43 NIV).

The voice of God in Acts

Acts provides us with insight into the lives of the apostles, the so-called "early church", and the first Christians. God speaking and the hearing of His voice play a vital role for all three groups. With Jesus having gone to be with the Father, the New Testament having not yet been written and dogma not yet having been developed, the believers find themselves living in utter dependency on their ability to hear God's voice directly through the Holy Spirit – they have nothing else[208]! The spiritual dynamic that the first Christians experience

---

206   Luke 9:30.
207   John 12:28ff.
208   First was the Word, then the book!

without the canon of the Bible or sophisticated spiritual growth programmes and dogmatic theology is impressive. The realisation that we can expect to be guided directly by God is one of the great lessons that the Book of Acts has to offer.

The heart of the commission

The reports in the Book of Acts begin with Jesus setting out the action plan for his followers. He is just about to ascend to be with his Father. In his final words he once again summarises what the disciples must prepare for. To this day, these words are seminal for all of his followers. You "will receive power when the Holy Spirit comes on you; and *you will be my witnesses* in Jerusalem, and in all Judea and Samaria, and to the ends of the earth." (Acts 1:8 NIV, emphasis KR).

His statement includes three answers to three questions that are presumably being asked by his disciples:

1. What should we do now? Bear witness to me!
2. How should we do it? Through the power of the Holy Spirit!
3. Where should we do it? First locally, then everywhere!

The statement: "you will be my witnesses" is central to Jesus' final, great commission. But what does Jesus mean by this? How exactly should we be witnesses? In order to understand this statement better, we must place it in the context of his life.

Jesus came to be a witness for his Father[209]. In order to accomplish this, he doesn't formulate his own thoughts into words, but rather speaks the words that the Father places in his mouth. "So whatever I say is just what the Father has told me to say." (John 12:50 NIV).

Jesus makes it clear to his disciples that he is sending them, *as* he himself has been sent. "*As* the Father has sent me, I am sending you." (John 20:21 NIV, emphasis KR). So the disciples should not go as witnesses of their own accord, in their own strength or by their own conviction, but should instead let themselves be guided and empowered by the Spirit of the Father.

---

209   John 3:16.

"You will be my witnesses" can thus be understood as a promise issued by Jesus, that the Father will act through the disciples. In order to be witnesses they should say what He says, go where He goes, and do what they see Him do. To be a witness for Jesus doesn't mean offering forward their best arguments in order to *convince* people, but rather to simply let God speak. The reports in the Book of Acts address this; God's voice speaking through the first followers of Jesus, "in Jerusalem, and in all Judea and Samaria, and to the ends of the earth", more specifically.

Hunting for signs of His voice in Acts

Below I will work my way through the book of Acts and will attempt to draw up a "map" plotting instances of God's voice spoken into the lives of the first Christians. In so doing I will note the passages in which God's voice is particularly evident. That said, it is only on rare occasions that God "speaks" audibly or with words. God "speaks" by revealing facts (as at Pentecost), by transforming people's character (as with Saul[210]), through angels, visions and through internal revelation, to name but a few examples.

In particular, I hope to show how God's voice can be heard *indirectly* in the reports found in the book of Acts. I intend to make clear how His voice – audibly and indirectly – serves as a *tool* with which to guide and transform the first followers of Jesus.

Wherever we can recognise God's voice speaking directly or indirectly, I have marked it in *italics* in the text.

Acts 1 – 2

After Jesus ascends into heaven, the disconcerted apostles are left "...staring after him..." (1:9, TLB). God relieves them from this uncomfortable posture and *speaks* through two angels, who appear to them and issue further instructions (1:10). God then *speaks* through the symbols of tongues of fire, storms and spiritual drunkenness (2:2ff). God very publically identifies those who belong to him - His supernatural touch and empowerment are a *message* to the entire city. Peter declares to those present that the event is God's fulfilment

---

210   Acst 9:21.

of the long since promised filling with His Spirit (2:14ff). At the same time, the Holy Spirit *speaks* by bestowing the gift of tongues upon the believers, who address those who happen also to be present. All of the foreigners who are there can hear and understand them, thus receiving an explanation of what God is doing in their own native language (2:5ff). As the early church is forming, God *speaks* to those outside the church through their lifestyle. Their love for one another, their willingness to help and the miracles that take place have a strong impact (2:42ff). We read of the reaction of those around them: "The whole city was favourable to them, and each day God added to them all who were being saved, (...)" (2:47, TLB).

Acts 3 – 4

During a visit to the temple, Peter heals a man who "was lame from birth" (3:2). When he begins to tell of Jesus, he and John are seized by the temple guard. When they are then interrogated by the High Council, God *speaks* to their accusers through the two apostles' supernatural fearlessness and knowledge of scripture. We read that "when they saw the courage of Peter and John and realized that they were unschooled, ordinary men, they were astonished and they took note that these men had been with Jesus" (4:13).

Acts 5

As the life of the early church takes form, Ananias and Saphira are deceitful, in that they make false statements regarding a donation (5:1ff). The Holy Spirit *reveals* the deceit to the apostle Peter, who confronts the married couple. Because they do not repent, the pair consequently die one shortly after the other, as the result of a divine judgement. The judgement dealt out by God is deemed by the church and all those who heard of it as a *strong word from God*. "Great fear seized the whole church, (...)" (5:11). We then read of how God *attests* to the apostles' message, in that he enables "many signs and wonders" to take place through them (5:12). Full of envy, the Jewish religious leaders imprison the apostles. However, in the night they are freed by an angel. Through this event *God speaks to them* and once again *confirms* their commission. The angel instructs them: "(...) tell the people all about this new life" (5:20).

Acts 6 – 7

Due to the huge growth of the church, seven additional leaders are appointed. One of them is Stephen. Because God acts through him very powerfully, he experiences particular resistance and is ultimately stoned. During the trial that precedes his execution, he is entitled to defend himself. With all eyes fixed on him, *God speaks to his accusers,* by lighting up Stephen's face, "(...) like the face of an angel" (6:15 NIV). At the end of his long and detailed defence *the Holy Spirit speaks to him through an open vision.* He sees heaven open and Jesus standing at the right hand of God. This image *speaks* of the supremacy of Jesus and succinctly summarises his extensive sermon (7:55).

Acts 8

On a missions trip to Samaria *the Holy Spirit speaks to Peter* about the false motives of Simon the Sorcerer and in so doing reveals his divided loyalties (8:18ff). God *speaks* to the evangelist Philip through an angel and instructs him to take an isolated desert road. There he meets an official of the Ethiopian queen. The Holy Spirit *instructs Philip* to draw near to him. As a result he is able to deliver the message of Jesus to the official, and he is baptised (8:26ff).

Acts 9 – 10

The following chapters are largely dedicated to the life and ministry of Paul. His conversion begins with Jesus *speaking to him personally and audibly* while journeying to Damascus. Those accompanying him do not hear Jesus' voice, *although they do see the bright light* and are rendered "speechless" (9:3ff, 22:9). Dazzled by the light, Paul is blind for three days, and does not eat or drink. *Through his three-day spell of blindness, God gives Paul two important messages*: through the physical, he reveals to him his spiritual blindness[211]. In addition to this, Paul endures three days of total fasting, and the darkness that is symbolic the three days following Jesus' death. As Paul is led, blind, to Damascus, *God speaks to a disciple* in the city (Ananias). He instructs him to heal Paul and to *reveal* to him important

---

211   "Jesus said, "I came into this world so that the world could be judged. I came so that the blind would see and so that those who see will become blind." (John 9:39 NIV).

details regarding his future. When Ananias carries out this instruction, *God confirms His message,* in that Paul is filled with His Spirit.

Likewise when planting the first churches with a view to spreading the gospel among the gentiles, the voice of God plays an important role. *God speaks through an angel* to the Roman centurion Cornelius and commands him to invite Peter into his home (10:3ff). Shortly before Cornelius' messengers reach him, *God speaks to Peter regarding His plans* through *an open vision and His audible voice.* As Peter reflects on what exactly this vision might mean, *the Holy Spirit speaks directly to him.* He informs him of the messengers and instructs him to follow them without worrying (10:9ff). As Peter shares the gospel in the home of Cornelius, *God confirms the message* in that the Holy Spirit falls on those listening in the same way as He fell on the disciples at Pentecost[212] (9:44).

Acts 11

Once back in Jerusalem, when Peter is obliged to justify his visit to Cornelius, he is scrutinised critically. However, when he reports back concerning the pouring out of the Spirit of God, the apostles see in this a *clear declaration from God* regarding the acceptance of the gentiles (11:18).

Following on from this, God then works so powerfully amongst the gentiles in Antioch that "a large group of people" (11:21) decide to follow Jesus. *In this way, God confirms what He had said before.*

Antioch thus develops into a spiritual centre. A number of prophets from Jerusalem (among them Agabus) visit the church. *Through Agabus, the Holy Spirit announces* a coming famine. Guided *by this word from God* the disciples make preparations for the crisis (11:27ff).

Acts 12

At around this time, King Herod begins persecuting the church in Jerusalem. Peter is imprisoned, but *God speaks to him through an angel* and frees him (12:11f). A short time later *God speaks judgement over Herod,* by striking him down with illness via "an angel of the Lord" (12:23).

---

212   Cf. Acts 11:15.

Acts 13

Following the visit of the prophets from Jerusalem, the church in Antioch themselves produce a series of prophets. *The Holy Spirit speaks* – presumably through them – to the leaders instructing them to send out Paul and Barnabas to fulfil their calling (13:1ff). In Paphos the pair encounter the magician and false prophet Bar-Jesus, who was attempting to prevent the proconsul in office there from coming to faith. *God delivers a sign of judgement through Paul,* which leaves Bar-Jesus blind for a period of time. The proconsul views the sign *as the voice of God and as confirmation of the message* that Paul brings, and subsequently comes to faith (13:11ff).

Acts 14 – 15

As they continue their travels, Paul and Barnabas reach Iconium. *Here God confirms their message* "by giving them the power to work miracles and signs" (14:3). After Paul and Barnabas have returned home, a discussion develops with some Pharisees who are followers of Jesus regarding the extent to which the newly converted non-Jewish disciples must follow the "Law of Moses". *God's blessings shown* to them, which happened without them having been circumcised or knowing the Mosaic Law, *are viewed by the gathered leaders as the voice of God* (15:4ff).

Acts 16 – 18

On his second missionary trip Paul is accompanied by Timothy. *God speaks to the pair by preventing them* from travelling on their initially planned route. As they travel on, *the Holy Spirit again speaks to them, telling them to avoid the destination they now plan to head to.* With God having now twice made it clear that he doesn't want them to go there, *he speaks to Paul through a vision in the night* concerning His will. Paul sees before him a Macedonian, who asks him for help. They immediately head for this region, convinced that God Himself *"has called them through this vision"* (16:6ff). On his travels Paul comes to Corinth. *There God speaks to him in a vision at night,* revealing to him His plans for the city and asking him to be fearless (18:9f).

Acts 19 – 28

On his third missionary journey Paul stays on in Ephesus. *God speaks in confirmation of Paul's message*, in that He performs "extraordinary miracles through Paul" (19:11). After further stop-offs, Paul makes his way back to Jerusalem. God continually *speaks* "in every city" (20:23) that he comes to regarding his impending suffering. When Paul meets with leaders of the church in Ephesus, *he prophesies to them of the coming of false teachers*, who will damage the churches following his departure. *God thus encourages them* to be vigilant (20:28ff). Paul travels on via Tyre. Here he discovers *that the Holy Spirit is speaking to the disciples about the problems he will soon face.* Whereas the disciples view the revelation they have received as a warning, Paul sees *in this word from God a further confirmation* of His will, and travels on undisturbed (21:4ff). In Caesarea he meets up with the prophet Agabus. *God also speaks through the prophet* regarding Paul's future suffering. Again Paul receives this prophetic word as affirmative, although others attempt to dissuade him from his final destination (21:10ff). On arriving in Jerusalem, Paul is actually arrested, as a crowd which has become violent attempts to kill him. The soldiers arresting him do, however, allow him to state his defence. In pleading his case, he tells of *how Jesus spoke to him in a vision* and commissioned him to preach to the gentiles (22:1ff). This statement causes a huge commotion and Paul is locked up by the soldiers. During his second night in prison *Jesus visits him personally and speaks to him.* He encourages him to be strong and courageous as his witness *and prophesies that he will also do so in Rome* (23:11). Following a period of imprisonment lasting at least two years, Paul is allowed to defend himself before the Emperor in Rome. The journey to Rome by ship is slow going on account of the weather and they are required to wait out the winter in a port. *God speaks to Paul* regarding "great dangers" facing the ship, the cargo and crew, but nonetheless the journey is to go ahead (27:10). His warnings fall on deaf ears. As the ship sets off again it is met with a terrible storm which renders it unable to manoeuvre. After several days battling the storm *God speaks to Paul at night, through an angel,* providing him with courage and issuing further instructions (27:23).

What can we learn from the first followers of Christ?

Becoming God's voice as a result of listening to Him

Just as the believers live out of the practice of hearing from God, they themselves become the voice of God within their environments. We read of how the people in Jerusalem are "(...) filled with awe" (Acts 2:43) at the miracles and at what they see in the life of the church community. As a result of their lifestyle they receive "the favour of all the people" (2:47). The subsequent and public realisation of God's will is like a sermon delivered to the entire city.

TEAM TALK: BECOMING GOD'S VOICE AS A RESULT OF LISTENING TO HIM.

God wants us to be His voice and not merely an echo.

1. What is the difference between "being God's voice" and "being His echo"?
2. Discuss among yourselves: In which areas of your life are you "His word", and where do you merely quote His Word? Where is the difference clear?
3. Attempt to describe the process of "becoming His word" in individual areas of your life.

Perseverance in listening to God

God speaking to the disciples is a common theme that permeates the book of Acts. Everything the first followers of Jesus do, they do prompted by the voice of God. However, because His word is often revealed in stages, they must at the same time be open to further revelation. It is often the case that this only comes when they begin to obey what God has already said. The first followers of Jesus do not need to understand God fully before they respond to His voice. We see this, for instance, in the sending of Peter to Cornelius and in the sending of Philip to the Egyptian official.

TEAM TALK: PERSERVERENCE IN LISTENING TO GOD.

1. Discuss among yourselves: How willing are you to remain faithful in following what you have heard from God, without having to grasp His message in its entirety?

2. In what areas are you currently finding it difficult to act faithfully due to only having a partial revelation? Share your thoughts with one another and ask God for breakthroughs regarding revelation in these areas.

3. Where have you found that faith in the small things has enabled you to receive greater things? What did this process look like? What were you able to learn?

Listening together

The leaders in Jerusalem also reflect together in order to deduce God's voice from the knowledge revealed to them. This is evident in the discussion regarding the Mosaic Law and the gentiles. They describe their findings and the process adopted in a co-written letter. "So *we all agreed...*" (15:25). "It seemed good *to the Holy Spirit and to us* not to burden you with anything beyond the following requirements..." (15:28). Their understanding of God's will in this matter is something they reach together.

MULL IT OVER: LISTENING TOGETHER.

Do you ever feel of lesser value because you require help from others in order to understand what God is saying to you? Rethink your attitude and stop feeling too ashamed to accept help. Who around you could help you to understand what God is saying to you?

Acting while listening

Whenever Paul cannot hear clearly where God is leading him, he follows the route that seems most probable to him, and at the same time is willing to be corrected by God. We see this on his second missionary journey, in that he alters his route twice. Twice he sets off on a specific course and then allows the Holy Spirit to dissuade him from continuing along the chosen path. He finally hears God clearly in a vision. Paul acts while listening, he seeks God's guidance and is also willing to hear the word "No" from the Holy Spirit.

TEAM TALK: ACTING WHILE LISTENING.

Has God ever told you "no" when you have chosen a certain path? Did you set off down this path anyway or were you obedient? How did you hear His "no"? What happened in the end? What were you able to learn?

Getting to know God while listening

The first followers of Jesus do not put themselves forward as experts in the matters of God, but rather as people who are in the process of getting to know Him. They continually seek God's guidance, showing humility rather than just jumping in with both feet. We see this when God speaks to Peter regarding the "purity" of the non-Jewish peoples[213] or when God speaks to Paul in the desert during his "conversion"[214].

MULL IT OVER: GETTING TO KNOW GOD WHILE LISTENING.

Every time God speaks to you, it should deepen your knowledge of who He is.

1. What are the last things God said to you[215]? If nothing comes to mind, ask the Holy Spirit to remind you.

2. What can you learn from the last instance when God prompted you to engage with learning more about who He is?

TEAM TALK: GETTING TO KNOW GOD WHILE LISTENING.

1. Study the steps that Peter took to better understand God's revelation. Start by reading Acts 10:10-25; Acts 10:44; Acts 11:4ff.

2. Study the steps Paul took to better understand what God was doing in his life. Start by reading Acts 9:3ff; Acts 22:6ff; Acts 26:12ff.

3. What conclusions can you draw from these two stories with regard to your own journey with Jesus?

---

213   Acts 10:10ff.

214   Acts 9:3ff.

215   Consider this: God also speaks indirectly through events, people, thoughts etc.

3RD MOVEMENT – CREDO

THE 'DOCTRINE' OF LEARNING TO HEAR

Chapter 9

Learning how to learn to hear

*"Everyone who has heard the Father and **learned** from him comes to me."*[216]

*"Take my yoke upon you and **learn** from me, for I am gentle and humble in heart, and you will find rest for your souls."*[217]

A fiasco and a game-changing word

At the beginning of the 1990s, shortly after the formation of the Jesus Freaks in Hamburg, our band was asked to play a concert somewhere in the south of Germany, supporting the band 'No-Longer-Music'. I still remember it well as the whole thing ended up being a complete fiasco: after weeks of practising and a ten-hour car journey, including a number of traffic jams, upon arriving at the venue we were informed that the concert was to be cancelled. There were only fifteen people there, including the musicians!

---

216 John 6:45 NIV, emphasis KR.
217 Matt 11:29 NIV, emphasis KR.

After a few bitter tears we decided to spend the evening with David Pierce and his band. They had just toured Mongolia and had plenty of stories to tell. One of the band members really stood out to me: he looked like a blonde version of William Wallace from the film Braveheart[218], but with even more muscles and tattoos! They called him Rocky (BAM!). It was rumoured that during the concerts in Mongolia he was always responsible for keeping the stage "free from demons". Although I couldn't really figure out what that was meant to mean, I took the stories on their word. During the course of the evening I asked him to pray for me[219] and in so doing was hoping I would receive a few "prophetic words". Once we had chatted for a while and the time came for his 'powerful prayer', he just said to me: "Kristian, every child of God must at some point **learn** to hear God for themselves, and to take responsibility for what they hear – for you this is that time!" This was not the cosy prayer or the promising prophetic word that I had expected. Still, deep down I knew that God had spoken. Rocky's instruction, "learn to hear God for yourself!" was exactly what I had needed. I knew: if I took this seriously, I would become like Rocky – or even better: I would be like Jesus!

Around 15 years later I experienced the story from the other side, with Eva. I had meet Eva several times before at church events; she generally seemed somewhat depressed. Every time we spoke she would ask me for an encouraging word from God. On this occasion, things went differently. I felt that inner prompting from Jesus: "Just tell her that she can hear me herself and that she should begin to trust her heart – she hears me in her heart." As I shared my thoughts, Eva did not hide her disappointment. I found this quite an awkward moment – I didn't want to disappoint, but I had to hold true to what God had told me.

A few months later I bumped into Eva once again. She seemed more self-confident and wasn't so sad any more – I believe she took God up on His invitation to personal encounter.

---

218   A film about the Scottish freedom fighter William Wallace, with Mel Gibson playing the lead.
219   See 2 Tim 1:6.

I have never heard God before...

A number of years ago, a friend who had known Jesus for quite some time complained to me with these words: "I have never heard God before!" He was frustrated that he had never before heard God, whereas I – as far as he was concerned – always heard God. I encouraged him to ask himself a few questions (see 'Mull it over') and proposed that over the next few days I would ask God to make Himself heard.

A few days later he came up to me, beaming with joy: "I now know that God speaks to me and I also know how He does it! It is this quiet, tiny little voice in my head – I hear it all the time, but I had always thought it was just my own thoughts."

I was surprised and delighted – a quiet, tiny little voice – did I hear God this way too? As I began to ponder this, it became clear to me that I too knew this voice – in exactly the same way, I too had taken it to be my own thoughts (how thoughtless!). That day we both learned to hear God better[220].

I meet followers of Jesus all the time who say that they don't hear God or even that they have never heard Him at all. These paradoxical statements can be explained in various ways.

Scenario 1: The person has actually never noticed God speaking to them personally. However, this also means that, contrary to what they themselves say, they do not know God "personally", but merely as a concept. Following Jesus does not mean copying the life of Jesus, but instead means allowing ourselves to be guided by the Father, as Jesus did. In short: hearing God and responding positively.

If we have not yet heard God personally, the information at our disposal may, however, lead us to believe that we do know Him[221]. If we bite into a piece of chocolate, the experience is extremely different to having mere knowledge of the ingredients. God is love[222].

---

220 Nowadays God speaks to me regularly using this soft, inner voice – especially when quick, intuitive decisions are required. I then ask a question, and often before I have fully thought this through, a small, quiet impulse hits me, prompting me in a certain direction. Many of my friends also hear from God in this way.

221 "But knowledge puffs up while love builds up (...)" (1 Cor 8:1 NIV).

222 1 John 4:16.

Love cannot be theoretically grasped, you have to experience it. When we hear God *personally,* information becomes recognition.

Scenario 2: The person has come to know God, however, the relationship has been broken off again. A break in a relationship can take place abruptly or through a subtle process. In the first instance we actively block ourselves off to God's voice out of anger, disappointment or the like. This can be in the form of a public decision or an internal vow. In the event that this is by means of a more subtle process, this is generally as a result of lethargy, loss of community with other followers of Jesus or idolatry (e.g. relationships or hobbies), which render us deaf to God.

If we have not heard God for some time, we should ask ourselves honestly whether or not our relationship with Jesus still exists. A love relationship without active communication is an illusion.

Scenario 3: The person knows God, but has never learned to hear His voice as part of everyday life, or to differentiate it from other voices. If a follower of Jesus claims not to hear God, this is the most probable scenario.

Following implies a connection – one goes before, the other follows. One condition is that the follower is aware of the movements of the one he or she is following. Without listening, there is no following – without following one cannot be a disciple of Jesus. Learning to hear God's voice on a personal level is therefore a fundamental part of following Jesus, yet it is something that is not generally taught to an appropriate degree. A lack of role models for a lifestyle of listening is highly detrimental to our spiritual development.

MULL IT OVER: I HAVE NEVER HEARD GOD BEFORE.

1. If you are unsure as to whether you have ever heard God personally before, you can address the topic more closely by considering the following questions: Why did you start a relationship with Jesus? At the time, how did you become aware of God's offer of relationship? Which ways and means did He use to reveal Himself to you and attract your attention? Write down what comes to mind.

2. Consider whether the same "perceptions", "impulses" "coincidences", "encounters" etc. inspire you nowadays. You are now on the trail for traces of God's voice in your life!

My sheep hear my voice

"My sheep listen to my voice; I know them and they follow me."[223]
"Jesus says, "my sheep listen to my voice". Doesn't this mean that I can already hear him? Why do I still have to learn this?"

This is an objection that I often encounter when I teach about learning to hear God's voice. Here Jesus uses the image of a sheep as a metaphor for his followers. If we take Jesus' comment out of context, we could actually read into it that his followers *have to hear him*. However, if this were the case we would also have to accept that they *have no option but to follow him*; the text does say: "they follow me". If we read the Bible in this way, we neglect the relational aspect between ourselves and God. Here Jesus isn't talking about a compulsion, under which the sheep finds itself, but rather is describing an ability or lifestyle.

A real sheep is also required to learn to follow the shepherd's voice. A newborn lamb slowly gets to know the shepherd by living in the flock, learning to listen to him and to trust him. External influences – such as distraction by other sheep, a wolf, stormy weather, exhaustion or illness – affect its ability to hear the shepherd. Even a mature sheep can lose sight of the shepherd and as a result can no longer hear. In the parable of the lost sheep[224] Jesus tells of how one of 100 sheep is lost and the shepherd searches for it and finds it.

God wanted everything between us and Him to take place on the basis of free will. It is God's desire that we love Him in freedom, without being manipulated or pressured. Jesus releases us into this freedom[225]. However, due to the freedom promised to us, we come to hear God organically. The process by which we time and again open ourselves up and decide to hear God's voice is referred to as "learning". If God always forced us to listen to him, this would rob us of our freedom and thus of the dignity that He himself has promised us.

---

223   John 10:27 NIV.

224   See Luke 15.

225   "So if the Son sets you free, you will be free indeed" (John 8:36 NIV); "The Spirit of the Lord is on me, because he has anointed me (...) He has sent me to proclaim freedom for the prisoners." (Lk 4:18 NIV).

Learning to hear as a door-opener

Like everything we experience in our relationship with Him, "hearing God" is something that we have to learn. In the same way as we learn to love God, to trust Him or obey Him, we have to learn to recognise His voice and understand what He is saying. Of all the things that we learn with regard to God, hearing God has special meaning. It opens doors to other aspects of our relationship with God. In the same extent as we have been trained to hear and understand God, we are equipped to follow Him – that is, to love Him, to trust Him, to obey etc. This is because our discipleship always takes the form of a response to His revelation and invitation. Only when we hear and understand these can we follow Him.

For many followers of Jesus, the need to learn within their relationship with God is foreign to them. Two contrasting theological approaches are particularly opposed to the notion of learning.

An "only in heaven" theology

This approach assumes that God's "supernatural[226]" intervention can no longer be experienced today to the extent that it was in the times of the New Testament. In the corresponding Christian tradition, we find Jesus' life and his work of reconciliation are detached from one another. Emphasis is placed on the fact that Jesus died to pay man's debt 2,000 years ago and that we now have access to heaven through his death and resurrection. With this comes the call to emulate Jesus' historical example of what it is to be a good person, in so far as is humanly possible.

Taking Jesus' supernatural lifestyle, on the other hand, as a physical model for our everyday life is something that the majority of people who subscribe to this way of thinking reject. The coming of the rule of heaven[227] through signs and wonders in Jesus' life is presented as a myth or as something that we cannot imitate.

---

226   What even is "supernatural" in God's eyes.

227   Depending on the translation, this is referred to as the Kingdom of God, the Kingdom of Heaven, the Rule of God etc. See also Matt 13:38; Matt 13:25; Luke 9:2 and many others. The coming of the Rule of God is the fundamental message announced by Jesus.

Although taking a historical look at Jesus' ministry can be thoroughly inspiring, to emulate this ministry is, by and large, considered impossible. We feel unable, unworthy or insecure. As a result, Jesus' statement that the Holy Spirit wants to be our teacher[228] seems odd or is simply unknown to us. N. T. Wright writes: "So instead of suggesting that we could escape the earth to go to heaven, Jesus' good news was about heaven coming to earth. And there are many people inside and outside the church who have never heard this news."[229]

A theological approach such as this, which pushes God's rule back to "heavenly times", destroys our motivation to learn from the Holy Spirit on a daily basis. If our main purpose is "that we get into heaven", learning processes and striving to gain a better understanding of God during our life on Earth, while allowing Him to work through us, become meaningless.

An "I can do everything now" theology

The opposite theological extreme can have just as detrimental an effect on our learning. Through the spiritualisation of our earthly existence, we can become convinced that our growth once filled with the Holy Spirit is solely supernatural and happens automatically through God's miraculous works. We celebrate Bible passages such as "I can do all this through him who gives me strength"[230] or point out that His Spirit transforms us "from glory to glory"[231]. We have a high level of expectation that we will see God's powerful intervention in our lives. However, to a certain extent, in so doing we have a tendency to turn a blind eye to the part of our being that is distinctly human and to the dynamic that exists in our world. We view Christ's miraculous works in us and through us in a manner that is "detached from the world".

---

228 "But the Helper, the Holy Spirit, whom the Father will send in My name, He will teach you all things, and bring to your remembrance all things that I said to you." (John 14:26 NIV).

229 Simply Good News: Why The Gospel Is News and What Makes It Good. Harper Collins, 2015, P. 7.

230 Phil 4:13 NIV.

231 2 Cor 3:18 NKJV.

Understanding forms of growth

In the beginning, my journey of faith was characterised by the "I can do everything now" way of thinking. I got to know Jesus within the context of a period of revival in Hamburg. A short time later the Jesus Freaks were established in the city and over the course of several months I experienced God's power, answers to prayer, miracles and people being freed from bondage on an astonishing level. Because this was the only form of Christianity that I knew, I lived with huge expectation and was continually searching for the "next touch of God". I expected that, through miraculous works, God would simply take difficult character traits, fears, prejudices and other attitudes away from me. I viewed church meetings like a visit to a car workshop: "Let's see what Jesus will find and repair today!" I therefore often asked people to pray for me and responded to every appeal in every church service.

As a result of my continual openness, I experienced spectacular encounters with God. However, at the same time, due to my one-sided perspective, my expectation was met with frustration and doubt – especially when after around 36 months, the sense of awakening around me started to taper off.

I increasingly wondered why my transformation into Jesus' likeness was progressing so slowly, in spite of the fact that I was continually searching for him? Why were powerful prophetic words not fulfilled immediately? Why did I stumble across chasms of unbelief within myself, even though I was continually asking God to fill me more? Why did I experience spiritual highs, and yet could fail entirely just moments later? Too many questions remained unanswered, and I became increasingly aware of God prompting me to add another element to my spiritual life – process-based learning. I now understand that God was calling me into a new spiritual season[232].

Because I had experienced Jesus in a predominantly spontaneous and impulsive manner during the initial years after I came to faith, I found it difficult to follow His command to learn. Driven by the excitement of my awakening, everything had functioned wonderfully – why couldn't it continue in the same way?

---

232   In: Gebet als Begegnung (Prayer as a Place, HGM Publishing 2009), Grainpress 2012, Charles Bello and I write about how one manoeuvres between different spiritual seasons.

In order that I could better assess my situation, I began taking a closer look at the lives of the characters in the New Testament. I noticed that apostles also went through highs and lows. Even in the life of Jesus, spiritual high points were followed by times of withdrawal and orientation.

Through a parable, it became particularly clear to me that following Jesus also entailed continual learning and the willingness to go through various spiritual seasons.

"So every teacher of the law who has *been taught* about the kingdom of heaven is like the owner of a house. He brings out both new things and old things he has saved." (Matt 13:52 NIV, emphasis KR). Here Jesus describes his disciples as being capable of bringing both old and new things out of life's treasures. So these are people who are constantly learning new things "in the school of the Kingdom of Heaven", and are willing to live in a process of transformation.

Today I no longer understand my process of becoming like Christ[233] merely as a miraculous event, but also as a lifelong learning process. Alongside the expectation that God will spontaneously bless us with supernatural spiritual growth, I have become just as willing to spend my whole life learning from Him and with Him.

This duality is also visible in creation: you were created supernaturally, but now grow in the natural. All healthy organisms are continually *learning* how to adjust to their environment. This ability is written into their DNA by the Creator. In just the same way, our supernatural and our natural growth are initiated and made possible by God.

My personal transformation in Christ is thus more like a mystery than a mathematical equation: **sometimes** it is a learning process, in which I say 'yes' to who God is and begin to think like God. As this takes place I behave more like Him and am increasingly transformed into His likeness. **At other times** He supernaturally transforms me through a special encounter, which would have taken years if journeyed as a learning experience – or would not have been possible at all.

In practice, both often go hand in hand. While I have no influence on supernatural growth, I can drive the natural development forwards through my willingness to learn from life. For me, living as a lifelong learner means accepting responsibility for the gift of life that I have been given.

---

233   Cf. Romans 8: 28-29.

TEAM TALK: UNDERSTANDING FORMS OF GROWTH.

Are you aware that both spontaneous, supernaturally gifted growth and the ability to grow spiritually "in the natural" come from God?

1. Cf. Phil 2:13 and Matt 11:29. What can you learn from these two passages? Do any other Bible passages on spiritual growth come to mind? Which form of growth do you focus on?

2. Can you identify periods of both forms of growth in your life? What happened? What started your growth phase in each case?

3. What does the notion that God is asking you to be willing to receive growth "supernaturally" from Him trigger in you?

4. What does the notion that God is asking you to be willing to grow by means of "lifelong learning" trigger in you?

Understanding our capacity for learning as an expression of our dignity

The ability to learn is a characteristic of our God-given dignity. My transformation to become like Christ is not like some great magic trick performed by God, but instead comes as the result of teamwork.

Team Jesus

Helen grew up within a setting marked by domestic abuse. Her parents demanded absolute obedience and brutally punished any deviation from this. In her relationship with Jesus she was driven by the fear that she might disappoint God and be punished by Him. However, the mere thought of a loving relationship with God made her feel even more insecure – she would rather have heard clear commands from Him. In one of our conversations, Jesus asked me to tell her the following:

"Helen, my team is incomplete without you! Please come and play on my team. Sometimes I will feed you the ball, sometimes it will be your responsibility to initiate

156

the play. If we are a team this means that failures and successes are lamented and celebrated together. Commands are for immature people – you have accepted me as Lord and have become mature enough to play with me, in my team. My dear Helen, please join Team Jesus!"

To this day I am still unsure as to what extent Helen was able to take these words on board, however, expressing these thoughts aloud broke down a whole series of religious walls within me[234]. Team Jesus – that's the team I want to be part of!

The notion of teamwork with Jesus is something I find fascinating! God doesn't just want to act through me, but rather together with me. The reports in the Bible testify to this. As such, God asks Adam to name the animals He has created[235] and uses prophets as His messengers[236]. In the same way, Jesus sends his friends out to minister in his name[237].

In God's decision to accept me onto His team, it becomes clear that learning from Him is not a matter of giving up my free will[238]. My unique character would be lost through the simple deletion or reprogramming of my personality.

God wants me as a partner. I can accept His offer and learn to work alongside Him.

---

234   Astonishing! For this reason God's word is also compared with a *double-edged* sword" (Heb 4:12 NIV, emphasis KR). If I pass His word on, it has just as much an effect on me as it does on my counterpart.

235   Gen 2:19

236   Is 6:8; among others.

237   Luke 10ff.

238   If this does mean giving up my free will, how then can I still decide to follow Him.

Learning to hear as a lifestyle – God calls disciples, not experts

*"Jesus called his twelve **disciples** to him and gave them authority to drive out impure spirits and to heal every disease and sickness."*[239]

Our society is more interested in good results than good processes. We define "ability" as the goal of learning. A learning process is deemed successful if we are able to permanently apply what we have learnt.

However, if we apply this perspective to our relationship with God, the result may be that we increasingly come to perceive this relationship as substandard. In this life we will not achieve the perfect relationship with God, only ever really seeing and understanding God in the form of a "dim reflection"[240]. Living with God is not about establishing oneself as an expert, whether for a short or a long period of time, but is rather about living as a disciple[241].

What does it mean to be a disciple? The word disciple is the translation of the Greek word "mathetes", which simply means "learner". Jesus thus called people who were willing to learn from him to be his followers. Learning to hear the voice of God is first and foremost about the process of triggering increasing mindfulness and expectation within us. These two attitudes are our strongest catalysts to learning.

If we analyse learning in relation to our topic, it makes sense to differentiate between the factual and the relational. The factual refers to our practical knowledge. Processes such as cycling, cleaning one's teeth and opening beer bottles with a lighter, can be easily learned.

It is a slightly different case on the relational level. Although you can have theoretical knowledge as to how a relationship functions, practice often gives us a better understanding. We then proclaim in astonishment that we *hadn't* understood how the relationship

---

239   Matt 10:1 NIV, emphasis KR.

240   "It is the same with us. Now we see a dim reflection, as if we were looking into a mirror, but then we shall see clearly. Now I know only a part, but then I will know fully, as God has known me." (1 Cor 13:12 GNB).

241   The Pharisees, who in Jesus' time were considered religious experts, were often harshly rebuffed by Jesus!

actually functions! The difficulty in making reliable predictions within relationships lies in the unpredictable dynamic and complexity that characterises the relationship, and in the influence of other unknown factors. If we come into a relationship with fixed assumptions, it is incomprehensible to us when the relationship (or partner) doesn't behave as we expect. Whereas on the factual level the focus is on activities that take place within a predictable context, relationships turn out to be more like an Indiana Jones-style adventure[242].

The relational level covers, for example, the complex interaction of elementary components, interpersonal relationships and hearing the voice of God. Due to their unpredictable nature, topics such as this have the tendency to be out of our control, guiding us, teaching us and defining us. If we allow ourselves to enter into this relationship, it is (generally) in the knowledge that we will never master or understand it. If we accept that what we are doing exceeds the capacity of our understanding, the resulting "adventure" can help us to push beyond our own limitations.

Learning to hear the voice of God takes place on the basis of our growing love relationship with Him. Just like our relationship with Him on the whole, it should really be viewed as art rather than science. In art the focus is more on the emotional connection between the artist and his work, and the joint path that emerges, rather than on precise and correct results. In the same way, learning to hear God is about going on a journey that develops and forms us, and is not about instantly becoming the finished article.

New life, new learning

When we consider a growing baby, it becomes clear that our life consists of a series of learning processes. Strictly speaking, everything that we actively do must be learned. No-one can speak or move all of their limbs in the proper manner immediately upon being born. Things such as eating, tying your shoelaces, withdrawing cash or spending money *wisely* must be learned.

---

242   The four Indiana Jones films (1981-2008, Lucasfilm) are definitely worth watching, with a view to weighing up your own willingness to take risks and your passion as you search for the treasures of the Kingdom of Heaven. The protagonist is continually placing his life on the line in order to uncover treasures and solve mysteries – a great role model!

The Bible explains that when we enter into a relationship with God, we experience a rebirth, which makes us spiritual babies. Initially, we experience our lives with God as immature and naive spiritual infants. We cannot yet align our minds to God's will or His works. The templates of our old experience and pattern of understanding cannot be superimposed onto our new lives with God, we must instead create new experiences.

"When I was a child, I talked like a child, I thought like a child, I reasoned like a child." (1 Cor 13:11 NIV).

On the fast track to sanctification

I remember how at the beginning of my relationship with Jesus I had the wildest theories about God and life with Him. I repeatedly tried to place the template of my "old way of thinking" onto my life with Jesus, which resulted in a great many misunderstandings. As a spiritual baby, without Christian roots, I understood practically nothing, which consequently produced a few humorous moments.

When a friend and I read about "sanctification[243]" for the first time in the Bible, we asked God, in all seriousness, to accomplish this feat in us over the next few months (a fast-track course as it were), in order that we could see more of Him.

Only after several years did it begin to dawn on me that sanctification was not something that God could dispense to me intravenously. It was about going deeper into my relationship with Him! By entering into His presence sanctification would take place on a continual basis in my life. Sanctification is the act of striving after the Holy One, and is not the pursuit of a moral high ground.

The "magic word"

In the first church environment I experienced there was also a lot of talk about the power of the Word of God. I watched other people carrying their Bibles into the church service with reverence. For these people the book seemed to hold some kind

---

243   "Make every effort to live in peace with everyone and to be holy; without holiness no one will see the Lord."

of magic – to me it was entirely unclear as to how I could activate the "power of these texts" – especially seeing as I could barely understand what I was reading. During a bout of flu I attempted to discover the link between God's word and healing. As a little experiment one night I placed my Bibles on top of me. I was expecting to experience "healing through God's word". The next morning, as I awoke on my "Bible bed", I realised that it was not just Bibles on top of me, but also "Good Morning, Holy Spirit" by Benny Hinn. A joke straight from God – with the hidden instruction that I should stop looking for formulae and instead seek the guidance of His Spirit. But I only came to understand this at a much later stage. Whoever has ears, let them hear!

Learning a Jesus-centred worldview and lifestyle poses problems for us, especially if we only come to know God as an adult. We have already gathered a great deal of life experience and our worldview is largely established. We are reluctant to return to ignorance, to the role of a student and a person in need. We can happily do without slipping back into the role of an infant and starting over entirely with regard to our values and practices.

When Nicodemus, an important scribe, comes to Jesus, he is astonished to be invited into precisely this process. "Jesus answered, "Very truly I tell you, no one can enter the kingdom of God unless they are born of water and the Spirit. Flesh gives birth to flesh, but the Spirit gives birth to spirit. You should not be surprised at my saying, "You must be born again." " (John 3:5-7 NIV).

Jesus' claim that everyone who wants to begin a relationship with God "must be born again", is confusing to those listening. One of the most intelligent minds of his time cannot comprehend these statements. Whereas Nicodemus feels as though he is being instructed to undergo a physical rebirth, Jesus is actually speaking about spiritual rebirth, which is only the beginning of a major transformation.

The implication of the path described by Jesus is that we must learn a new way of thinking in most areas of life. Things that previously seemed meaningful and worthy of our attention all of a sudden lose their value on account of our new perspective. Other things that previously appeared meaningless now hold high value for us. Our scale of values adjusts to match that of Jesus, under the guidance of the Spirit of God[244]. If we pursue

---

244   Sanctification!

this process, we will experience our love for God becoming deeper. Paul describes the effects of this change of perspective in his own life: "But whatever were gains to me I now consider loss for the sake of Christ." (Phil 3:7 NIV).

Relearning how to hear

The process of relearning through God's presence that I have described also applies with regard to hearing. In our childhood we learned how to listen to our parents, friends and teachers. Later we learned how to listen to lecturers, politicians, expert opinions, media reports and also to ourselves. Without the need to be consciously aware of it, it is often the case that we have even become accustomed to listening to the voices of impure spirits. Many of our inferiority complexes and addictions find their roots here[245]. In the same way as we have learned to listen to those voices, we must now learn to listen to God – and at the same time unlearn a host of hearing patterns.

Relearning when it comes to "hearing" is helped along by our study of His written word and our mindfulness towards His presence in our everyday lives. Engaging with what He has already said creates expectation, encourages mindfulness and fosters our understanding of His omnipresent voice. Our perception of our surroundings is, so to speak, somewhat selective. Our thoughtlife serves as a selective filter. Whatever occupies my thoughts is what I will see. If I preoccupy myself with God, I will become increasingly aware of God in my everyday life – if I preoccupy myself with a make of car, I will notice this brand on the roads more and more often.

Seeing what we want to see

A few years ago when we wanted to buy a new car, I was really preoccupied with the whole thing. In the end it came down to a choice between two models. Suddenly I got the impression that everyone else in Hamburg had decided to drive these two models – everywhere I looked, there they were! I felt like I was on-trend, and that my choice had been confirmed. When I shared the observation with my friend

---

245   Do I actually do what I want to do? If not, am I perhaps fulfilling someone else's will!

Daniel, he remarked politely: "Perhaps you are just seeing what you want to see?" I felt a bit stupid – he was of course right! The trend I had noticed only existed in my thoughtlife.

Energy!

It often becomes clear that relearning requires additional energy. Continuing to operate in our old patterns is simpler; it gives us a sense of security and conserves energy. God's invitation to relearn is therefore frequently initiated by a special encounter with Him or as the result of a vision. It is in grace that He acts this way, in order to generate in us a determination and motivation to relearn. If we do not see the new land into which He wants to lead us in front of our eyes, it doesn't make sense to us to expend energy in getting to this destination. The process of relearning is therefore not concluded with a new discovery or encounter with God, but is only just beginning. It should be noted: the preview that He grants us is but an invitation to the party, and not the party itself!

We can say that we have learned a new practice when it becomes a fixed part of our everyday activity. Astonishingly, when it comes to our relationship with God this is also precisely the point at which He leads us into a new learning process. This is part of His promise: as long as we follow Jesus, the Holy Spirit will "teach us Jesus".

Learning on the job!

Below I will illustrate, *where* and *when* we learn from God and what might prevent us from learning.

How Jesus teaches his friends

The gospels provide us with a glimpse into the lives of twelve young men, whom Jesus personally calls to follow him. Within the shortest period of time, he leads them into a major learning process, as a result of which their entire world is turned upside down. As one of Jesus' closest friends, Peter plays a special role in the accounts. If we explore the passages in which he is involved, it becomes clear that his subsequent, special position as an apostle is not as a result of his vast wisdom, high level of intelligence or loving approach. What sets Peter apart is his capacity to repeatedly get up each time he falls down. He is a master in the art of "Failing Forward"[246]. He is willing to be corrected by Jesus time and again and, above all, he is willing to learn from him.

When Peter hears Jesus' command to follow him in order to become a fisher of men[247], he has no idea that choosing to follow will shatter his entire concept of living. He is entirely unaware that in so doing he is set to become one of the leading figures in the greatest adventure of all time[248].

Jesus' invitation to Peter appears unexpected, issued right in the middle of his working day, without an introductory conversation, internship, traineeship or prior submission of an application. Peter had presumably planned an entirely normal day as a fisherman and was most likely looking forward to going out for a beer with his friends after work.

---

246   This refers to the ability to apply lessons learnt from one's own errors in order to gain future success. See also, "Failing Forward: Turning mistakes into stepping-stones for success", John C. Maxwell.

247   Matt 4:18.

248   The spread of the Kingdom of God on the Earth – it doesn't get any bigger than that!

But when Jesus speaks to him, everything changes: Peter hears not just words, but eternal life[249]. This life appears before him[250] and he cannot resist the internal urge that Jesus' words trigger within him. God's voice unearths a deep longing inside him!

Peter follows and takes the first of many courageous steps away from his family relationships, his career, his hometown – and he does so without looking back[251]. God's voice proves to be the force in his life that defines his calling.

A few days later, as Peter reflects with Jesus on his new calling, the following scene can be imagined playing out:

> "Jesus, how can I actually *learn* to be a fisher of men? Can I do an apprenticeship (3 years) or some sort of advanced training course (10 months)? Do you do a weekend seminar? Do you have a book, or at least a handout?" "No", answers Jesus, with a smile. Jesus loves Peter's questions and his curiosity. "The handout is something that you will write yourself at a later stage! But with regard to *learning*: you will learn to be a fisher of men as we do it, for even I only do what I see my Father do, and this is what I am going to teach you.[252]"

---

249   "Simon Peter answered him, "Lord, to whom shall we go? You have the words of eternal life" (John 6:68 NIV).

250   "The life appeared; we have seen it and testify to it, and we proclaim to you the eternal life, which was with the Father and has appeared to us." (1 John 1:2 NIV).

251   One might suppose that Tolkien drew from this scene in his saga "The Hobbit". Tolkien's story begins with the wizard Gandalf searching for the hobbit Bilbo Baggins and inviting him to become part of a daring expedition. Their goal is to find a long-hidden treasure and (presumably) in so doing to kill a dragon. Bilbo initially forcefully declines the invitation. However, Gandalf's words have unlocked in him a longing for fame, adventure and the chance to do something special, and act like Valium in counteracting his concerns and fears. At this point he could have had no idea what his courageous step would mean for himself and his descendents, indeed that his nephew Frodo (see: The Lord of the Rings) will ultimately, as a result of a pioneering decision, rescue all of the citizens of "Middle Earth" from the dark lord Sauron. He simply notices that life is calling him and that a door has opened, through which he can escape the mediocrity of his existence as a hobbit.

252   John 5:19.

On the road with Jesus

The life of the disciples encourages us to learn to follow Jesus *by just doing it.* Jesus calls simple people, without a great deal of life experience or spiritual training, to walk alongside him as his representatives. After just a few months he commissions them and sends them out to announce and embody God's Kingdom.

Would you have allowed a Peter, or a Judas, to publically advertise on your behalf? I wouldn't! Jesus' disciples fail[253], argue[254], want to commit religiously justified mass murder[255], steal[256], are prideful[257], are void of understanding[258], allow demons to speak through them[259] and turn away from Jesus when faced with persecution[260]. It is clear that in the Twelve Jesus called not capable, but in fact somewhat inept disciples. However, just as clear is their willingness to learn and their determination to keep going. These characteristics are the true reason they are selected. God doesn't commission people who are ready to go, He commissions people who are ready to learn.

The successful cave dweller

In light of the story of the calling of the Gerasene[261] this becomes all the more clear. From the perspective of a church leader, who attempts to carefully select his leaders by drawing on the advice of Paul[262], the way Jesus goes about things is utterly bizarre to me, crazy actually. In an isolated region, Jesus meets a man who is possessed by a legion[263] of demons and who lives in tombs. It is reported that this man had not worn any clothes for some time, and was continually shouting and hitting himself with stones[264]. What's more, he

---

253   Matt 16:14.

254   Luke 22:24.

255   Luke 9:54.

256   John 12:6.

257   Luke 22:24.

258   Matt 16:9.

259   Matt 16:23.

260   Matt 26:56.

261   Luke 8:22ff; Mark 5:1ff.

262   For example, 1 Tim 3:2 and Tit 1:7.

263   At the time of Jesus a Roman legion consisted of approx. 5,500 soldiers.

264   What a terrible neighbour – it was little wonder that he was forced to live in tombs!

wouldn't let himself be restrained and was able to break chains. While those who lived in the area feared the man, Jesus does not seem fazed by his behaviour. He views the situation through the eyes of the Holy Spirit, seeing not his condition, but his potential. Jesus is compassionate, shows acceptance, frees the man from the spiritual "parasites" and provides him with clothes. For the residents of the region this is a step too far. They presumably think that Jesus has freed the man with the help of a greater demon and are therefore all the more afraid. It will not have been the first time that people have reacted to Jesus' intervention in this way[265]. They ask Jesus to leave the area.

The Gerasene experiences a two-fold touch from Jesus: Jesus sets him free and sends him out. When it comes to the freeing, we have barely any problem – it seems natural, and "biblical". In many Christian communities he would be treated in just the same way; deliverance is part of Jesus' core message[266]. But who among us would then have sent this formerly possessed man out immediately, as an evangelist to the entire region? As someone who had lived in tombs, hit himself with stones and was host to a vast number of demons, he presumably had a few things to work through! At the very least a little pastoral care, community and training wouldn't have gone amiss. "Keep yourself as closely connected with the church community as possible and visit all of our courses!" would have been our advice. Jesus does something that is, in our eyes, unthinkable. He allows the man *to go out on his own*, sending him out directly as an evangelist in spite of the fact that he had asked to go with Jesus.

"Then all the people of the region of the Gerasenes asked Jesus to leave them, because they were overcome with fear. So he got into the boat and left. [38] The man from whom the demons had gone out begged to go with him, but Jesus sent him away, saying, [39] "Return home and tell how much God has done for you." So the man went away and told all over town how much Jesus had done for him." (Luke 8:37–39 NIV).

How could Jesus do something so irresponsible? What theological training did the man have, what practical experience of the faith? He had presumably only spent a few hours with Jesus, perhaps a few days. His message as an evangelist was consequently a simple one: "I was possessed, Jesus set me free – it's really worthwhile believing in Jesus!"

---

265   Mark 3:22; Luke 11:15; Matt 9:34.

266   Luke 4:18ff.

Everything else he had to *learn while on the road* – just like Jesus. We can deduce that the man was unbelievably successful in the fact that the next time Jesus visits the region a great welcome is extended to him and he brings in a huge harvest. Matthew tells us this of his second visit: "Jesus left there and went along the Sea of Galilee. Then he went up on a mountainside and sat down. [30] Great crowds came to him, bringing the lame, the blind, the crippled, the mute and many others, and laid them at his feet; and he healed them. [31] The people were amazed when they saw the mute speaking, the crippled made well, the lame walking and the blind seeing. And they praised the God of Israel." (Matt 15:29–31 NIV).

What a huge change in comparison to his first visit! Mark and Matthew also both report that there Jesus fed 4,000 people with seven loaves of bread and a few fish[267]. Doors that had previously been closed were opened wide as a result of the "lay preaching" of the delivered Gerasene.

God trusts us

God calls us His disciples, messengers and friends, even though we have no idea what it is really all about! He doesn't appear to worry about our stumbles and failures. He has faith in His ability *to speak to us*, and in our ability *to listen to Him* and *learn from Him*. God does not assess our condition, but rather our potential to develop – Jesus lies hidden within each of us.

Living as a new creation is a lifelong learning process. We learn how to live this new life as we live it. It isn't about what we actually do, but rather that the new dimensions of our being begin to define our actions. We learn how to live like Jesus by "living with Jesus" – there is no other form of training planned. The Holy Spirit acts as a teacher within us. He guides and teaches the followers of Jesus in the same way as he did with Jesus. "But the Advocate, the Holy Spirit, whom the Father will send in my name, will teach you all things and will remind you of everything I have said to you." (John 14:26 NIV).

What's great about this form of learning is the permanent proximity to our teacher. If we allow him to, he will make use of each and every situation we encounter to bring us deeper into the truth. Thus, every moment in our lives can lead to spiritual growth.

---

267   Mark 8:1ff and Matt 15:32ff.

What can I learn today?

At the start of 2012, I asked God for a few words of guidance for the year, to help me stay on course. One of the sentences that God gave me was this: When you suffer injustice, ask yourself: what can I learn from this situation? I really wasn't too pleased that God had dropped a hint that I was to suffer injustice! Nonetheless, I would use this word as a compass to guide me throughout the course of the year. It enabled me to find an alternative way to deal with injustice in various situations, and in so doing, to overcome.

This word has recently come to life for me once again: a tyre slasher has been terrorising our neighbourhood for a few weeks. One morning I once again discovered that my bike tyres had been punctured. As I patched up the four (!) holes, I ran over in my mind what I had, up until this point, considered as possible means of preventing this from happening: 1. I had wondered to what extent physical violence against the perpetrator could be justified. 2. I had placed my bike under God's protection. 3. I had advised my neighbour as to what measures we could take together. Thus far, none of these had shown any effect. As I stood pondering, I noticed that the Holy Spirit had suddenly given me compassion for the perpetrator. I considered how lonely and broken a person would have to be to go around slashing bicycle tyres at night. I came to the conclusion that this person was presumably him/herself a victim of violence.

The following Bible passage sprung to mind: "(…) bless those who curse you, pray for those who mistreat you." (Luke 6:28 NIV). What could I learn from this injustice towards me? Compassion! As I patched up each of the four holes I prayed that the culprit would experience a blessed encounter with Jesus, and I resolved to pray for the perpetrator any time this happened again. The attacks decreased in frequency – however, there would continue to be new opportunities to confront injustice suffered in a Christ-like manner.

MULL IT OVER: LEARNING TO LISTEN AS A LIFESTYLE – GOD CALLS DISCIPLES, NOT EXPERTS.

What prevents you from learning new things from God?

1. What are your best excuses when God tries to lead you into new learning processes? Write down your excuses and ask God to give you His perspective on each. Write down His perspective beside each excuse. Also consider which answer the Bible offers for each of your excuses and write it down beside the excuse.

2. Discuss your findings with a friend.

TEAM TALK: LEARNING TO LISTEN AS A LIFESTYLE – GOD CALLS DISCIPLES, NOT EXPERTS.

1. Each ask God what He is currently teaching you and write down some key words. Share what you have heard with one another. Are you surprised by God's answers or had you expected something similar? How can you respond responsibly to God's current teaching plan for you? Share your thoughts with one another.

2. Read the story of the calling of the Gerasene together[268]. What do you think about Jesus' approach? Would you have allowed this man to speak on your behalf or given him a position of responsibility in your church? Why/why not?

3. What hope does Jesus' behaviour towards the Gerasene hold for each of us?

4. How could Jesus' behaviour change how we act towards "broken people"?

---

268   Luke 8:22ff; Mark 5:1ff.

Chapter 10

Overcoming learning barriers

When God invites us to learn from Him, His objective is always to deepen our relationship with Him. Alongside questionable theologies and a simple lack of the realisation that we should be learning from God, there are numerous other factors that prevent our learning processes. Self-awareness is the first step to overcoming barriers. As such, I will now identify some learning barriers and look at strategies by which we can overcome them.

Learning barrier 1 – Fear of failure

The fear of making mistakes and therefore being punished or exposed can pose a powerful learning barrier. For this reason, some of us live out our discipleship according to the motto: 'If I don't do anything, I can't do anything wrong'. However, this assumption in itself is 'wrong' and is borne of fear.

In the parable of the talents, Jesus tells of a rich man who entrusts three of his servants with money, in order that they might generate a profit. Whereas two of them make good use of the money, the third buries it and cannot present a profit to his master upon his return.

The servant justifies his disobedience as being down to fear. " 'Master,' he said, 'I knew that you are a hard man (...) So I was afraid and went out and hid your gold in the ground. See, here is what belongs to you." (Matt 25:24–25). Even though the servant does not embezzle the money and does give everything back, a harsh punishment awaits him, while the other two are rewarded[269].

This parable can teach us a lot about how God acts and also tells us that we must be able to justify our decisions before Him. In this regard, it becomes clear that God requires all people to multiply the gifts that He gives them, and that fear of failure is not accepted as justification for disobedience.

Our fear of failure is particularly evident when God guides us into learning processes and confronts us with thoughts and steps that are unknown or unfamiliar to us. It goes without saying that we will make more mistakes, both when learning things and once we have already mastered them. God is entirely clear on this. He knows that we only learn by making mistakes[270]. His love offers the perfect framework within which to try things out, make mistakes, turn back and start over.

It annoys me when Christian celebrities, authors or leaders keep quiet about their failures and learning processes. In so doing they are creating the illusion of someone who successfully follows Jesus without ever having had to experience the problems and challenges that we struggle with on a daily basis. The truth often comes to light when their masks fall off, in the form of sordid revelations and scandals. Our world does not require role models in the form of "infallible" superstars who can do everything, have no weaknesses and never make mistakes. It requires transparent role models. People who are willing to live as "lifelong learners", "forward-falling failures" or "broken healers". Lifestyles such as this are possible, provided we do not leave the learning environment of God's love, acceptance and forgiveness.

269　Matt 25:15ff.

270　Thomas Edison is known as the inventor of the light bulb. Various sources report that he required 1,200 – 2,000 attempts to produce a permanently illuminated light bulb. When asked of his frequent failures, he stated that he did not fail more than 1,000 times, but rather found 1,000 ways in which *not* to permanently illuminate a light bulb. This attitude is something we can learn from as we follow Jesus.

Learning barrier 2 – unclear objectives

*If I am unclear as to why I am travelling and where the journey is
headed, it is very difficult to set off in the first place!*

"Why does God continually lead me into learning processes – where is this all going?"
The answer stated by many followers of Jesus is that He simply wants to make us "better
people". But what does a better person look like, when is he better and what comes after
that – an improvement on the improvement?

The vague notion that God wants my "improvement" is not an inspiring incentive to
consent to partake in a continual learning process. Paul states that the actual objective of
our learning is to be transformed so as to be more like Jesus. "(...) in all things God works
for the good of those who love him; (...) For those God foreknew he also predestined to be
conformed to the image of his Son, that he might be the firstborn among many brothers
and sisters (...)." (Rom 8:28–29 NIV).

Here it is worthwhile considering this: Why does our Father want to form Jesus within
us? What would this mean for us and those around us? In the same letter Paul provides
an indication as to what purpose our becoming like Jesus should fulfil. "For if, by the
trespass of the one man, death reigned through that one man, how much more will those
who receive God's abundant provision of grace and of the gift of righteousness *reign* in life
through the one man, Jesus Christ!" (Rom 5:17 NIV, emphasis KR).

The Holy Spirit does not guide us through learning processes in order to bring about a
moral improvement in us, but rather to mature us and equip us to live out our calling
– this is what being a child of God is all about! Jesus' maturity is evident in his ability to
recognise and carry out the will of his Father. "Very truly I tell you, the Son can do nothing
by himself; he can do only what he sees his Father doing (...) For the Father loves the Son
and shows him all he does (...)." (John 5:19-20 NIV).

The objective of our learning is thus that we mature in order to rule with our Father.
Maturity means living in connection with the Father, like Jesus. The more we learn to be
and think like Jesus, the more we can take up our original gift – lordship over creation.

This approach to living together with the Father is the goal of all learning in the Holy Spirit. In Jesus we see an image of what our life could look like – God wants to enable us to live how Jesus lived. This is the goal to which every divine learning process ultimately leads.

Learning barrier 3 – Following your own learning plan

The tendency to determine ourselves what we want to learn is another learning barrier. This can easily take place if we detach ideas or topics that we find particularly exciting from our discipleship[271] and thus begin to define our learning objectives ourselves. We reject God's curriculum and only learn what we ourselves deem to be important[272].

Our self-defined learning objectives are generally comprised of two categories of topics. We want to learn, *what comes easy to us* – and *what seems to us to be morally and systematically worth striving after*. Our own learning objectives can have "good" content, and can from the outside in appear very spiritual. However, they ultimately amount to rebellion against God's guidance.

The path of least resistance – learning what comes easy to us

It is only natural that we attempt to grow in areas that we find easy and in which we have already developed. Here we experience more rapid success and are not required to strive to such an extent. For this reason, amateur athletes who want to perform to a high level fall into the trap of training their "favourite" parts of their bodies more than is necessary, and neglecting others[273].

In the same way there are followers of Jesus who have reached a high level in one area of their spirituality (e.g. intercession, Bible study or street evangelism), but are visibly underdeveloped in others.

---

271 It is not the follower who determines the destination, but the one who is being followed.

272 The Pharisees were experts at designing their own learning plans, and at shining in areas that they had declared to be important. Jesus criticises them harshly for this.

273 A friend of mine met a guy at a fitness class who had worked out his biceps to such an extent that he was unable to perform a warm-up exercise whereby you were required to clap your hands with your arms outstretched.

If we allow our learning to be guided by the Holy Spirit, He will ensure that we experience balanced growth. However, this can mean that we are required to train a "muscle" that is poorly developed. Although this appears less attractive at first, in the long term it results in major spiritual growth, as only God knows what we really need[274].

Amending the curriculum

I am well aware of the temptation towards self-defined learning! At a time when my spiritual life was not at a world-class level, I urgently asked God: "Teach me to love You again!" A few days later I received an astonishing prompt in the form of His voice speaking to me internally: "Kristian, *I* want you to learn to love yourself." It instantly became clear to me that I had no concept what it was to "love myself". Initially I had no idea how I could carry out God's will. In the days that followed I noticed that many of my problems were created or developed as a result of my inability to love myself. I was thankful for God's adjustment of my curriculum.

Since this time, I have developed the habit of praying the following prayer: "Dad, what do you want to teach me just now?" I often combine this prayer with a written spiritual exercise or pray it during a prayer walk. It is a great way to synchronise my learning with God's teaching plan.

Learning systematic rules, rather than relationship

Wherever we are, we find ourselves tempted to adjust to the circumstances, which could also be referred to as "systems". Regardless of whether it's a neighbourhood, a church community or a family, in every "system" we find internal rules that determine whether or not we are successful. If we want to be successful within this system, we attempt to do the right thing and to avoid doing the wrong thing.

So, too, in our relationship with God, the temptation is also to seek out and define systematic rules. We do this for ourselves personally, but also as a church community.

---

274   "And he is not served by human hands, as if he needed anything. Rather, he himself gives everyone life and breath and everything else." (Acts 17:25 NIV).

It is astonishing how much people love to define moral and systematic boundaries[275]. This is because it gives us the impression that we can determine between good and evil, and helps us to make sure we are on the "right" side.

Of course, the formulation of simple commandments or principles of belief do also bring security, and this is not always entirely negative. Many fundamental defined values, such as generosity, faithfulness, courage and worship help us to live a godly lifestyle, without having to constantly weigh everything up again.

However, at the same time there is the risk that we end up living independently of God, in that we follow these commandments more than we follow His voice. What actually sounds like a paradox was nonetheless the major error committed by the Pharisees and the Sadducees in Jesus' day.

The "system" that Jesus models out to his friends is extremely dynamic, flexible and is continually in a state of development – it is called "relationship with God". Jesus doesn't teach his disciples to recite a collection of commandments. He teaches them to live as he himself lives.

Hearing God is key to his everyday life: he follows his Father's voice rather than adhering to a rigid set of rules. This hearing not only forms the basis for his relationship with God, but also elevates it to a higher dynamic.

The following formula is evident in the example of Jesus: it is not adherence to defined rules, but rather our ability to recognise and implement God's desired direction that determines the level of our relationship with Him. Paul describes it like this: "For those who are led by the Spirit of God are the children of God." (Romans 8:14 NIV).

Jesus' secret: relational obedience

In our culture, and particularly in German-speaking countries, society is permeated with rules, standards and laws, and this is what holds things together. Many of us are therefore used to operating within a marked "legal mindset", including in our relationship with God. We ask ourselves: what is right? What is wrong? What is forbidden and what is allowed?

---

275   We love secretly bypassing these boundaries just as much.

What do you do, what don't you do? However, in the "system" modelled by Jesus, commandments and rules are not rigid, but are instead activated by *relational obedience*.

As such, Jesus leaves his friends with one fundamental instruction. "A new command I give you: Love one another. *As I have loved you, so you must love one another.*" (John 13:34 NIV, emphasis KR). We find Jesus' command to love expressed in various forms[276], but the basic message is always the same: just love!

When Jesus commands his disciples to love, *as* he loved them, this poses the question: *How* did Jesus love his disciples? The answer can be found on a relational level: Jesus always loves his disciples in the same way the Father does, as Jesus says that he only does what he sees the Father do[277].

If we hear Jesus' command without having the accompanying relationship with the Father, we miss the actual purpose of Jesus' command – to convey relationship with the Father.

Although we find commands right through the Bible that reveal God's will to us, and even though Jesus also leaves us with a command, our goal is never to learn commands or systematic rules, but rather relationship. God's commands lead us into relationship and protect this relationship, but they should never replace it.

In every situation in our lives we must therefore *re-hear*, what "the commandment" means *in this specific instance*.

> What does it mean for a child who is abused at home to honour his parents?[278]

> What does it mean in a globalised and networked world to accept responsibility for my *neighbour*?[279]

> What does it mean for a wife who suffers violence at the hands of her husband to love her "enemy"?[280]

---

276   Matt 5:44; Matt 19:19; Matt 22:39; Mark 12:31ff; Luke 10:27; among others.

277   John 5:19.

278   Matt 15:4.

279   Luke 10:30ff.

280   Luke 6:27.

The process can be compared with a satellite navigation device: the device requires a satellite connection in order to calculate locations, routes and destinations. On our last holiday in Britain, our Sat Nav refused to establish a connection with the satellite somewhere in Wales. We were forced to realise that a Sat Nav is only helpful to the extent that it is under the guidance of the satellite.

When connected to the Father's voice, God's commandments direct us down the correct path.

Learning barrier 4 – Pressure to succeed

If we feel God placing us under pressure to succeed, this is usually as a result of the concern that we might disappoint him and thereby be deemed unworthy. Behind this lies the notion that God's acceptance is dependent on our ability.

Many marriages start with the hope that the partners will stick to a shared agreement and, if they do change at all, it will only be for the positive. However, each new day is unpredictable. It quickly comes to pass that one, or both partners fail to adhere to the rules and arrangements – in marriage vows this is the "for worse". If we have built our marriage on the positive behaviour of our spouse, then their failure is often the beginning of the end. However, if we are willing to allow change, failure and detours on the part of our partner, then the relationship has a chance of long-term success.

In no way does God make his faithfulness dependent on our behaviour[281]. His 'yes' to us can endure a great deal, for He doesn't look at the moment, but instead focuses on our development.

In our loving relationship with him, "learning to hear Him" and "getting to know Him" go hand in hand. Both are processes that can last our entire lives. It is just as much a mistake for us to sit back and wait on growth as it is for us to lapse into actionism and performance-based faith. We must allow God to set the tempo and we must then adhere to that tempo.

---

281   "...if we are faithless, he remains faithful;... for he cannot disown himself." (2 Tim 2:13 NIV).

In my first few years with Jesus I felt a huge amount of stress as a result of the internal pressure to grow spiritually. At some point it dawned on me that, because God's plan is perfect, I could not accelerate growth processes – in fact I could only slow them down[282].

God isn't in a hurry with me. He relaxes in our relationship and is not reliant on me learning quickly. He knows in advance how long He will need to bring me to the place of His will. He knows my future, for He designed me. As a result, my learning with God can take place within an atmosphere of love and acceptance – in a place where He calls me child and likes to be referred to as 'Dad'.

Nowadays I spend less time thinking about my own failure: Jesus declared that his success is my success and has claimed my failure as his own. His works free me from any pressure to success that I feel towards God – and any that I impose on myself.

Learning barrier 5 – Traumatic learning experiences

In the spiritual environment that I found myself in a strong emphasis was placed on the "supernatural" and the immediate receipt of God's blessing. Spiritual changes were often "released" in conjunction with personal prayer and the laying on of hands. I liked the way in which this was received and found it to be extremely practical. During ministry times[283] I had many supernatural experiences, was empowered and felt God's presence.

However, after a while my faith became somewhat imbalanced, as I was lacking in understanding with regard to internal learning processes and the deepening of my relationship with God.

I increasingly lived under a "pressure to receive". If, following the laying on of hands, a conference or a special time with God, the expected change or touch from God failed to materialise, I became frustrated and began troubleshooting for mistakes: did I have hidden sin within me, did I have too little faith or had I missed the moment – or did God

---

282   At the time, God said to me: Do you seriously believe that you can speed up what I am doing with you? Stop grumbling all the time, things are going quicker than you think!

283   Times of prayer, during which people receive blessing, generally for specific topics.

simply no longer want me? By adopting a one-sided theological framework I was living in real spiritual stress.

It was at that time that God began speaking to me about the topic of "learning", and to be honest I wasn't particularly open to it! As a teenager, as a result of having had poor teachers and a sub-substandard school system, school had left me traumatised when it came to learning[284]. For me, school-based learning was always associated with pressure and the fear that I would not be able to learn something, and consequently be viewed as a failure. The authoritarian demeanour of some teachers was like poison to my childlike appetite for learning. Upon leaving school, I made an internal vow: no more school – no more teachers – no more learning!

God did not let Himself be affected by my resolution and, at the time, He declared to me: "Kristian, I want you to learn a few things from me. You are under no obligation, but if you do not want to learn from me, you will not see me and my Kingdom in the way you want to see it". His communication on this subject took place over a longer period of time, by speaking to me internally, through people, thoughts and a series of Bible passages[285].

He had pressed the right buttons in order to motivate me: I was ready to see Him and His Kingdom, to break every internal vow and admit the contrary. As a result I began to open myself up afresh to learning.

God showed me that the presence of His Holy Spirit in my life was the key to learning. "But the Advocate, the Holy Spirit, whom the Father will send in my name, will teach you all things and will remind you of everything I have said to you." (John 14:26 NIV). He also spoke to through a recurring dream and helped me to understand that the core of all of my learning from Him would be the strengthening of my relationship with Him. By way of illustration, I will summarise the dream below.

The test within the test

I enter a classroom and sit down at a table. Other pupils are already sitting at their desks. There is also a mean-looking teacher there. Tests are handed out. Everyone

---

284 Luckily not all people experience this in the same way.

285 John 6:45; Eph 5:17; 2 Pet 3:18.

appears to know what they should write, but I am completely unprepared. I cannot understand any of the questions and feel utterly overwhelmed. Thoughts are shooting through my head: Why did no-one tell me about the test? Why do I have to take a test about things I have never heard of?

Once I had experienced this unpleasant dream several times, I finally asked God for an explanation and for resolution. I closed my eyes and in my mind returned to the room in my dream. I noticed the insecurity and the frustration and asked God: What now? This time I saw Jesus standing in the classroom beside me – up to this point I had been concentrating so much on the test that I had barely noticed him. He winked at me and said: "Every answer can be found in me." I gathered all the courage I could muster and then simply wrote "Jesus" right across the test paper. Jesus took the sheet and handed it over to the teacher – he no longer appeared quite as gloomy as before, in fact he even looked friendly. As Jesus approached him, their similarity became clear – they were Father and Son! Jesus gave Him the test, but the Father simply smiled and didn't even look at it. He said: "Jesus, what you give me I don't even need to check!" I was completely taken aback – everyone else in the room was still writing - trying to pass the test in their own strength. I had passed simply because I had learned to place my trust in Jesus.

Through the dream I came to understand that learning from God was not about passing a test, and thus being deemed a good or a poor student. Instead, with every "test" God wanted to teach me to look to Jesus – that's how you pass. My childlike eagerness to learn had been restored!

MULL IT OVER: BARRIERS TO LEARNING.

1. Ask God whether there are general learning barriers within you and write them down. Speak out forgiveness (if possible in the presence of a friend) towards people or institutions that have caused these in you.

2. Ask God for forgiveness if you notice an inner reluctance to learn from Him. As a second step, ask Him to restore your ability to learn.

TEAM TALK: BARRIERS TO LEARNING.

1. Consider which positive role models your have with regard to learning, and share them with the group. What in particular do you like about the way these people approach learning?

2. Take a look at the five barriers to learning. Can you add any additional barriers? Which learning barrier represents a particular obstacle to you? Consider and discuss: How did this barrier develop and what sustains it?

3. For each learning barrier work together to develop strategies that could help you overcome them.

4TH MOVEMENT – CODA

THE PRACTICE OF LEARNING TO HEAR

Chapter 11

Learning to hear – first steps

*"The majority of followers of Jesus are actually unaware of the
distance between them and God."*

A few years ago, when I heard John Wimber say this, it really struck home with me. I noticed that in many areas of my discipleship I allowed myself to be satisfied with mediocrity. I had begun to measure my spirituality based on those around me, and no longer on Jesus. In comparison to other followers of Jesus I classified myself as successful – however, when I turned my eyes back onto Jesus[286], my distance from God became painfully apparent.

In order to grow in our relationship with Jesus, we must be our most honest critics and our most consistent encouragers. Unfortunately, our churches are full of followers of Jesus who have never matured beyond the level of a spiritual infant. Growth generally ceases as the result of an unwillingness to learn and embrace change. Instead of taking risks and venturing down new and perhaps uncomfortable paths, we prefer to repeat the same, often empty, rituals in the hope that at some point we will once again see a positive result.

---

286 "Therefore, holy brothers and sisters, who share in the heavenly calling, fix your thoughts on Jesus, whom we acknowledge as our apostle and high priest." (Heb 3:1 NIV).

In order to justify our failure, we develop theologies that are not based on the experiences of people in the New Testament, but rather on our own experiences.

Only when we risk taking an honest look and lining our behaviour up alongside Jesus can we really recognise our true spiritual status. Without this integrity it is not possible to grow in Jesus.

The recognition of our spiritual powerlessness can be the beginning of an accelerated development process. In my relationship with Jesus I have gone through various times of accelerated spiritual growth. These are times of particular grace, although each time I am still required to say 'yes'.

When I heard the above quote from John Wimber, I heard God's call to me and began to reach out to Him afresh. In order to seek out God's presence in my everyday life, I began to wrestle over **four questions**. These were intended as a means by which to sharpen my ability to hear.

First of all I asked myself *how* (1) I can expect to hear God's voice. To this end, I studied God speaking to people in the Bible, to my friends and to myself.

This was then followed by asking *when* (2) I can expect Him to speak and *what* (3) He might speak about. Here, too, I studied the Bible: what did God talk about when speaking to people in the Bible stories I read?

Finally I also pondered *how I could process what He said to me in a productive manner* (4). Once again I found helpful tips in the Bible and in the works of some authors who address the topic of "contemplative prayer".

These four questions provide the communicative framework for every long-standing relationship. In a partnership it is particularly important to be aware of the basic way in which one's partner communicates. Being deaf to our partner's "language" is the best path to a crisis. On the other hand, if we have clarity regarding the ways in which the other person communicates, this creates a good growth environment for our ability to mutually understand one another, like a communicative greenhouse as it were.

Below I will present my findings regarding the four questions. However, I would encourage anyone reading to take these steps themselves in order to experience profound growth.

It is worthwhile noting down your findings. To this end, I have provided list of more specific questions in the "Mull it over" section.

How can I expect God to talk to me?

As has already been pointed out, learning to hear God speak is more of an art than a science. However, when it comes to asking how God communicates with us personally, it is important that we come to a clear conclusion. Without this clarity, there is no basis for the learning process. Learning to hear is then like trying to hunt partridges without having any idea where to find them. Clarity regarding the "how" increases our mindfulness, tunes in our receiver und and establishes a framework of expectation.

Jesus models an incredibly intimate relationship with his "Daddy"[287]. Such a close relationship with the all-powerful Creator of the universe is a challenging example to follow. Self-doubt is amplified: Why should someone who has endless options to choose from choose to be near me, of all people? Our insecurity can express itself in the form of a rather formal relationship and style of communication with God – I have experienced this myself.

"Kristian, please stop calling me *Lord* all the time!"[288] When God abruptly interrupted me with this interjection during a prayer time, I was shocked. "But Lord, that is unbiblical!" As I was talking, I noticed that my answer was not the smartest. As I pause to listen, I heard a quiet voice inside my head:

"Kristian, you have accepted me as Lord and you do not doubt that I am the boss, and that is good. But you do doubt my fatherhood – start calling me Dad, and you will experience me more as a dad."

---

287   Mark 14:36.

288   This happened via His "internal voice".

As I then began to change my choice of words, the image I had of God also changed. I began getting to know the heavenly Father introduced to me by Jesus as a child – it doesn't get any better than that![289]

Nowadays I often notice that my relationship with Jesus is becoming increasing unbureacratic and uncomplicated – God's love sets you free[290]. It's glorious! I want to lead people into a simple, genuine and deep love relationship with God. Therefore I am continually emphasising that the communication expressed between myself and God is an expression of our intimacy – no-one else has to understand what we share with one another! My love relationship with him can be as individual and unique as I myself am.

This emphasis can of course also lead to extremes, which keep me from the actual goal. For example, in that I begin to assume that God's voice is behind every little event, and as a result I get lost in endless attempts to find meaning in things. In the same way, I overshoot the mark when I specify that God should only speak directly to me and that I no longer accept Him talking to me through other people. Our personal and unique love relationship with God must be embedded in the Biblical Christian tradition[291] and in community with other followers of Jesus[292]. What we experience with God will likely not be exciting enough to be classified as 'church history' in 2,000 years time.

Jesus himself demonstrates this two-fold consistency in that he lives out his relationship with God within the living tradition of the people of Israel, and in his relationship with his friends. If I study God's individual communication with me, I should therefore place it within the context of the experience of biblical role models and the people around me. If I take an average based on what they did and what I am currently doing, I can establish a balanced level of expectation for myself.

---

289   I later summarised this exchange of thoughts using the following disassociation of the well-known Wilhelm Busch quotation: Once you accept the Kingdom come, you can openly carry on.

290   "So if the Son sets you free, you will be free indeed" (John 8:36 NIV).

291   "Remember your leaders, who spoke the word of God to you. Consider the outcome of their way of life and imitate their faith." (Heb 13:7 NIV).

292   "The Lord God said, "It is not good for the man to be alone." " (Gen 2:18 NIV).

Analysing God speaking to people in the Bible

We shall first study how God speaks to people in the reports provided in the Bible. The Bible is full of accounts of God speaking to individual people or to groups of people. Some of His paths of communication are difficult to comprehend, and will perhaps even seem unacceptable or foreign to us.

There are presumably not too many of us who would expect God to speak to them through an animal. Balaam will likewise have been surprised when God spoke to him through an ass[293]. It must have been rather humiliating for the famous prophet to have been (publicly) instructed by a donkey.

Or take, for example, the Wise Men from the East, who hear God's voice through a rising star. This reveals to them the time and place of the birth of Jesus. God confirms Jesus' calling to Mary and Joseph in the appearance of these three foreigners, through what they say and through their gifts[294]. It is amazing that God uses them to honour the birth of His son, and to speak prophetically to King Herod and to the parents of Jesus[295].

It is also strange that God speaks through the High Priest Caiaphas. Caiaphas prophesies, seemingly without himself understanding the blessing that the death of Jesus will bring to the people of Israel[296]. He belongs to the group who later condemn Jesus and hand him over to Pilate. One of Jesus' strongest accusers, and someone responsible for the murder of Jesus is thus used as God's mouthpiece.

The rainbow[297] is another mysterious way in which God speaks. God continually speaks to humanity through this "natural phenomenon", without the majority understanding its message. God's communication through angels, colours, symbols, miracles, wonders of

---

293   Num 22:28.

294   Matt 2:1ff.

295   The term used to refer to the Wise Men in the original texts was "magoi". This term can be translated as sorcerers, astrologers or fortune tellers. However, it also allows for the possibility that they were scientists, as at that time there was no recognised difference between astronomy and astrology. Regardless of their professional classification, they do not belong to the people of Israel, but rather represent the heathens, that is people who – in the eyes of the Israelites – do not know God.

296   John 11:50f.

297   Gen 9:2ff.

nature, plagues and creation itself[298] are among other ways He speaks that we often find surprising.

When I noticed the diverse range of ways in which God talks to people in the Bible, I noted the following in my spiritual journal: *"God doesn't change – He is reliability personified[299]. He spoke to human beings from the very beginning and will always continue to do so. The ways in which He speaks are as diverse as the people to whom He speaks. Every person and every generation can hear God in a way that they understand Him."*

Analysing God speaking to people around me

Secondly, I asked friends of mine how they hear God's voice. Did they have certain listening habits, or had they developed a love language with God? Many said that they hear God through music, nature, the Bible, other people or thoughts and internal pictures. Others experience God's voice more as an intuitive prompting and an internal knowledge.

Chatting with friends, our children or our partner about our listening habits is particularly worthwhile, as we can interpret what they say within the context of their lives. Learning from one another functions particularly well this way. Indeed, sharing with your spouse on this topic can lead to astonishing discoveries.

Colour consultation

On a visit to Austria, a married couple invited me to breakfast. As we sat at the table, God began to speak to me internally about the wife. He said: "She sees colours on people." I didn't exactly know what I should do with this information, so I waited a little and then simply asked her: "Do you see colours on people?" She didn't seem surprised at my question and answered: "Yes, that happens." Her husband looked back and forth between us in disbelief, as if we were part of a secret conspiracy that had selected *him* as a sacrifice. Then he splurted our: "You have never told *me* that!" She replied, a little uncertain: "*You* have never asked me either." I smiled into my

---

298   Psalm 19:2.

299   "Jesus Christ is the same yesterday and today and forever." (Heb 13:8 NIV).

bread roll and pondered how to rescue this uncomfortable situation. I encouraged the wife to look deeper into the gift and to ask God about what the colours meant. That day I probably – unintentionally – kick-started the spiritual exchange between the two of them.

I have myself often experienced how my own 'listening horizon' has been expanded by other people. I love to observe how other people listen to God, and I intentionally spend time with prophetically gifted people in order to learn from them.

When number plates speak

When I got to know my friend Shane, he told me that God regularly spoke to him through numbers. I was surprised – this concept was as of yet unknown to me. Over the next few days, on a few occasions, he pointed out number combinations that we encountered and in each case decrypted for me what God was saying to him through these numbers. While travelling to Hanover on a ministry trip, we asked God for a special word for the group. While I was parking, he pointed out the number plate of the car in front: JO 316. "This is the message for this evening – John 3:16.[300]" I was astounded – God had answered through a number plate!

Analysing God speaking to me

Having studied how people in the Bible and our friends hear from God, we will now address the question as to how *we* hear God ourselves.

First of all we will make a list of ways in which we have already heard God in the past.

Then we can also ask ourselves whether or not a personal language of love has developed between ourselves and God and how this is expressed. This refers to a particularly personal form our communication, which no-one else understands.

---

300   "For God so loved the world that he gave his one and only Son, that whoever believes in him shall not perish but have eternal life." (John 3:16 NIV).

By making a list of ways in which He communicates with me, I became aware that God often speaks to me through internal pictures, internal words of knowledge, that quiet inner voice or simply through His presence. On top of all this, He also speaks as I write in my spiritual journal.

Regarding the question about a love language, it struck me that God gives me everyday encouragement through combinations of numbers, fragrances or songs that spring to mind.

Secondly we shall consider whether there are specific occasions or places where we hear God particularly strongly or frequently.

For me this is the case when I am travelling, especially in aeroplanes, and as soon as I find myself alone in nature[301].

Thirdly we shall consider whether there are people in whose presence we find it easier to hear God[302]. It may be that these are people who have a special gift for hearing God, or are simply very encouraging or spiritually open. If we identify dynamics such as this, we can intentionally ask these people to spend time with us or to coach us.

I have a host of people like this around me. When I am near them I notice a spiritual pull, similar to when overtaking a lorry on the motorway and suddenly surging forwards upon entering its slipstream. Conveniently my wife Kim is one of them. Many of my directly inspired worship songs were written in her presence.

My findings

Studying God speaking to people in the Bible, to my friend and to myself has opened up exciting new dynamics to me.

When studying the people of the Bible, my biblical understanding underwent an astonishing transformation. In the past I had always approached the Bible with an extremely serious attitude and enormous respect. This went so far as that I actually felt

---

301   Out of this realisation, I developed the practice of going on prayer walks, which enrich my spiritual life immensely. I address this topic in greater detail in "Gebet als Begegnung" (Prayer as a Place HGM Publishing 2009), Bello/Reschke, Grainpress, 2012.

302   See 1 Sam 10:10ff.

guilty when there were sections I did not understand – I was afraid I could not love God without having understood "His Word".

As I now saw for myself how vibrant God was in His communication with the early church, it became evident to me that these followers of Jesus didn't even have access to a finished Bible through which God could speak to them!

They lived in a distinctly "oral tradition" and in a best-case scenario only had access to the Old Testament texts in written form. The first followers of Jesus were thus capable of following without having understood the Bible, or without even owning one!

My surprise at myself knew no end: by adhering to biblical guidelines I had attempted to achieve results that the characters in the very same Bible actually achieved by means of a direct relationship with God.

This notion was entirely new to me, and was extremely liberating as the pressure of being required to understand God's book was lifted off me. I was able to radically follow Jesus from where I was, with the conviction that I could contribute, without having to do everything "right".

My perspective on the Bible changed and I grasped how I could learn from the experiences of the early followers of God – God's word came to life, and brought life. It was no longer a corset that I had to force myself into, but instead was a flowing river that would pull me along whenever I dared to jump in.

Likewise, when studying how God spoke to my friends and to me myself, I was in for a surprise. I was not able to identify a standardised template for communication with God. On the contrary, it became clear to me that His communication is something that is highly personal to each individual. God's communication varies depending on the depth of the relationship, the life situation, the environment, the topic or the objective He wishes to fulfil. God appears to favour the communicative media that are already active in our life. For this reason, His personal communication can often appear strange to those on the outside looking in, whereas it is perfectly understandable to the recipient.

As such, He speaks to people with a mathematical gifting through numbers, to nature-lovers through nature, to visually gifted people through films or perhaps colours, and

193

to people who are doing the cleaning, through the vacuum cleaner. God transmits at the frequency at which He created each of us, or in contexts that make sense to us in a particular moment.

MULL IT OVER: HOW CAN I EXPECT GOD TO SPEAK TO ME?

1. Answer the following questions in writing and share your findings with someone else.
   - How did people in the Bible hear God?
   - How have your friends heard God in the past?
   - How have you heard God in the past?
   - What have been the 3 main ways He has spoken to you?
   - What love languages are there between you and God?
   - Are there places where you have heard God particularly well?
   - Are there people in whose company you hear God particularly well?

2. What conclusions can you draw based on your findings?

3. Also consider: Can God talk to you through everything that He wants to use? Allow Him to communicate with you actively through everything. To this end, you can make use of this prayer: *"Dad, I allow you to speak to me through everything. I lay down my attempts to control your voice and ask for forgiveness for times I have done this. Please be the Word*[303] *in my life – speak through everything, at all times, and about every subject."*

TEAM TALK: HOW CAN I EXPECT GOD TO SPEAK TO ME?

1. Answer the questions (see above) in writing and discuss your answers. What strikes you in particular?

2. Discuss among yourselves: Do you see a connection between the 3 main ways God speaks and you/your personality? What conclusions can you draw about how God speaks to people?

---

303   "In the beginning was the Word, and the Word was with God, and the Word was God. He was with God in the beginning. Through him all things were made; without him nothing was made that has been made." (John 1:1–3 NIV).

3. Does anyone else in the group hear from God in a way that you would like to learn? What is it? Consider together: Which learning steps could you take to tune in to this form of communication?

4. Discuss among yourselves: Can God speak to you through any method He chooses? How would you react, for example, if God were to speak to you through a donkey, a person who you don't actually like, or a wonder of nature? Would you listen and accept His word?

When can I expect God to speak to me?

Sometimes during the welcome and announcements at church services we hear prayers like this: "God, help us now to leave behind all of our thoughts from the past week and to meet with you." I find prayers like this almost unbearable! They paint a picture of a defeated army, returning home after a terrible battle. Let's be honest: if my week was so void of God's presence that I have to leave it behind me on a Sunday, then my life is not headed in a great direction. Can we only hear from God in church gatherings? Do we really believe we will be able to meet with God on a Sunday if we lose sight of Him for the rest of the week?

What would my relationship with my family look like if I limited my communication with them to one day a week? And from another perspective – what sort of father would God be if He only spoke to me in special church meetings?

In this section we will put our personal expectation to the test. Ask yourself:

When do I really expect God to speak to me?

In season and out of season

"Preach the word; be prepared in season and out of season."[304]

The translation of this verse sounds perhaps a little old-fashioned here, but it really appealed to me. Here the Apostle Paul encourages Timothy to pass on the message of Jesus in radical fashion, "when it is easy and people want to listen and when it is hard and people do not want to listen".

One of the things I love about God is that He does not require of us things that He Himself does not do. If we take the scripture seriously, we can therefore expect Him to speak at precisely these times – whether it happens to be convenient for us or not! God's voice speaking to His children knows no temporal limits. He doesn't sleep, He doesn't take holidays and He always has something important to say, for He is always there to draw us close to Him[305]. If we were to fall into the assumption that God only speaks to us in "spiritual moments", we must understand that for us – if His Spirit lives in us – there only are spiritual moments. It's not religious somersaults that make our lives spiritual, but rather the presence of His Spirit.

Jesus is continually following the Spirit of God, and thereby makes his everyday life an act of service to God. As his followers we are invited to do exactly the same[306]. If we only hear from God at special Christian events, then our relationship with God is not compatible with our everyday, and should be rethought.

"God, allow me to hear you – in season and out of season!"

I know that this attitude is a challenge in the hustle and bustle of everyday life – nonetheless, I want to live in this way and to continually expect His voice.

In order to focus myself on this, while eating breakfast I ask God to speak to me during the day and to interrupt the flow of my day should this be necessary. When going to sleep

---

304   2 Tim 4:2 (NIV).

305   "And I, when I am lifted up from the earth, will draw all people to myself." (John 12:32 NIV).

306   "For those who are led by the Spirit of God are the children of God." (Rom 8:14 NIV).

I hand over my sleep to Him and expect Him to speak and act during the night[307]. Habits like these and the awareness that the solution to my everyday chaos is just "a word from Him" away are my greatest allies in remaining open to His voice.

Learning to hear God's voice in the everyday

Our everyday life offers a perfect environment in which to learn to hear God. There are situations every single day in which we need God's guidance. If we learn to hear His voice in the ordinary things, like buying a pair of shoes, looking for a car parking space, cooking etc., we are then also trained to follow His guidance when facing more significant challenges. The degree to which I hear God's voice in my everyday correlates with the amount I will be able to hear Him in crisis moments. Here are three examples from my everyday life.

Maple syrup

I still had a little tomato sauce left over from the pizza topping from the previous day. Pizza sauce should be rather strongly seasoned in order to guarantee that the pizza has the right flavour when cooked. Today it was pasta on the meal plan and I wanted to use the rest of the sauce for it. When cooking I noticed that the sauce was too heavily seasoned to work with my pasta. I tried a few tricks; nothing would work. Shortly before resorting to throwing the sauce out, I asked, almost jokingly: "Jesus, how do I get this sauce to taste right?" I then heard the quiet, internal voice say the word "maple syrup". After a little hunting, I found a bottle of maple syrup – I didn't even know that we had it. I added a little syrup, tasted and was completely flabbergasted – the sauce tasted amazing! I was delighted with my pasta, and God was delighted at my delight.

---

307   "...For the Lord provides for those he loves, while they are asleep." (Ps 127:2 GNT).

Journey with a detour

Leif was two years old when he and I flew together for the first time. I had already set our passports and tickets on the table at around midday, just to make sure I didn't forget them. I showed Leif the photo in his passport once again – he found it funny to discover his picture in the little book. A friend drove us to the airport. As we were saying goodbye, I reached into my bag once more to check the passports and tickets. I saw my passport, my ticket and Leif's ticket, but something was missing – Leif's passport! Presumably he had been playing with it and then left it somewhere around the house. I jumped into the car and we raced back from the airport in record time. I ran the calculations in my head: in order to catch the flight I had a window of five minutes to find the passport. I tried to squeeze some information out of Leif as to where the passport had been left[308], but he declined to make comment – the silence of the otherwise talkative child seemed revealing. I ran into the flat, tore apart the sofa cushions (a perfect hiding place), pushed the sofa and tables around, rummaged around underneath the carpet, turned everything in Leif's room upside down – no passport. I now knew that it was too late and there was no point bothering to go any further. I said: God, this is the last chance – can you help? Internally, I heard the word "Wastepaper" and the phrase "You don't need to hurry on the way back to the airport". I ran into the kitchen – the passport was lying underneath a pile of wastepaper – what had Leif been thinking? I sprinted back to the car and rushed to the airport. Just when the check-in was closing, I arrived at the desk with Leif in my arms, pulling our bag behind us, completely out of breath and sweating. The woman behind the desk gave a friendly smile. Unfortunately your flight is delayed by one hour. You don't need to hurry on the way to the gate!" "You don't need to hurry" – the words rang in my ear – someone had already said that to me today.

Farewell via SMS

A young man from my church was going through a difficult time and I was making every effort to help him through. One day I received the following text message from

---

308   A difficult process with a two-year-old in tow.

him: "I'm done, faith doesn't work, church is annoying, leave me in peace, ☹☹☹…". It makes me unbelievably angry when people announce decisions such as this via SMS or email! In a mix of rage and concern, I dialled his number, not yet sure if I wanted to have a go at him or encourage him (ideally both!). Suddenly I heard the still small voice in my head: "Do not call – he needs time now." Perplexed, I set down the phone and answered: "I hope that's you, Jesus!" Six months later the person came up to me and apologised for the abrupt break in relationship. Without knowing about my conversation with God, he said: "Thank you for not contacting me back then – I needed space and time to think things through, and you gave me both."

God is active everywhere and at all times. I can and should expect Him to speak to me everywhere and at all times. When doing life with an invisible God, this posture of expectation is something we have to practise. The joy His voice brings and our need to hear Him motivate us in this task.

TEAM TALK: WHEN CAN I EXPECT TO HEAR GOD SPEAK TO ME?

Share stories of times you have heard God's voice completely unexpectedly. What happened? What were you able to learn from God through it?

What can I expect God to speak to me about?

I enjoy chatting with my son Leif. If we are out and about, we talk a lot about our surroundings. Sometimes this is a particularly beautiful sky, a sports car, an advertisement, or people who behave strangely and stand out to us. I ask Leif what he thinks about things or attempt to explain what we see from my perspective. Sometimes I use a story as an explanatory aid or refer back to a previous experience. By communicating with me, he comes to know and understand our world. I believe that our heavenly Father adopts the same approach with us.

How important am I God?

When I talk about how much God loves to chat with us, I am often left looking into perplexed eyes: "What does God want to talk to *me* about?" Comments such as this blow my mind – about everything, of course! God wants to tell me who He is and He wants to tell me who I am. He wants to be acknowledged by us and he wants us to see ourselves as He sees us. And He also wants to explain an entire universe to me! He wants to bestow honour upon us as we unpack and claim possession of creation, His great gift to us.

Solomon describes it like this: God's greatness becomes evident in that He can conceal things, but the honour He bestows upon kings becomes evident in the fact that they can uncover things[309]. The kings he is speaking about, that's us! God has called you and me to rule over the Earth. I am permitted to study and uncover the secrets of life – this is where the honour He bestows upon me becomes evident.

If I am genuinely unsure what God might like to talk to me about, this can only mean that I believe myself to be uninteresting and insignificant in God's eyes. The opposite is true. To Him, I am the most important thing in the whole universe! My value to Him cannot be overestimated. Everything God created, He created for *me*. God doesn't need air to breathe, and he doesn't need the Earth to live in. A seemingly endless quantity of colours, forms, flavours, animals, plants and stars are of no use to Him. Everything we recognise as falling under creation, He created for my good and for my pleasure – I am at the centre of all He longs for!

In worship times we sing about the incredible greatness, glory, power and sovereignty of God. And it is true – He is the absolute greatest, the boss of all bosses, the ruler of all rulers, the superstar among superstars! Nothing comes close to Him, He is in a different league to everything else that exists.

Yet, the Father's eyes looking at us reveal another perspective altogether. In the life, the death and resurrection of Christ we discover that *we* are the focal point of His yearning. We are given an indication of the unbelievable significance that we have in His eyes. Our value is evident the cost that He was willing to "pay" for us. Our value is equal to the life

---

309   "It is the glory of God to conceal a matter; to search out a matter is the glory of kings." (Prov 25:2 NIV).

of His son – each of us is worth one "Christ". The Father set this as the price for us[310]. I find that this concept alone provides enough of material for discussion with God to last for half of eternity.

God loves details

God created the world to be unbelievably detailed. It has more intricacies than we could ever grasp. God conceived and implemented each of them – He loves the small details! This makes it so clear that, for God, there is no topic that is too small or too insignificant to discuss. God is not just the God of major decisions, but also of the microcosm of our everyday lives. If we grant Him access, He will open up a whole new level of relationship with Him. If we allow Him to advise us when doing the shopping, cooking, putting on make-up or playing sport, we will learn of the close intimacy He desires. Discovering His presence in the little things in our lives makes it clear how unfathomably He loves us and cares for us.

He chooses His own topics

Allowing God to speak into the finer details of our existence is not without risk. Let's take a look for a moment at how Jesus chooses topics of conversation: he is shameless and has no regard for taboo. He doesn't worry about the rules of language, but he is hard-hitting and wins every argument.

I regularly find that God says things all of a sudden; things that would never enter my mind as a topic of conversation. This includes confronting my "secret" negative thoughts.

Freedom for the nose

God interrupted[311] me, speaking via His internal voice, in the middle of an intense prayer time. "Kristian, why don't you like your nose?"

Me: "Oh, God, I like my nose alright..."

---

310   Matt 20:28.

311   Perhaps my prayer wasn't as important to Him as I thought?

God: "No Kristian, you don't like it. What would it be like to make peace with your nose – after all, isn't it from me?"

Right from my childhood, my nose had actually always been something I was internally preoccupied with (who told God that?). I made peace with my nose by thanking God for it. Since that day I haven't wasted another moment thinking about my nose – how awesome is that?! If only it were always so simple!

He chooses my topics

In the same way as God speaks about content of His choosing, He also speaks about topics that are relevant to me. If it is important to me, then it is important to Him - because I am important to Him. There are no topics that God considers unimportant if they are our topics.

If I am standing in the supermarket and don't know what I should buy to eat, I ask Him what I should cook. When I am buying clothes I ask Him to direct me to things that would look good on me. I ask Him to show me where a parking space is or where I have left my wallet. I ask Him why my head is sore, why I'm in a bad mood and so on and so forth. I love hearing from Him about how life works, and He loves explaining it to me.

When I describe it this way it perhaps sounds as though I always immediately hear an answer to my questions. This is by no means the case. However, I am in a process of relationship with Him and am learning from Him. And the more regularly I seek His voice, the more often I hear Him.

Beer belly

A few years ago I looked down at myself and, speaking more to myself than to God, I said: "God, somehow or other I have developed a bit of a belly." That internal voice swiftly and mercilessly issued its analysis: "Kristian, if you are really asking how that happened, it's the beer!" God was right – two weeks without beer and the belly was gone!

What is still holding me back?

When we planted a church in Hamburg in 2008, spiritually speaking I felt in really good shape. As we walked through our neighbourhood praying, the following conversation unfolded: "God, I want to give myself to you more – what is still holding me back?"

The internal voice answered: "Arrogance and pride, my son. You take yourself much too seriously." Wow... I really wasn't looking for such a precise answer!

MULL IT OVER: WHAT CAN I EXPECT GOD TO SPEAK TO ME ABOUT?

1. Consider: Are there topics about which you do not want to hear God's opinion? Write down any that come to mind and what the reasons for your attitude might be.

2. Reconsider your resistance and, when you are ready, turn away from it. Remember that the power to change comes from the living word of God, spoken to you. Begin viewing His promptings as seeds of change. Actively give God permission to talk to you about any subject, at any time. Because we can easily fall back into non-Christ-like listening patterns, it is good to grant this permission out loud now and then.

How can I process what God says in a productive manner?

Gathering and harvesting – the spiritual journal

Gathering the words that God says to me has become the most important strategy in learning to understand God. In January of every year I purchase a notebook and attempt to carry this with me at all times. In this book I write down prayers, thoughts, spiritual exercises, sermon ideas, dreams, impressions, drawings – put simply, everything significant that comes out of communication between me and God. For the sake of clarity, I write my thoughts, prayers, spiritual exercises and ideas at the front of the book. Things God says to me (dreams, impressions, promises) I write at the back[312]. Each time I note down the date and location, and in some cases a heading.

In December I bring in my harvest. First I read everything and underline sentences that stand out to me. These 25-30 sentences I then type up in a document on my computer, stating the respective dates. This harvest does take up two working days, but it is extremely worthwhile. For every year since 2006 I have a document that allows me to check what the main prompts God gave me that year were. This way, I can trace the consistency and faithfulness with which He speaks to me over the years.

What are the advantages of writing down His words?

Understanding the long path He walks with me

God's work in our lives often takes us by surprise – however, from His perspective it is not spontaneous, but rather part of His eternal plan with us. God has always known where He wants to go with us and how He will bring us there. Some of His processes draw out over periods of years of decades[313] and can only be recognised retrospectively. For me, this retrospection has only become possible since I began archiving God's words spoken to me. I recognise His targeted and constant commitment in my life. Many thoughts He places in my head still turn out to be inspirational and life-bringing months later. By remembering His personal promises, my faith is strengthened and my future path laid out before me.

Jesus experienced this very thing. It must have encouraged him when reading the texts of the prophets to see that God inspired the writing down of details regarding his mission and life, long before his birth. Their prophecies inspire him and sketch out his commission[314]. They help him to see his place in history and strengthen him in his darkest hour[315]. If Jesus needs help understanding his Father's long game, how much more do we need it?

---

312   I simply turn the book "upside down" and start writing.

313   See Moses and Joseph.

314   Luke 4:17ff.

315   Psalm 22:2; Matt 27:46.

204

Preparation

By recording his words I have noticed how some dreams and thoughts only make sense months or years later – i.e. they were a form of preparation.

At the beginning of 2011 God opened my eyes to a series of dreams that I had in January 2008. Although I had regularly thought about these dreams over the subsequent three years, I had only ever been able to understand fragments of them. They foresaw a number of difficult events that I would go through, and were thus encouraging to me when I found myself "caught up in the whirlwind". God had seen my future and had prepared me in order that I could stand firm.

Mary also experiences the same thing. Following the birth of Jesus she receives a series of prophetic words relating to her life and calling. Shepherds tell her of how angels had announced to them that, in Jesus, the Messiah had been born[316]. A few weeks later Simeon speaks similar words of confirmation to her in the temple[317]. He also prophesies that she will endure great pain, as Jesus will be met with resistance. Shortly thereafter, the prophetess Hannah likewise confirms Jesus' calling[318].

These words prepare Mary and help her to believe in Jesus later on, when he experiences rejection and is murdered. We read that Mary "pondered [the words of the shepherds] in her heart", that is to say, she attempted to understand their meaning. She gathered God's words and could later "harvest" them when the announced events came to pass. It is not without reason that Mary is one of the last to remain waiting at the cross, and one of the first to meet Jesus after his resurrection. She was well prepared.

Testing and seeking clarity regarding His words

Paul writes that we should test prophetic words[319]. The importance of this instruction increases in keeping with the potential level of consequence that God's words could

---

316   Luke 2:17ff.

317   Luke 2:28ff.

318   Luke 2:36ff.

319   1 Thes 5:20.

have[320]. A test is rarely completed instantly, but instead takes time. Only by writing His words down can we allow time to pass without forgetting what God said to us.

At the same time, a process of clarification takes place as we write things down, as we are forced to transform spiritual impressions into words and statements[321]. If a spiritual impression proves too confusing to write down, I take this as a sign that it probably doesn't come from God[322].

Building a treasure chest

Presumably each of us is aware of times during which the voice of God seems far off and his presence barely tangible. Our memories of God's work in the past then seem puzzling or are overshadowed by negative images. In times like these it is essential that we have a testimony that we can refer back to. My spiritual journey is such a testimony. Reading the described encounters with God and the impressions He has given me awakens new courage and faith within me. On several occasions I have discovered promises or words from Him that I had completely forgotten, and have then begun thanking Him all over again.

In spite of my detours, God's path for me is constant – His blessed work in the past thus shows me what I can expect from Him in the present[323]. If we do not have a clear picture of His faithfulness in our past, it is difficult to develop faith for our future.

---

320   If I believe that I have heard from God that I am meant to marry a worship leader from my church, this clearly would require a greater level of testing than when He reminds me to pick up flowers for my wife when I'm at the shops.

321   Sometimes I attempt to draw an impression if I am finding it difficult to express in words. A few strokes of a pen can often say much more than words.

322   However, this is only a rule of thumb. Paul reports that when a man he knew was raptured into paradise, he "heard inexpressible things, things that no-one is permitted to tell." (2 Cor 12:3 NIV). Thus, there evidently exists a type of divine revelation that is difficult to write down or even speak aloud.

323   Incidentally, this also applies when reading the Bible!

TEAM TALK: HOW CAN I PROCESS WHAT GOD SAYS IN A PRODUCTIVE MANNER?

1. Discuss among yourselves: How have you processed what God says up to this point? Have you written it down, noted it, forgotten it ...?

2. Consider together: Do any other benefits of keeping a spiritual journal spring to mind?

3. Can you remember the promptings or words that you have heard from God over the last 12 months? Discuss among yourselves: Have you given them their attention? What fruit came from His words?

Summing up – Learning to hear, first steps

Can I impose rules of communication on God?

Every follower of Jesus would agree that God is inconceivable, uncontrollable and all-powerful. Nonetheless, we are often unwilling to expect God's voice within these descriptions. On the contrary, we have an internal list of paths, places and times at which God is permitted to speak up[324]. What would happen if I were to instruct Kim that she could only communicate with me at specific times and specific locations? I wouldn't even like to imagine!

Does God fit within my framework?

God wants to speak to us through **everything**; He wants to talk to us **everywhere** and He wants to talk to us **at all times**. His works are an expression of this: they reveal Him and His character everywhere and at all times[325]. The only way for me to limit God's voice is by limiting my expectation.

Each of us has an internal framework of expectation, in which the voice of God is received and accepted. If God reveals Himself outside of this framework, we are deaf to His voice, we cannot assign it to a specific box, we find it laughable or even threatening. If, for example, we are of the opinion that God would not speak to us through an angel, through natural

---

324   What does your list look like?

325   Romans 1:19f.

phenomena, scents or animals, then this belief becomes fact – He can't. Our expectation filter does not allow His voice to get through.

God reserves the right to speak in every conceivable and even yet to be conceived ways. He makes use of all the options at His disposal – and every option is at His disposal! To limit God speaking to us amounts to us wanting to control Him. No-one is yet to manage this.

What is my responsibility?

As in every relationship, the framework of communication between us and God is dynamic and grows as the relationship grows. With increasing revelation our responsibility to process what He says well also increases. This brings us to the tension between revelation and responsibility, and to the next chapter.

Chapter 12

Inside revelation – mastering the three stages of hearing from God

All people hear God.
Some of them recognise that they are hearing God.
Some of those who recognise that they are hearing God understand
what He is saying.
Some of those who understand what He is saying, follow His voice.

God's voice and our responsibility

Several years ago, an acquaintance of mine told be about a time when she came into difficulty as a result of misinterpreting the voice of God. She had entered hastily into a relationship, which turned out to be a real nightmare for her. When on one occasion I was using her example to explain how important it is not only to hear God, but also to learn to understand Him, one listener contradicted me forcibly. He countered: "God is all-powerful. If He wants me to hear and understand, He can simply make me!" The notion that it is possible to misinterpret God's voice, to process it incorrectly and thus have to suffer the consequences, did not make sense to him, and clearly made him fearful.

His comment stuck with me, and prompted me to reflect: God speaks – but to what extent is it our responsibility to hear and understand what He says? How are His revelations and our responsibility to understand Him and act accordingly linked?

It is without doubt true that God, on account of His omnipotence, could cause me to hear Him completely, understand and act perfectly in accordance with His will[326]. But does He want to interfere in my life in this way? Has He not instead opted to create room for relationship, rather than enforcing influence with all of his might?

On the cross, God chooses powerlessness[327] and pays an unbelievably high price to make a love relationship with me possible. His wish is that I make decisions out of love for Him, in the same way He does. This love is not a spontaneous emotion, but rather means giving Him my "everything", in order to get to know Him and follow Him. Doing this is my responsibility and entails the possibility that I will hear incorrectly, misunderstand and make mistakes. God is neither frustrated nor angry when I make mistakes – they are part of the love relationship that He himself designed. On the other hand, if I work on the basis of an image of God whereby God "coerces" me into understanding Him – and maybe even to act correctly – the love relationship He desires is snuffed out again.

Three stages of hearing from God

It thus becomes clear that we bear a partial responsibility for the relationship. Below I will examine what exactly this entails. The first step towards accepting responsibility for the relationship occurs in that we become aware the God communicates with us, even though there is the chance that we will misunderstand.

Knowledge of our fallibility when listeni.ng serves as a safety belt and also reveals to us that God does not want to provide us with information, but instead offers relationship!

---

326   Who can say they have never wanted this to happen?!
327   Matt 26:53ff

If we understand God incorrectly, this happens unintentionally – a classic misunderstanding occurs. Misunderstanding when listening to God often occurs because we mix up the various levels on which He talks to us, or are not even aware of their existence. It is helpful to differentiate between the *hearing*, the *interpretation* and the *application* of what God is saying.

The first time I visited the Slot-Art Festival in Poland, I experienced over lunch how these three stages are linked. Once I had found the food stands on the festival grounds, I was struck by the complexity of the Polish language as I read the menus. I couldn't even begin to decipher what meals were hidden behind the characters on the menu!

The menu did indeed reveal to me that there was food available, but not what sort of food this was. I could not interpret the revelation and thus could not apply the information. It is the same with the voice of God, when we do not understand Him and therefore cannot follow His words, or at least not in a productive manner.

Below I explain the three stages in detail.

Perceiving God's voice

"Like an earring of gold or an ornament of fine gold is the rebuke
*of a wise judge to a **listening** ear."*[328]

Every follower of Jesus expects to hear God's voice within a certain framework. This framework, and as such our ability to perceive God's communication, is determined by our *expectation, mindfulness, our knowledge of God* and *our desire to be close to Him*.

If my impression of God is that He is rather distant, then my **expectation** that I will hear Him will be low. If I tend to divide my life into spiritual and secular activities, I will expect Him to speak primarily at church services or during other "holy" activities. While on these occasions my **mindfulness** is correspondingly high, it lies dormant throughout the rest of the week.

---

328   Prov 25:12 GNB, emphasis KR.

The degree to which I am familiar with God's character is expressed using the phrase **knowledge of God**. Jesus' knowledge of God is evident in his limitless trust, his faithful following and his assurance regarding the love of his Father. In the fact that he can say, "the Father loves (me)[329]", he defines a previously unknown dimension of relationship with God. Through his knowledge of the fatherhood of God, Jesus reveals to us the climax of the revelation of God that develops throughout the Old Testament. This experience of the love of God ultimately results in the increasing **desire to be close to Him**.

My communicative expectation is based on the content, quantity and time of the communication. The more intimate the relationship in question, the greater the scope of the shared communicative framework. In a short-term or superficial relationship, the communicative framework is therefore rather small.

Because God's interest in us extends beyond all measure and because He knows everything about us and is always with us, our expectation when it comes to communication with him cannot be large enough. If we want to grow, we can intentionally *nourish* our expectation, our mindfulness, our knowledge of God and our desire to be close to Him. Spiritual exercises, rituals, moments of reflection, Bible studies, prayer meetings, home groups or similar habits all help us in this.

Jesus himself lives in constant expectation and mindfulness towards his Father. His knowledge of God and his desire to be close to God are unlimited. His relationship with God is not part of his life, but rather his life is part of his relationship with God.

Jesus not only hears God in his everyday life, but his everyday life is actually formed as a result of hearing God. He allows his Father's voice to orchestrate his life. Everything he does happens as a result of his Father's prompting. Jesus explains this in an argument with the Pharisees: "(...) the Son can do nothing by himself; he can do only what he sees his Father doing, because whatever the Father does the Son also does." (John 5:19 NIV). As followers of Jesus it is precisely this lifestyle that is our inheritance and goal.

---

329   John 5:20.

Learning to interpret God's voice

Interpreting God's voice is not in the same league as merely hearing – here it's all about understanding.

The importance of not only hearing one another, but also understanding, recently became clear to me all over again when visiting a friend who has a dog. He sat beside us and began blinking at us. "Do you see how he is blinking at us?" she asked me. "He wants out – that's how he lets us know."

To be honest, I had thought he had something in his eye. Because my friend knew her dog better than I did and was familiar with its body language, she could interpret its communication without any problem. Although we both noticed that her dog was communicating, only she was able to understand him – and as a reward could then go out with him.

Our ability to interpret God's voice, that is, to understand, depends first and foremost on our knowledge of His character. In addition to knowledge of His character, mentors and our willingness to invest time and energy are crucial factors when it comes to learning to understand Him. If we do not invest any time following and pondering over His revelation, we will miss out on the full benefit of His words.

The first time I read in the book of Romans that God can be "understood from what has been made"[330], I didn't actually understand this remark. I looked at the trees in my garden and tried desperately to see God in them – to no avail! Only years later did the fog lift, when I came to understand that God had made creation for *me*. He didn't need it – I, on the other hand, was urgently in need of things like air, nutrition, water and sunlight. By creating such a beautiful and diverse living space, God communicates His desire to care for me, but also His generosity[331] and love[332].

---

330   Rom 1:19ff.

331   Creation contains more than we need or ever will be aware of.

332   If we want to show someone we love them, we give them something beautiful.

213

If I look at plants now, I can interpret what I see within the context of my current, expanded knowledge of God, and in them I see the Creator communicating with me.

When looking at the sea, His boundless strength and the depth of His character become clear to me.

A glance up to the stars often makes me shiver – the infinite greatness and wisdom of God appears to shine through them.

The unique nature of every human being shows me His creativity and attention to detail. Whereas previously I was not even certain that God spoke through His creation, today I can even understand what He is saying. As a result of my understanding – that is, by applying this understanding – thankfulness, worship and an awareness of God's presence are growing in my life.

Hearing does not mean understanding

"Just because I hear a dog barking, does not mean that I understand him."

When, on a boat trip, Jesus warned his disciples against the 'yeast' of the Pharisees and Sadducees; they misunderstand him spectacularly! "They discussed this among themselves and said, "It is because we didn't bring any bread." Aware of their discussion, Jesus asked, "You of little faith, why are you talking among yourselves about having no bread?" " He explains to them that he was talking about the teaching of the Pharisees and not about their baked goods[333]. The disciples had understood Jesus' words – but not his message.

Each of us who are getting to know God better learns to hear Him and to understand Him. This means that we not only learn to hear the words God is speaking, but also to grasp their content and meaning. We know from communication between two people that hearing and understanding do not always take place at the same time. The gospels show us that the very same applies to our relationship with God.

---

333   Matt 16:5ff.

It is often the case that the disciples do not understand Jesus' parables and ask him for clarification *later on*, when they are alone with Jesus[334].

When Jesus washes Peter's feet, Peter doesn't understand the interaction. Jesus predicts that he will *later* come to understand what the washing of his feet means[335].

In the same way, we read that the disciples are only able to make sense of some of Jesus' comments *after* Jesus has been resurrected[336].

Even if we do not immediately understand everything God says, we can be certain that He also wants to explain what He says. The "exploration" of what He says is sometimes like a treasure hunt, during which we come to know Him more profoundly. Increasing understanding of His voice thus births increasing intimacy between us and Him.

Learning a life of listening

A lifestyle of listening is an ongoing journey, which cannot remain stuck in the purely theoretical. We can compare living a lifestyle marked by hearing God with a muscle – it is well known that muscles deteriorate when are not put to use. If we do not develop our ability to hear God into a permanent lifestyle, or if we fail to provide His word with fertile soil in our everyday lives, our ability to hear Him will slowly but surely dwindle away.

Sometimes I experience this very phenomenon and God has to once again remind me of His voice and His revelations, as I have lost hold of them. I then read about past spiritual encounters in my journal – in my own handwriting, which move me incredibly and seem almost unfamiliar to me, as if I have never actually experienced them before. I am truly thankful that God is always gracious as He leads me down the same process of realisation, time and again. In this way, previous revelations are brought back to the front of my mind for me to process all over again.

In a world marked by distance from God, revelation has the tendency to evaporate away. God is aware of this and is therefore continually in the practice of reminding us. Obviously, you only need reminding if you have forgotten in the first place. This is one of the tasks of

---

334   Mark 4:10.

335   John 13:7.

336   John 2:22; John 12:16.

the Holy Spirit. "But the Advocate, the Holy Spirit, whom the Father will send in my name, will *teach* you all things and will remind you of everything I have said to you." (John 14:26 NIV, emphasis KR).

Regardless of whether we are experts in hearing and understanding God, this does not mean that we will automatically remain as such forever. Steps backwards with regard to the ability of people or groups of people to hear God are described at length in the Bible. The author of the book of Hebrews describes his intended readers as people who "by this time (…) ought to be teachers" and accuses them of "no longer trying to understand" – they have become hard of hearing. They once again require the "elementary truths of God's word"[337]. This group has obviously taken steps backwards in their ability to hear and understand God.

In the first letter to Timothy, Paul talks about Hymenaeus and Alexander, who rejected a good conscience[338]. This refers to people who hear God's voice, but who have stubbornly ignored it and have thus become indifferent.

In the case of the prophet Jeremiah, we read of a threat of judgement over the nation of Israel, because it no longer listens to God[339].

Even if we have just hit a spiritual bull's eye, this is far from a guarantee that we will understand future revelations. In the lives of the disciples we can see how moments of great revelation go hand in hand with moments of human short-sightedness[340].

---

337 "We have much to say about this, but it is hard to make it clear to you because you no longer try to understand. [12] In fact, though by this time you ought to be teachers, you need someone to teach you the elementary truths of God's word all over again. You need milk, not solid food!" (Heb 5:11–12 NIV).

338 "(…) holding on to faith and a good conscience, which some have rejected and so have suffered shipwreck with regard to the faith. [20] Among them are Hymenaeus and Alexander (…)." (1 Tim 1:19f NIV).

339 "These wicked people, who *refuse to listen* to my words, who follow the stubbornness of their hearts and go after other gods to serve and worship them, will be like this belt—completely useless." (Jer 13:10 NIV, emphasis KR).

340 This was also the case with Adam and Eve.

For instance, Peter recognises Jesus as Christ and just moments later – inspired by Satan[341] – he attempts to prevent him from going to the cross. "Simon Peter answered, "You are the Messiah, the Son of the living God." Jesus replied, "Blessed are you, Simon son of Jonah, for this was not revealed to you by flesh and blood, but by my Father in heaven. (…) From that time on Jesus began to explain (…) that he must be killed. (…) Peter took him aside and began to rebuke him. (…) Jesus turned and said to Peter, "Get behind me, Satan! You are a stumbling block to me; you do not have in mind the concerns of God, but merely human concerns." " (Matt 16:16–23 NIV).

How does interpretation function in everyday life?

Interpretation means asking what the God-given revelation is intended to mean to me. At first this seems more complicated than it really is. We continually test our communication with regard to its meaning on a daily basis. If we see someone we know on the other side of the road raising their hand in our direction, this can have various meanings: perhaps he is greeting us, warning us, or maybe just stretching his arm (without actually having seen us at all). We generally interpret communication such as this within a few milliseconds, as we have an experience-based template to which we can refer.

If we come across a new environment, group of people or culture, we must acquire an internal grasp of the individuals present in order to be able to intuitively "read" their communication. Our relationship with God is similar – the more we know His character and nature, the better we can interpret and understand His communication. On the other hand, if we have crude misconceptions about God, these will taint our interpretations accordingly.

Pictures, symbols, parables etc.

Interpretation is particularly necessary when God speaks to us symbolically, through internal pictures, visions, dreams or the like. If I ask God where I can find a free parking space and his response is highly specific ("There is a free space in front of house number 3 on

---

341   Not bad: Here the rock on which Jesus builds his church serves as the personal mouthpiece of Satan. So for those of us who, as a result of demonic inspiration, have ever spoken utter rubbish in the name of God, there is still hope!

Abbey Road."), I don't really need to interpret what He is saying, but can instead act in an equally specific manner. However, if in responding He directs my thoughts towards a house in our neighbourhood, I must interpret that there is presumably a space for me in front of this house.

> In 2003 I received a picture from God showing two hands passing a baby to me, and a voice said: 'I want to give you a new child!' My initial, impulsive interpretation was that it referred to the planting of a church. As I reflected and prayed I became increasingly convinced that God was encouraging me, to plant a church. Four year later when, in the midst of planting the church, I found myself going through a difficult phase, a friend of mine shared the following impression with me: "I see you once again in the pain of childbirth." She couldn't have described the process of planting the church any better. I immediately interpreted that in the symbol of this pain, God was speaking into the situation regarding the planting process – He had previously used a similar image – and I felt encouraged.

The interpretation of a word from God delivered in symbolic form can be thoroughly challenging and can cost time and energy. In Acts 10 we read of how God spoke to Peter through a highly symbolic vision. In the vision he sees a sheet descending from heaven, containing all sorts of animals – which were considered unclean for Jews. God commands him three times to kill the animals and eat, but Peter strongly objects, citing Jewish dietary restrictions. When the vision comes to a close, Peter "wonders" as to what it should mean – that is, he attempts to find an interpretation. His pondering is initially without success. We read on as to how two men appear and ask Peter to accompany them to the home of Cornelius. The text reads: "While Peter was still thinking about the vision, the Spirit said to him (…)", "Do not hesitate to go with them (…)"[342]. It is still unclear to Peter what God was trying to say through the "sheet of creepy crawlies". Only when he arrives at the house of Cornelius, after a three-day journey, does he receive full understanding of the revelation: "Then Peter began to speak: "I *now* realize how true it is that God does not

---

342   Acts 10:19f.

show favoritism." "[343] Thus, in this case there are three days and a great deal of pondering between God speaking and Peter gaining understanding.

When John receives parts of his revelation, this also takes places in the form of symbols, which he does not understand at first. An angel interprets for him. "But the angel said to me, "Why did you marvel? *I will tell you* the mystery of the woman and of the beast that carries her, which has the seven heads and the ten horns." (...) *"Then he said to me,* "The waters which you saw, where the harlot sits, are peoples, multitudes, nations, and tongues." (Rev 17:7 and 15 NIV, emphasis KR).

Here John requires external help in order to reach understanding. This is also the case for some of the prophets of the Old Testament during their visions[344].

Even the disciples of Jesus required that he provide an interpretation for his parables and pictures. Jesus taught a lot in public using parables, and having withdrawn he provides his disciples with a full interpretation. "But when He was alone, those around Him with the twelve asked Him about the parable." (Mark 4:10 NIV).

Obstacles to interpretation

It is not surprising that different people have differing interpretations of the same word of God. Our image of God, our knowledge of God, prior experiences with His voice or our social background are just some of the parameters on which we base our assessment. Generally speaking, we can say that we do not interpret God's word as it "is", but as we "are". This also becomes clear in the example of Peter, as he interprets God's voice speaking through the animals, reptiles and birds, within his own Jewish cultural framework[345].

Various levels of understanding

In order to clarify this, we shall look at a story from John 12. Jesus finds himself in a crowd and prays aloud to his Father, who responds audibly so as all can hear. Jesus prays: " "Father, glorify your name!" Then a voice came from heaven, "I have glorified it, and

---

343   Acts 10:34, NCV, emphasis KR.

344   Jer 1:11; 1:13; Zech 6:4.

345   In contrast, many people from Asian cultures would have accepted the offer with thanks.

will glorify it again." *The crowd* that was there and heard it said it had thundered; *others* said an angel had spoken to him. *Jesus* said, "This voice was for your benefit, not mine." " (John 12:28–30 NIV, emphasis KR).

The text describes three groups of listeners, who hear God's words simultaneously, yet come to completely different interpretations regarding their origin and message. The first group are referred to in the text as "the crowd". Upon hearing the voice of the Father they think it is a natural phenomenon, concluding that it is thunder they have heard. This group contains people with little or no spiritual expectation. Perhaps they had come to hear Jesus out of philosophical interest, saw him as a good person from whom they could learn, or perhaps as an organiser of cultural events. In any case they had no great expectation that spiritual events would take place in the presence of Jesus.

The second group is referred to as "others", and they assume God's voice to be the voice of an angel. In contrast to the first, this group has spiritual expectation, but no knowledge of God. Although these people assume that heavenly beings are responding to Jesus' prayer, the unique relationship between Jesus and the Father remains hidden to them. They perhaps view Jesus as a prophet or miracle-worker, but not as someone who would receive an audible response from God.

The third group consists only of Jesus. He not only hears the words, but also knows by whom they are spoken and can interpret their message. Jesus turns to the crowd and attempts to explain to them that they have just listened in on a powerful encouragement from God. He says: "This voice was for your benefit, not mine."

I am touched by the fact that God clearly wanted to encourage all of the people there to believe in Jesus, using His voice. However, Jesus is the only one who understands the full magnitude of the statement. Could it be that it is often a similar case with us? God speaks to us and wants to bless us, but instead of being encouraged, we get out our umbrella?

Here are two examples of times I have heard God speak, have understood and been encouraged.

God speaks through a storm.

In 1999 I attended a discipleship school in Southeast Asia. One evening we were praying for a persecuted people group. Having started praying, things quickly got straight to the point. We began to feel God's love for these people and some of us wept in compassion, inspired by the Holy Spirit's presence in that moment. It felt as though we were on the verge of some form of spiritual breakthrough, as suddenly a violent storm broke out directly above our building. With the first roll of thunder, the girls shrieked in fear and the power cut out[346].

I was excited that God had responded to our prayer with this magnificent sign[347]. When I was talking about it with a few students, however, I was met with puzzled looks – they could not see any logical connection between the thunder (directly above our building!) and our prayer. I was bewildered, as for me the connection was crystal clear, and so I finally asked out school leader. "Is it possible that God wanted to confirm our prayer through the thunder?" He looked at me with eyes that had seen a great deal over several years of mission in Asia, and said: "Of course, that was His 'Amen' – God is like that!"

God speaks through digital watches.

I was driving with my friend Manuel to a meeting, at which a crucial decision for an important project was to be made. As we arrived at the venue, we asked God once again for His favour. In this moment I noticed on the number plate of the car in front of me the numbers 555[348]. I said: "God will give us overflowing grace!", pointed to the licence plate and explained the series of number aloud. Manuel's smirk revealed to me that he found my thought great, but that he could not entirely follow.

---

346   To be honest, it might not have been just the girls who shrieked – it was dark, so difficult to tell. In any case they all shrieked *like* girls.

347   "Then the Lord will appear over them; his arrow will flash like lightning. The Sovereign Lord will sound the trumpet; he will march in the storms of the south." (Zech 9:14 NIV).

348   In my love language with God this combination means overflowing grace.

The meeting went as well as it possibly could have – the doors were opened wide for the project! As we travelled back the next day, I looked at my watch – the time read exactly 5:55. Manuel and I took a deep breath and enjoyed a moment in complete awareness of being seen and cared for by God.

Applying God's voice

When we recognise and interpret God's communication, the question remains as to whether and how we convert this into action.

Are we always required to act when God speaks?

If we are asking ourselves whether every word from God must be followed by an action, then the answer is no. Indeed, communication between human beings does not always contain a call to action. Likewise, this is not always the case with God. The main reason why God speaks to us is because this is an expression of His relationship with us. Friends talk with one another. They share their knowledge, their thoughts, feelings, stories or desires.

Another reason why God speaks is the creative effect and seed-like nature of His words. Through His words, God places thoughts, visions or processes of change within us. When this happens, we don't always notice it the same way. God's words may only have meaning or bring fruit much later, once they have matured.

At his baptism, when Jesus heard his Father's voice say: "You are my Son, whom I love"[349], at first God's revelation has no direct application, but it does plant a seed. A short time later, when Jesus being God's child is called into question by the Devil, in the wilderness[350], the words previously heard bring Jesus security in his position – the seed sprouts and its effect unfurls. In this account, revelation, interpretation and application are temporally disconnected.

---

349   Mark 1:11.
350   Matt 4:3.

Sometimes we are required to act when God speaks!

All that said, God's voice may also require a 100% specific response, for example intercession, the passing on of His word, simple obedience or something else altogether.

No room for interpretation

When I was at an event and looked around the room, my gaze came to rest on one specific person, and Jesus said to me internally: Give him the contents of your pocket[351]. There wasn't much to interpret in this, instead I was being prompted to carry out a specific action.

A seed is planted and a process begins

As already mentioned, in 2001 when God offered me the "new baby" in a short vision[352] and I interpreted this as an invitation to plant a church. In the same moment I heard Him say[353]: "I can only fill up empty hands." It suddenly became clear to me that planting the church would cost me my leadership responsibility and relationships within the Hamburg Jesus Freak community. My interpretation of what He was saying, through pictures and His voice, initiated a difficult separation process. Twelve months later we finally left the community and connected with the Altona Vineyard, who in 2008 sent us out as a church-planting project[354].

Here God's voice did involve a call to action and at the same time planted a seed within me, as after the vision the topic of church planting never left me and, for that matter, grew in me over the years that followed.

We can thus see that God's word can contain a mixture of seeds that will not sprout until a later time, and direct calls to action.

---

351   It was money, not a used tissue.

352   Here I am not referring to anything spectacular, just moving images seen with closed eyes.

353   By means of His internal voice.

354   There were actually seven years between God's invitation to plant a church and the planting of the church itself! God was simply not in a hurry. I, on the other hand, felt like Brad Pitt in the film, "Seven Years in Tibet", who has to wait for seven years before he can hold his son in his arms.

The pain of application

When we come to apply what God has said, we are required to exercise more faith than when hearing or interpreting. The integrity of our discipleship and out willingness to take risks, suddenly become evident in such moments.

A missed window of opportunity

During an internal flight within the USA a female soldier sat beside me, who appeared to be en route to deployment. A strong thought suddenly sprung to mind: 'Tell her I will protect her, she will return without injury and I will also look after her mother.' I was completely shocked at this direct order and felt totally overwhelmed. At the same time I could tell that this might be an important word for this young woman. I struggled with this prompt from God right until we landed. Upon disembarking from the aircraft it was clear that my window of opportunity to talk with her was tight. As I stood behind her I suddenly thought: 'I have nothing to lose here!' As this thought came to mind we became separated in the crowd, and I could no longer find her.

All that was left was for me to apologise to the Holy Spirit. The limitations of my willingness to follow His voice was painfully laid out in front of my eyes.

Please send someone else...

While out jogging I ran past a couple running in the opposite direction. As they drew level with me and I looked at them, I suddenly thought: "The couple are considering having an abortion – tell them that the child will be a great blessing to them." I felt as if I had been struck by lightning, and was completely out of my depth. The memory shot into my head of how a few weeks before I had asked God to use me as His messenger in everyday life. And yet right now I had no desire to talk to these strangers about such an intimate subject. At the same time it was clear to me that under certain circumstances, a human life could depend on my courage. My head was spinning and I finally asked God: "Please send someone else – I can't do it." A "moderate[355]" peace fell on me and also the awareness that I still had a lot to learn.

I wanted these to be the only stories of this kind that I had to tell!

However, if, in speaking to us, God wants to prompt us to carry out an action, the window of opportunity for obedience is not always so small. At other times God has spoken to me over periods of months before I was ready to act – better late than never![356]

Discipleship is spelt R.I.S.K[357]

We all know doubt, indecision, fear of change or the cost of discipleship. Although we hear and understand God, the fruit of His words is often lost in the battle with these Goliaths. When inhibited by them, we limit our pursuit of Jesus to activities in which we do not actually need God, and intentionally let opportunities that are outside of our spiritual comfort zone pass us by.

This is tragic! What sense is there in hearing and understanding God, if we do not allow our lives to be directed and changed by His voice? At the end of the day, God is not interested in keeping us informed, but rather wants to transform us and those around us. The integrity of our discipleship is not seen in the fact that we carry around a Bible or pray weighty prayers. It is only in close combat, when our high-risk faith requires painfully specific action, is its true nature revealed. If we want to follow Jesus we have to be his voice *and* his hands. Had Jesus kept silent hid himself away from obeying God's word, none of us would today be able to get to know the Father, in all of His multi-faceted character.

---

355   God forgives immediately – forgiving yourself takes time.

356   Matt 21:28.

357   Here I have altered the famous quote from John Wimber, "Faith is spelt R.I.S.K" slightly.

TEAM TALK: THE THREE STAGES OF HEARING FROM GOD

1. Were you aware of the three stages of hearing God's voice (hearing, interpretation, application)? Which of the concepts discussed are new to you?

2. Share stories in which you have mastered the three stages and some in which you have failed to do so. What were you able to learn from these events?

3. Which of the three stages is most challenging to you? Why? What exactly do you find difficult?

4. Consider what would help a person who has difficulty with hearing, interpreting or application to develop further. Draw up an action plan with steps for each of the three stages.

Chapter 13

Uncovering communication blockades

*"Great peace have those who love your law, and **nothing** can make them stumble."*[358]

Thus far we have grappled with the fact that God is a God who speaks and is seeking relationship and that human beings can hear Him. We shall now delve deeper into the question as to why we nonetheless often find it difficult to hear Him.

In so doing, we will shed light on circumstances that act as blockades. For the purpose of clarity I have subdivided these into *emotional, practical* and *external obstacles*. Each of these obstacles can occur in varying intensity and in extreme cases can mutate into a longstanding relational blockade between us and God.

Emotional barriers are generally rooted in our upbringing, our social background and internal injuries we may have suffered.

In contrast, *practical obstacles* refer mainly to issues regarding how we lead our lives: Do we have time, space, peace and quiet in order to hear from God?

---

358   Ps 119:165 NIV, emphasis KR.

External obstacles can be of a spiritual nature (e.g. impure spirits or curses) or may be to do with our current social and cultural environment.

Movements in one of the three areas of constraint can break down or reinforce barriers in one of the others. If, for example, I give God more time to speak to me (lack of time is a practical obstacle) emotional barriers will also be broken down as a result of the increased time in His presence. On the other hand, emotional obstacles can also be reinforced if I continually open myself up to an environment that does not share the values of Jesus (external obstacle).

Below I will begin by addressing obstacles on an emotional level. These can be divided into two main categories: *obstacles that developed as a result of our relationship with our parents*, and *various fears*.

Emotional obstacles: Our relationship with our parents

When learning to hear the voice of God, it seems essential that we become aware of how and what was communicated within our families. Some of us grew up in an emotionally unstable parental home. Perhaps we experienced our father as domineering or absent (emotionally or physically) or maybe our mother as overexerted, fearful or disappointed and withdrawn. A scenario such as this would bring typical patterns of communication with it, under the influence of which we grew up.

The manner in which we experienced communication with our parents creates a basic framework within us with regard to how we view communication with people and God. In this respect, two basic developmental patterns can be observed:

No basic trust in our own personal value has been imparted to us and we hear what others say against a background of mistrust, assuming they are being critical.

A basic trust in our own personal value has been imparted to us, and we also speak this value out over others and listen to them in good will.

When we get to know God, we unintentionally bring with us the communicative framework from our childhood and begin expecting God to speak within this framework. In order to be set free, we must become aware of how our parents formed our expectations and our ability to communicate. Letting go of destructive hearing patterns is a process that can last for years, with the support of many prayers and processes.

However, in the same way I have also experienced that in a fleeting moment God can restore a lost or warped ability to hear.

I have put together a list of five different types of parent. These are based on experiences and observations. They can occur in mixed form or as variations, and should be used as guidelines to help us understand our communication with God.

Type 1 – The overwhelmed parent

Our parents can be overwhelmed for the most varied of reasons. For example, it may be as the result of raising children on their own, financial need, emotional loneliness or illness. In such cases, communication with our parents can have a negative or world-weary aftertaste or may be accompanied by unforeseeable emotional outbursts or accusations. Perhaps our parents also intentionally attempt to ignore or play down important subjects "so as not to burden us". As a result, being overwhelmed can also birth highly results-oriented communication within the family – you only talk about the most essential topics.

The perception that our parents are overwhelmed can trigger the desire in us to want to compensate for their hardship. Because they do not accept any responsibility, we jump in on their behalf. We grow up with the feeling of being needed and holding responsibility – we fulfil an important task. Fulfilling this role can leave us emotionally isolated. Our own needs are suppressed, or in some cases not even recognised in the first place. Either way, it is generally the case that we are unable to express them. We learn to avoid problematic topics in conversations, engage in small talk and want to keep our parent's mind off the real issues. It can also be the case that we withdraw, as we do not want to annoy or burden them. We feel responsible for their situation or consider ourselves a burden to them.

Our perception of God: God is incapable.

With regard to our relationship with God, this can mean that our main directive is to avoid burdening Him with our problems. Internally voiced phrases such as: 'God has other things to do' or 'there are things that are more important to God' are lies that define our everyday lives. We carry within us a subconscious feeling of worthlessness and do not believe that God will meet us in our lowly position.

Because we have not experienced parental care and provision, we also find it difficult to ask Him for help. As a result of having grown up within a responsibility vacuum, we have not experienced reliability and security and therefore have little trust in God's intervention. The notion that He reveals Himself as a "Father" who is capable of taking full responsibility for His creation – and our lives – seems foreign to us. Our prayer focuses primarily on "God's" concerns – we want to help Him.

Type 2 – The absent parent

Absence can be both physical and emotional. If our parents were frequently absent during our childhood, we will not have experienced a great deal of confirmation and attention from them. We grow up questioning whether they are actually interested in us or not. We learn to get by on our own and to form our own opinions. Our defining sense in life is one of loneliness or the idea that we are not important, valuable or loved. We compensate by "doing everything on our own" or by entering into a dependent relationship with someone.

Our perception of God: God is distant.

In our relationship with God we are unsure whether or not God is there (for us) and wants to talk to us. We sense an internal question mark when it comes to selecting topics of conversation and are unsure what an appropriate level of communication might be. In some instances, we view the fact that we have learned to get by "on our own" as a strength, which we could lose again in the event of too much interference from God. We continually ask ourselves whether God really loves us. We perceive Him to be silent and find it difficult to believe that He hears us and answers.

Type 3 – The abusive parent

Abuse within the parental home can take place on many completely different levels. Physical, verbal or emotional abuse by our parents often results in deep trauma. In the case of physical or verbal abuse, offence is committed against us either by means of contact or spoken word. Emotional abuse, on the other hand, is much more subtle and complex.

It may be the case that our parents want something that is "actually good" (e.g. a relationship with God) for us, but force us into it using non-Christ-like methods such as pressure or fear. This would be classified under religious abuse.

Perhaps as a child we notice that our presence merely serves to counteract the loneliness or boredom of our parents. Or perhaps we are pushed by our parents on account of our giftings: they actually only encourage us in certain areas so that they themselves feel successful. Or we find ourselves used as a tool for blackmail or as a buffer between arguing parents. What we are left with is a deep insecurity regarding our own value and purpose in life – this can also be expressed in the form of (auto-) aggression and anger. Domestic abuse can also result in a person placing strong boundaries between themselves and their own parents or other authority figures or in internal self-abandonment.

Our perception of God: God is unpredictable.

If we come from a background such as this, doubt regarding His love and His motives are pre-programmed into our relationship and communication with God. We are unsure as to what God's plans for us really are. We assume that there are ulterior motives behind what He says to us and weigh up His words carefully. We attempt to read hidden messages between the lines in order to prevent assault.

Although we sense a longing for God, we find it difficult, and not particularly desirable, when He draws near to us. This response pattern expresses our emotional ambivalence towards God – on the one hand we seek Him and long for Him, but on the other hand we reject Him completely. Driven by considerably insecurity towards God, we repeatedly try to find out whether God is good or evil.

If we have experienced abuse within the family setting, we can often find it difficult to separate good and evil, as the ones who abused us were at the same time "loving" and caring parents.

Type 4 – The performance parent

If we grow up in a performance household, we learn at an early stage that excellent performance and intelligence will see us through in life. Weakness, doubt and thoughtfulness are rejected or rationalised by our parents. Conversations among the family are intentionally directed by the parents and mainly address important and ambitious topics such as politics, art, economics or sport. We experience recognition and emotional proximity as a result of fulfilling our parents' expectations and as a reward for good performance. There is a prevailing tendency to talk down about people who are less "successful". As a result we are continually trying to classify the world according to who is "successful" and who is a "failure", and this habit is also transferred onto ourselves.

Our perception of God: God wants to improve me.

If we grow up in an environment such as this, a highly religious mindset can prevail within us, which leaves little room for God's compassion and love. We assume that the reason God speaks to us is actually to improve us and point out mistakes. We view God as the great teacher and ourselves as perpetual students. We suffer from the continual feeling of being schooled or even turn away from God for fear of failure, convinced that He wants nothing to do with our weaknesses.

We assume that there is a "right way" to live with God. We feel guilty when we fail Him or good and strong when we practice the faith successfully. We have no notion of how God works differently with each individual, and instruct others to copy us. Our communication with God is similar to our communication with our parents – one-dimensional, compulsive and results-oriented.

Type 5 – The gift-giving parent

In some instances, gift-giving parents offer the child what appears outwardly to be a wholesome family environment. As a result of their own emotional inadequacy, they communicate with the child through expensive gifts and excessive generosity rather than personal closeness. It can often be the case that they themselves grew up in traumatic poverty (e.g. the post-war generation in some parts of Europe following the 2nd World War) and now want to give their child what they were lacking.

As a child we love the presents, but at the same time there is the sense that the parents are "buying their way out", that is, fulfilling material desires rather than offering closeness. As the child, inside we are emotionally undernourished, whereas outwardly we have everything, and so we often try to fill the growing internal emptiness with external experiences and increased consumption.

Our perception of God: God is my ATM

As a result of all of this, the ambivalence towards our parents described above is something we also experience with God. A strong expectation develops in our relationship with God that He will bless us with material things and that our desires will be fulfilled immediately. On the one hand we expect material blessing, but on the other hand, this type of blessing does not show us that God really loves us.

The most important thing in our communication is the satisfaction of our needs. If God does not meet our expectation, we become stubborn and are insecure – doubting His love for us.

MULL IT OVER: OUR RELATIONSHIP WITH OUR PARENTS.

1. Which of the described parent types (or which combination) best matches your experience in childhood?

2. Lay your findings down before God and ask Him to reveal the blockades and perceptions of God that have developed in you. If necessary, engage in the process of forgiving your parents. Here it may help to ask for assistance from a friend or spiritual coach.

TEAM TALK: OUR RELATIONSHIP WITH OUR PARENTS.

1. Describe in your own words what the communication in your family was like. What do you remember as being positive and what as negative?

2. Identify strengths and weaknesses in your communication with God.

3. What conclusions can you draw when comparing your communication with God and that in your parental home?

4. Where did communication in your parental house define your communicative expectation towards God?

Emotional obstacles: Fears and concerns

"Fear needs me to survive – the opposite does not apply!"

Our fears can represent huge obstacles when learning to hear the voice of God. They cloud His speech, contaminate it and place it in doubt. They act as filters, only allowing certain information through, or preventing us from grasping the truth entirely. Fear towards God can only have an impact if we are not resting in God's love and acceptance. We then fear *hearing God* just as much as we fear *not being able to hear Him*. We fear *misunderstanding Him* or that *it might not even be God's voice that we are hearing in the first place.*

Fear of misunderstanding God

If we are afraid of misunderstanding God, this can result in us closing ourselves off to His personal voice and only allowing Him to speak indirectly. Church leaders, spiritual teachers, pastors or authors then serve as verifying authorities of God's voice and His will. If necessary, particular expectation is placed on our own church leadership to hear God's will for us and to convey this to us. As such, we palm off our responsibility to the "experts".

Unfortunately there are actually some leaders who allow themselves to be forced into such a role, or even just fall into it themselves. Such an allocation of roles will sooner or later result in the leader burning out, in disappointment or even spiritual abuse. The attempt to generate security by having the "pros" hear for us is condemned to failure and completely rules out God's actual aim of entering into a personal relationship with us. Added to this is the fact that our self-elected "experts" are just as likely to make mistakes as we are. If we just think of the Pharisees – they were the ones who pretended to understand everything and were considered the religious authorities in their day. Jesus casually refers to them as "the blind leading the blind[359]".

There is no reason for us to fear misunderstanding God. In fact there is no longer any reason for us to fear at all. As far as mistakes are concerned, these are probably unavoidable, as God alone is perfect in His ability to hear and understand Himself.

We are filled with the Holy Spirit and the "mind of Christ[360]" – these facts are of immeasurable value! That said, they reveal our potential rather than automatically enabling us to understand God perfectly. Anyone who manages to get out of bed in the morning will make mistakes in the few hours that follow and will attempt to correct the mistakes of the previous day. We are simply not perfect. God know our fallibility – He can see every mistake that we will ever make. Nonetheless, He chooses to have relationship with us. Our acceptance is not based on our success, but rather on His sovereign resolution. If we find in ourselves the fear of misunderstanding (and failing) Him, this speaks to uncertainty regarding His love, acceptance and forgiveness. He wants to take this uncertainty away from us.

As God's children we need not fear anything or anyone – including God! "There is no fear in love. But perfect love drives out fear, because fear has to do with punishment. The one who fears is not made perfect in love." (1 John 4:18 NIV).

---

359   Matt 15:14.
360   1 Cor 2:16, NIV.

Christ took the punishment for my past, present and future failure upon himself and when I accept that Jesus has taken my place, I become, so to speak, "un-punishable[361]" [362]. If I understand this, my fear disappears while thankfulness blossoms.

Fear should not guide us in any situation in life. It is good to have people around us who tell us this from time to time, as Paul does with Timothy. "For the Spirit God gave us does not make us timid, but gives us power, love and self-discipline." (2 Tim 1:7 NIV).

Recognising the truth in the fragments of the mosaic

Paul writes that when we hear God's voice we only ever have partial understanding. "For we know in part and we prophesy in part." (1 Cor 13:9 NIV). Viewed this way, we always hear Him slightly incorrectly– or at least not 100% correctly. We are not capable of fully appreciating God's revelation, so long as we do not see Him "as he is"[363] – until then everything happens in "faith"[364]. This is something we must accept.

Fear of hearing God incorrectly is something that we ultimately only conquer by stepping up and giving things a try. We follow His prompting and afterwards evaluate the result. Only in this was can we determine whether we have heard God or not.

As is also the case in other areas of life, mistakes can be our best learning tools, if we assess them with honesty, humility and humour. God looks at our hearts. If we give our hearts over to Him, He will use our failure in hearing Him as a way to bless us and to transform us to be like Jesus. "And we know that in *all* things God works for the good of those who love him, who have been called according to his purpose." (Rom 8:28 NIV, emphasis KR).

---

361 "Through the cross, Jesus introduced something into the world that we still don't understand. He has made each and every one of us un-punishable. We are un-punishable." Danny Silk, Culture of Honor, Destiny Image, 2009, P. 80.

362 Incidentally, being un-punishable does not mean that my misconduct does not have negative consequences on myself, those around me and my relationship with God. If I continually and intentionally act contrary to God's will, I cause suffering and cause God's love in me to go off the boil. (See also Matt 24:12).

363 1 John 3:2.

364 "(…) and everything that does not come from faith is sin." (Rom 14:23 NIV).

TEAM TALK: FEAR OF MISUNDERSTANDING GOD.

1. Are you familiar with the fear of misunderstanding God? Is it something you have ever experienced yourself? What happened? What led to you misunderstanding God? Which "safety belts" could have prevented your misunderstanding?

2. How would your relationship with Jesus develop if you were to begin to avoid personal communication out of fear that you will misunderstand God?

Fear of hearing the enemy

At a workshop, as I was encouraging those in attendance to seek God's voice in their everyday lives and to follow His prompting courageously, two of the participants seemed increasingly distraught, as was evident in their whispering. Finally one of them said: "What you are inviting people to do here is actually really dangerous – don't you know that the devil also speaks to us?"

I had to prevent myself from laughing in order to avoid showing the person up, and thought to myself: In any case he has already spoken to you, and you listened!

Fear of hearing the enemy actually prevents followers of Jesus from living a life marked by hearing the voice of God. This seems illogical to me for two reasons. First of all, fear should not influence any of our decisions. Secondly it is clear that we all hear negatively inspired prompts, thoughts, messages or voices on a daily basis. This applies all the more depending on how much time we spend watching TV, flicking through magazines, surfing the Internet or – talking with people! We encounter many prompts of the accuser[365] in the

---

365   Incidentally, Satan is not the name of the devil, but rather a description of what he does, and can be translated as accuser or enemy.

form of lies[366] or strongholds[367], however, these do not affect us provided the enemy has no hold[368] over us.

We read the following of Jesus following his temptation by the devil in the wilderness: "When the devil had ended all the temptations, he left Jesus *for a while* and went away." (Luke 4:13 TLB, emphasis KR). Thus, after his baptism Jesus gets a *little break* from being tempted by the devil. Based on other reports in the New Testament, we can also assume that Jesus was pestered, attacked and tempted by the enemy throughout his entire life. Why should it be any different for his followers?[369]

Our question is therefore not whether we *hear* the enemy, but rather whether we *listen* to him, i.e. follow his "voice". Jesus heard the devil, but he never followed him. I go into this in greater depth in the chapter entitled "Learning to distinguish God's voice".

TEAM TALK: FEAR OF HEARING THE ENEMY.

1. Have you ever noticed that impure spirits have communicated with you directly? What happened? What did they prompt you to do or think and how did you react?

2. Put together a list of Bible references in which unpure spirits speak to Jesus or the disciples[370]. Study what the impure spirits say in each case and how Jesus and the disciples react.

3. Compile a list of demonically inspired advertisements/commercials and ideologies. What features do they share? How are they communicated?

---

366   In John 8:44 we read this of the devil: "When he lies, he speaks his native language, for he is a liar and the father of lies." (John 8:44 NIV).

367   "The weapons we fight with are not the weapons of the world. On the contrary, they have divine power to demolish strongholds. 5 We demolish arguments and every pretension that sets itself up against the knowledge of God, and we take captive every thought to make it obedient to Christ." (2 Cor 10:4–5 NIV).

368   "I will not say much more to you, for the prince of this world is coming. He has no hold over me." (John 14:30

369   "The student shares his teacher's fate. The servant shares his master's!" (Matt 10:25 NIV).

370   The gospels and the book of Acts are well suited for such research.

Fear of not hearing God

Paradoxically, the fear that we might *not* be able to hear God is also one of the reasons why we avoid direct communication with Him. And in actual fact: If we ask God to speak to us on an important occasion and do not hear Him, this can trigger great frustration and irritation. I am well aware of the unpleasant feeling of not hearing God and nonetheless being forced to make important decisions. We feel as though left behind, unloved and unjustly treated. We suddenly become aware of how dependent we have become as a result of our decision to live by His guidance.

Refraining from hearing God

When, out of disappointment, followers of Jesus no longer seek God's direct communication, this is often off the back of a long period of waiting on His voice or hearing incorrectly. Sometimes in such situations we even swear internal oaths, which as a result become actual obstacles to hearing[371].

Having withdrawn from the practice of hearing, we justify ourselves with statements such as: "My faith had gone off track at the time", "In my charismatic phase I, too, thought that you can hear from God all the time" or the like. Our faith is thus controlled more by logic, pre-formulated creeds or Bible passages and quotations from spiritual leaders that we find easy to digest. If the disappointment runs very deep, it may come about that we prefer to operate within "self-contained" (i.e. controllable) philosophical or humanistic belief systems. It can also, as a result, come about that we look for a self-contained set of rules in the Bible – if we actually still read it – and no longer for living inspiration.

However, "secure faith" such as this cannot hide the fact that we have lost sight of Jesus as a model for hearing God's voice. Inner troubles or the fear of being disappointed again have become relational barriers between us and God. Accompanying people through such valleys of disappointment requires love, time and prayer. Here we do well to avoid trying to talk away the disillusionment that has developed, but should instead listen and bear one another's loads.

---

371   "If you don't tell me whether ... you really love me/I should enter into this relationship/this job offer is for me/ ... I'll never listen to you again!"

TEAM TALK: FEAR OF NOT HEARING GOD.

1. Have you ever internally withdrawn from God on account of not having heard God speak on a matter you deemed important? What happened?

2. Were you able to overcome the disappointment? What helped you in this? What did you learn about God and about yourself?

Fear of hearing God

While some of us worry that God could not speak to us, others fear the exact opposite: that God could speak! Here the underlying concern can be that God might condemn or reject you. It can also be a fear that God's words may result in either considerable or even just minor inconvenience for us. Both assumptions could constitute reasons for avoiding His voice. Thus, Adam and Eve's initial reaction to their guilty conscience is to hide from God, who lovingly calls out to them.

A while ago, when I asked my friend Leonardo what God had said to him recently, he answered: "I don't know – I am kind of out of the way of hearing Him speak. I am not sure that my current lifestyle is in keeping with a relationship with God." I was astounded: Leonardo had experienced God's faithfulness, his guidance and love, often in spectacular fashion. His answer revealed a deep-lying fear that he would disappoint his heavenly Father, or even be rejected by Him.

In particular, fear of hearing God can be found in people who have an awareness of God, without knowing Him personally. It manifests itself in the form of a vague feeling that at some point we will have to give account of ourselves to an unpredictable judge. The logic of the inner lawyer reasons: "Provided that I do not hear "the loving God" clearly and am uncertain that He actually exists, at the end of the day He cannot punish me severely – I didn't know what I was doing!"

However, followers of Jesus who have grown up in a strict religious environment can also fear hearing God personally. This is especially the case if the strict statements made by preachers, spiritual leaders or even people's own parents have been sold as the direct word of God during their childhood. When God's **holiness is emphasized** and His grace overlooked, we are smothered by the idea of a heavenly Father who subjects us to continual moral scrutiny and is constantly pointing out faults. It is only natural that you would not want to hear such a person unless absolutely necessary.

Finally, the fear that God will ask too much of us can result in us not wanting to hear Him. And to a certain extent this fear is not unjustified, seeing as by definition God overexerts everyone who meets Him, and the same goes when people hear His word[372]. "For the word of God is alive and active. Sharper than any double-edged sword, it penetrates even to dividing soul and spirit, joints and marrow; it judges the thoughts and attitudes of the heart." (Heb 4:12 NIV). The letter to the Hebrews describes God's voice as being alive, full of power, unbelievably sharp, penetrating and as being the judge of all things. In short: God's voice doesn't leave anything unchanged. We live in the tension that an encounter with His word can, as it were, mean the death of our ego[373] and its healing.

I myself must admit that God's voice regularly brings me to the limit of my capacity – however, I have learned to love it! What He says to me challenges me immensely and is often *"too good"* for me to even believe. Sometimes He says that He loves being close to me or thanks me for my faithfulness – to hear something like that from the Creator of the universe brings me to tears! If He says something like that to me, I feel like I am gazing into the starry heavens – it is much, much, much too much. It doesn't matter what I have already heard from Him in the past, what He is saying in the present is always more unbelievable, bigger and brings even more change – even more of God.

Hearing God's voice is always a stretching exercise for our status quo. Our own concepts as to the meaning of life prove too small and are torn down by Him, one by one – some people call this sanctification, others call this asking too much.

---

372   For God "is" what He says – His word (see John 1:1).

373   John the Baptist describes this process wonderfully: "He must become greater; I must become less." (John 3:30 NIV).

His voice is continually expanding our faith horizon and takes us out of our comfort zone. Following His voice means a loss of control, as we hand over control to Him. Anyone who begins living as someone who listens to God cannot stay the same, but will instead become increasingly more like God.

TEAM TALK: FEAR OF HEARING GOD.

1. Are there topics that you would rather not hear God talk about? Make a list and share with the group: What are the topics? What is the worst thing that could happen as a result of God speaking?

2. Consider: Have you had similar fears with other topics in the past? How did you dispel your reservations? What exactly happened?

3. Has God ever said something to you that was simply too good to believe? Share with the group.

External obstacles

External obstacles refer to barriers relating to our respective surroundings. They can be characterised by culture, family, your stage of life or even political systems. This type of obstacle can easily be overcome by means of a change of location, as a result of becoming more mature or through a change in culture.

Distraction

We live in a world of 10,000 voices. I recently stumbled across an article on the website "MediaÖkotest.de" on the subject of advertising, which states: "According to various communications researchers, the average German is thought to be bombarded with between 2,500 and 10,000 advertising messages each day."[374] Although the article does

---

374 An article in Wirtschaftswoche from 2012 (!) referred to a figure between 5,000-10,000 advertising messages that we are exposed to each day. Source: wiwo.de/unternehmen/dienstleister/werbesprech-werbung-nervt/6519856.html.

later point out that what ultimately constitutes advertising is subjective, the figures are extreme. Over the course of a single day (15 hours) we are (if calculating conservatively at 5,000 advertisements) met with an advertising message on average every 10.8 seconds, although there are indeed busier and quieter period distributed throughout the day. Advertising reaches us through clothing, car brands, outdoor advertising, our mobile phones, apps, Internet banners, the radio, TV, when shopping, and on the list goes. Very few of us experience the enjoyment of regular advertising-free moments.

However, advertising represents just one of the information channels that we have to hear and process on a daily basis. Added to this there is the enormous flow of general information we receive nowadays.

If panda triplets are born in China[375], we find out about it a few seconds later via Twitter, Facebook etc. And even if we avoid the use of social media networks, "important" news such as this still reaches us via the 'shopping radio' in the supermarket or the restless information screen in the underground. Regardless of whether it's tabloid news or a global event – never before have we been fed so much information in such a short period of time. In a nutshell: the distraction available to us, especially in major cities, is phenomenal!

It is by no means a sin to stay well informed, however, all of these stimuli fill our thoughts, trigger emotions in us and ultimately determine what we do. And let's not forget: the majority of these messages attempt to drown one another out by means of volume and intensity – in order to make it through to us ahead of the other information.

As a general rule[376] the voice described in this book behaves completely differently. It is a patient and friendly prompt; it is not envious, pushy or conceited. It is a call that never behaves tactlessly, never looks out for its own interest, is not resentful and never loses control. A call that does not delight at injustice, but instead celebrates the truth. A voice that always bears with us, always believes in us, always hopes for our best and stands by us through all our confusion – it is the voice of our God[377].

Nowadays immense distraction represents a massive obstacle to hearing God's voice.

---

375   Source: Spiegel online,12.08.2014, 15:58.

376   There are also moments when God speaks almost unmistakably – however, I personally have only ever experienced this a select few times.

377   Paraphrased based on 1 Cor 13:4-7.

Let's go back to the time of Jesus or Paul for a moment. The Bible's protagonists travelled on foot or by horse, generally through deserted landscapes. On their travels they had plenty of time and peace to pray, to meditate and to hear from God. They did not know the noise of cars, aeroplanes or machinery. Their mobiles phones never rang, they didn't stop to check their emails, they didn't have the latest nonsense delivered to them via twitter, and were not attacked by billboards or other visual messages. Because they were exposed to much fewer stimuli than we are today, what they were exposed to could have a much more intense impact.

Of course people at that time also had numerous challenges to overcome, which could distract them from hearing God[378], but nonetheless they without doubt lived in an environment with less stimulation.

In major cities we can now observe many people wearing headphones on the streets. This seems to me to be an intentional attempt to shield oneself from the noise around them. A self-determined audio impulse (e.g. music, a podcast) thus drowns out countless, irritating ambient impulses. The widespread wearing of sunglasses, caps or hats is also, as far as I am concerned, an attempt to escape from the flood of stimulation, if only for a short period of time. To the residents of major cities it is somehow or other already clear that they are living in a state of "over-stimulation", however not many can come up with a helpful solution to this realisation.

Hearing God among the 10,000 voices.

If we want to hear God's voice in our everyday lives, we must manage to filter His voice from among the other voices that tussle for our attention, or reduce the number of distracting messages, at least for a time. Neither approach works with immediate effect, but must instead be practised and ideally become a fixed part of our lives. Many of us are so used to noise, multi-tasking and the constant flow of information, that we experience fear and withdrawal symptoms in the event that the communication and information media cut out. The terms "Internet dependency" or "social media addiction" are now often-addressed topics in reputable publications[379].

---

378   Wars, famines, political unrest, illness etc.

379   Googling the term "Facebook addiction" produces 25,100,000 hits. Source: Google, accessed 04.2016.

In the summer of 2013 I organised a "silent retreat" with some of my friends. We met in a monastery to be silent together and give God space for three days. After just a few hours, on the very first evening, I startled one of the participants as she was fiddling on her mobile phone. She was clearly ashamed that she could not maintain the silence and apologised vehemently. "I have to send a few SMS to wean myself off again, otherwise I won't manage it – the silence here is unbearable."

When our hearing capacity is exhausted.

If we try to spend time with God in the evening, after a full day, it is difficult to open ourselves up to hear His quiet voice. The inflationary impulses from the day have filled us up in such a way that we honestly do not want to hear *another voice*[380].

If we are performance-oriented people, the abundance of daily impulses, resulting in the development of an inability to make it through the "quiet times", produce anger within us, which, in turn, distracts us from God.

Simple strategies for controlling distraction.

Here, I have put together a few simple tips, which can help us to reduce distraction. Continual distraction decimates our ability to hear God's prompting. Thus, if we cut the distracting factors out of our everyday lives, and in so doing create space, it gradually becomes easier for us to hear God's voice.

Unreachability

To be unreachable is to withdraw from any external influence and to be entirely "by oneself". This concept is particularly beneficial for those of us who work in social professions, and who are extremely helpful and empathetic.

Plan for fixed times during the day at which you are unreachable[381]. You can begin with short periods of time, using specific activities, such as driving to work, going shopping or

---

380 Interestingly, for many this is the time that they switch on the television, in order to "switch off" and get some rest.

381 During these times you should switch off your mobile phone, your telephone and computer, even disconnect your doorbell if possible.

playing sport to practise unreachability. At the same time you should make sure to avoid multi-tasking during your allotted period of unreachability – just be "present with yourself"!

The media clear-out

Uninstall Facebook, Twitter etc. from your mobile phone. You can intentionally set aside some time in the evening to follow the important events happening in the lives of your friends. This frees up valuable moments on an hourly basis, which you can spend with Jesus and by yourself[382].

First input

Try to begin the day with a short prayer, by reading a Bible verse or by listening to a worship song. Apply the "piggy back" method and use, for example, your time in the shower to pray[383]. Keep a Bible in the bathroom and on your dining table and read a verse as part of your morning ritual.

Your first thoughts of the day will go with you and mark the day.

Tying up loose ends

When going to sleep, consider which was the most life-giving moment of the day and which was the most life-draining. Thank God for His presence and faithfulness in both situations[384]. This exercise ties up loose ends regarding your thoughts throughout the day and will help you find inner peace for the night ahead.

---

382 A very simple study on mobile Facebook use came to the following conclusion: "It can be (...) said that the majority of users check their news feed at least once per hour (during the day) via smartphone." Explanatory note KR. How would our relationship with Jesus develop if we were to check the Holy Spirit's newsfeed every hour instead of checking Facebook? Source: http://bjoerntantau.com/studie-so-exzessiv-nutzen-facebook-user-den-mobilen- newsfeed-30072014.html.

383 If you are too tired, pray in tongues.

384 This exercise is also known as "the Examen". A detailed guide on this is described in "Gebet als Begegnung" (Prayer as a Place, HGM Publishing 2009), Bello/Reschke, Grainpress 2012.

The energy window

If you want to spend a fixed time with God each day, place this within an energy window, i.e. a time when you have capacity, strength and a clear head. Oftentimes, prayer is last on the list and only takes place once everything else had been checked off. This is of course also the time when we are exhausted and extremely easily distracted. One of the main reasons behind frustrating times of prayer is that we simply select the incorrect time or place[385].

TEAM TALK: "DISTRACTION" AS AN OBSTACLE TO HEARING GOD.

1. Which of the exercises aiming to control distraction (*unreachability, the media clear out, first input, tying up loose ends, the energy window*), can you imagine yourself implementing?

2. What about it do you find promising? What exactly could it change in your everyday life with regard to the topic of distraction?

3. Have you ever tried one of the exercises (or something similar) before? What were your experiences? What functioned well and what did you find difficult?

The enemy

The devil has made it his task in life to build up obstacles between us and God. In so doing, he actually tries to remain in the background himself. His most successful strategy in the western nations is to sell himself as a character from a fairytale and to control people indirectly using false world views, patterns of thought, money or other people. In so doing he disguises himself as the "Angel of Light"[386] and uses good things such as success, prosperity, health, spirituality or partnership in order to establish false gods and to manipulate people in their worship.

---

385   Whereby there are of course various types of prayer, that is, encounter with God. In moments when we have no energy, we can also encounter God without exertion, by means of soaking, listening to worship music, listening to sermons, through art or the like.

386   See 2 Cor 11:14.

His main strategy against us, as followers of Jesus, is to call God's word into question, or to sow seeds of doubt. Because he cannot trump God's voice, he attempts to temper it or to discredit it by making objections[387]. The sowing of doubt regarding God's word is a clever strategy, which has been effective since the time of Adam and Eve. "Now the serpent was more crafty than any of the wild animals the LORD God had made. He said to the woman, "Did God really say, 'You must not eat from any tree in the garden'?" " (Gen 3:1 NIV).

During the temptation of Jesus by the devil, we find the same tactic being used. Twice in Succession the tempter speaks to Jesus with the same starting question. "The tempter came to him and said, "*If* you are the Son of God (...)." (Matt 4:3 NIV, emphasis KR). With this question he attempts to place self-doubt in Jesus regarding his sonship, which the Father had just recently spoken out over him.

Getting to the bottom of doubt

If we follow Jesus, we will not lead a life without doubt and temptation. As already discussed, Jesus was continually challenged by the enemy during his ministry – why should we have it any different?

Our knowledge of the fact that the enemy will cast doubt is our best insurance against succumbing to this doubt.

Doubts have a life of their own and, should they become embedded, can develop into a huge blockade to God's voice. In order to be proactive in combating doubt, one helpful approach is to develop the habit of occasionally composing a list of the doubts we encounter.

Doubt often hides[388] behind unclear emotions or confused thoughts. By writing them down we can make ourselves aware of our doubts and clearly name them. After the now

---

387   We are familiar with this unholy approach from parliamentary debates, where the time allotted to speakers and those listening themselves are often exhausted as a result of speakers adopting a mindset that says, "because nothing better comes to mind, I will attack the previous speaker".

388   "For nobody knows, but nobody knows, my name is Rumpelstiltskin!" In the story of Rumpelstiltskin, the evil dwarf gains power over a maid and intends to take her baby from her. The dwarf allows the maid three attempts to guess his name – if she succeeds he will spare her baby. On discovering Rumpelstilskin's real name, she is freed from his control. If we can to put a name on doubt, and thus confront it, this is often the beginning of gaining freedom from it.

specifically named doubt, we then write a short statement about God's faithfulness or a promise in His word regarding our doubt.

We then receive God's forgiveness for our distrust, and ask Him to remind us of His faithfulness and His good plans for us.

We can see this "technique" in some of the psalms, where the psalmist identifies challenges and doubts, places God's faithfulness in opposition to them and then hands over his next steps to God in faith[389].

Let us now take a closer look at how doubt forms. Before we can doubt, we first require a worthwhile promise. In the story of Adam and Eve, this much is made clear: God assures Adam and Eve of His provision and love, and the enemy then attempts to sow doubt regarding God's good intentions. In the same way, Jesus is first confirmed as God's child and then the enemy attempts to cast doubt. Therefore, doubt will only attack us when we hold a promise that is worth doubting. If I have the flu I would hardly expect the enemy to sow doubt and say: "Are you really sure that you feel poorly?" He would, however, sow doubt regarding the fact that God is healing me.

So if we hear a worthwhile promise from God, it may be that over the next few hours and days we encounter doubt regarding the content and reality of His communication.

This may indicate a strategy of the enemy aiming to pour cold water on what God is saying, or it may simply be the result of habitual doubt. If we act against this and hold firm to God's word, the doubt gives way and our faith is strengthened. If we follow the doubt, we lose the fruit from what God says.

If we develop an awareness of the fact that great doubt[390] is probably a form of opposition to a great promise of blessing, we can actually make use of it, as viewed in this way it is an indication of God's good plans for us.

---

389   Ps 57, Ps 61 u. a.

390   Here I am talking about doubt as a negative demonic or spiritual force. An inner objection can also be a signal from the Holy Spirit urging caution.

TEAM TALK: "THE ENEMY" AS AN OBSTACLE TO HEARING GOD.

1. Are you familiar with the feeling of having doubt regarding a divinely appointed matter? What exactly happens when you encounter doubt – is there a progression? Does doubt in your life always feel the same?

2. Share your strategies for overcoming doubt with one another.

3. Tell stories of times you have conquered doubt and times when you have succumbed to doubt. What did you learn from this?

Our environment

An environment that belittles spiritual longing or paints it as a foolish craze can present a considerable obstacle to spiritual growth and discipleship marked by hearing God's voice.

The accusation of being out of touch or impulsive generally comes from followers of Jesus who are not prepared to live out their faith in an area of risk themselves. This is why their "faith" appears to function so well: they have reduced their discipleship to activities that require little or no faith in the first place.

Followers of Jesus who continually make decisions that distance themselves from God in certain areas of their lives can also distract us from God's will or pull us into their slump. Habits such as pessimism, grumbling, ungratefulness or being generally spiritually lukewarm are extremely contagious!

Because our environment defines us, we should be aware of the environment in which we are spending the majority of our time. How close we get in friendships or relationships is something we have to decide for ourselves in each individual case. However, withdrawal from all friendships with people who doubt, are broken or have unanswered questions is not a good solution. As the salt of the Earth[391] we are called to add flavour to the world. This can only happen if we are part of this world. Jesus spent his entire life with doubters and question-askers, but never allowed himself to be led astray by them.

391　Matt 5:13.

Prior to his death, he prayed for his followers: "My prayer is *not* that you take them out of the world but that you protect them from the evil one." (John 17:15 NIV, emphasis KR). It is therefore not escapism that is called for, but rather wisdom in dealing with the powers of this world.

Don't apologise to me...

"Jesus is stupid, I hate him, he is just horrible..." Petra was a good friend of mine who had been following Jesus for many years. Due to childhood pain, she repeatedly suffered from emotional breakdowns, which those around her found somewhat challenging to deal with. She stood in my living room and had been repeating her insults for several minutes. I had been slowly getting annoyed and was genuinely furious: she was insulting my best friend, speaking out lies about him and I was being forced to listen. Because I knew of her inner pain, I was showing compassion, but the time had now come to put a stop to it. "Petra!" I said, in a caring yet purposeful tone, "Jesus is my best friend, he saved my life and I love him with all my heart. If you do not stop insulting my friend, then we cannot go on being friends." She gulped. I myself was astonished at my bluntness, but I had said exactly what I wanted to say. After a brief pause, she said, "OK, you are right, I apologise." "You don't need to apologise to *me*," I replied with a smile.

Beyond social boundaries!

Anton had already been walking with Jesus for many years. He was a faithful husband, he tithed, and was active within the church community – he was recognised as a Christian. All in all, it was pleasant spending time with him and we had developed a friendship. However, he had a problem – he always spoke negatively about people. He did it so matter-of-factly that it was at first difficult to recognise, however, it always left a bitter after-taste. His gossip had a spiritual component: If you listened to him, you yourself began to think negatively about the people he was targeting, and you began doubting their motives. At one meeting he selected two of my best friends to be on the receiving end of his jibes. I suddenly heard the Holy Spirit say through me: "Anton, you are a great guy and you are my friend, but I can no longer bear how you talk about people. Please quit it when you are in my presence!" Wow – I could tell that he really didn't like my request – this type of criticism went way beyond his social boundaries! The relationship deteriorated over the coming months. I later heard from my friend, who he had been targeting that day, that he had talked just as negatively about me. Sometimes you just don't know what is going on!

TEAM TALK: "OUR ENVIRONMENT" AS AN OBSTACLE TO HEARING GOD

1. Have you ever found yourself pulling someone else down with your unbelief or unchristlike behaviour? What happened? Were you able to apologise and make things good again?

2. Are you jealous of people who experience "more" of God than you do? Put together a list of strategies in order to conquer jealousy.

3. Has God ever asked you to cut yourself off or distance yourself from people? What happened? What were you able to learn?

Practical obstacles

The final category we will look at is practical obstacles. This involves parameters that we can relatively easily influence and refers mainly to practical adjustments in the way we lead our lives or in our perception. I will only touch briefly on this, as the identified obstacles are addressed in greater detail elsewhere in this book.

A superficial relationship with God as a practical obstacle

Our interpersonal communication can range from deep, intimate exchange with our partner, best friend or another person we trust, to empty small talk.

The intimacy of the relationship thus controls the depth of the communication – deep communication requires a deep relationship. This insight can generally[392] be applied to our

---

392   In the Bible there are some exceptions involving people with exceptional callings, who God guides in special ways. For example, in the case of the prophet Samuel we can already see how, as a small child, without a mature relationship with God, he regularly hears clearly from God.

relationship with God. The ability to hear and understand God's voice develops in relation to the quality of our relationship with Him. If we want more intense communication with God, our relationship with Him must become more intense.

The deepening of our relationship with God takes place as part of a process, which we can influence by intentionally getting to know God and by being attentive and obedient.

If we allow ourselves to be satisfied with a superficial relationship with God, we will not experience profound communication with Him.

Levelling out

I have been getting to know Jesus since 1989. I have experienced times of fiery devotion to God and some fairly average times, however, I have also experienced a number of seasons of spiritual stagnation and levelling out. Levelling out can occur when we stop measuring our spiritual experience against Jesus and instead measure it against his other followers. By doing this we subconsciously fall into the situation whereby we are following them more than we are following Jesus.

> "Hold on a minute, Kristian – don't paint us worse than we actually are. Compared to other churches in Hamburg we are quite awakened!"

I had been feeling frustrated for quite some time about the development of our church. My sense was that it was increasingly less about Jesus and more about realising our own goals. What had brought us to this point? Just a few years ago I had experienced God's fire within the very same group – regardless of what we were doing, Jesus was always at the centre. What had happened for us to stop putting the focus on him? As I shared my concern regarding the development with my friend Ford, his response (see above) indirectly revealed the problem: As a group we had begun to focus on Christians rather than on Christ. As a result we were no longer celebrating the King of Kings, but rather ourselves.

A lack of role models

The term 'levelling off' would suggest that we have previously experienced profound discipleship. However, due to a severe lack of positive role models, a great many followers of Jesus may never advance into this reality.

If we feel at home (or grew up) in a more traditional Christian context - where possible pre-formulated prayers, repeated rituals and weekly biblical interpretation by the "experts" define church life - due to ill-conceived devotion, and although it may indeed frustrate us, we consider this the God-appointed norm.

In churches such as this there is often an ambivalence between our longing for "more" and our holding on to the tradition that ensures the cohesion of the church community. People lack an image of what this "more" might look like in their own spiritual context – so it is not so much that there is a lack of desire for spiritual depth, but rather that there are no contemporary examples that we can emulate. Unfortunately, their awakening is actually often blocked by the church tradition.

On the road to Ephesus, Paul meets a group of disciples[393], who have (only) received "John's baptism". When Paul asks them whether they received the Holy Spirit "when [they] believed", they answer in astonishment: "No, we have not even heard that there is a Holy Spirit." (Acts 19:2 NIV).

Because the texts expressly describe this group as disciples who had come to believe, we must assume that they really were following Jesus – even if only from within their limited spiritual context. They were not lacking the will to follow, but were instead lacking role models for a Spirit-led life. Perhaps the message of Jesus regarding knowing him as a result of having "heard of him" only reached them through the grapevine.

They had grasped the message in faith, but had no model for a life under the guidance of the Holy Spirit. In Paul they find a mentor and make a huge step forwards in their experience of God. They are then baptised in the name of Jesus: "When Paul placed his hands on them, the Holy Spirit came on them, and they spoke in tongues and prophesied." (Acts 19:6 NIV).

---

393   Acts 19:1.

Lack of practice as a practical obstacle

Our relationship with God is based on both supernatural and natural growth. While He is indeed the Giver of Gifts[395], we can train and strengthen what He has entrusted to us – this comes about as the result of *practice*. Whereas in the case of sport, hobbies, our job or in our marriage the connection between success and training is clearly evident to us, we seem happy to neglect to practise our spirituality – and we are then surprised at the lack of results[396].

The reason why Jesus brought disciples around with him was so that they could learn to do what he did. Jesus continually gave his disciples opportunities to practise. He used everyday events, provided them with a framework and a goal, and then left them to it. He then chatted with them and evaluated their findings. For example, we can observe this process in the sending out of the seventy-two disciples[397] and on the occasion of the multiplication of the loaves[398]. Jesus uses both situations to allow the disciples to practise.

If we are not prepared "to practise with Jesus", there is the risk that we will lose that which has already been entrusted to us. The writer of the letter to the Hebrews reproaches the

---

394 0 = extremely superficial. 10 = the depth of relationship that Jesus had.

395 "Every good and perfect gift is from above, coming down from the Father of the heavenly lights (...)." (James 1:17 NIV). See also 1 Cor 4:7.

396 When John Wimber was asked why he experienced such an extraordinary amount of healing through prayer, he always replied that he had prayed for more than 1,000 people before the first was healed. Source: Interview with Robby Dawkins, vineyardchurches.org.uk/resources/articles/high-risk-high-rewards.

397 Luke 10:1ff.

398 Matt 14:15ff.

recipients' lack of practice. He describes them as followers who are in need of milk and cannot tolerate "solid food", as would be expected were they developing appropriately[399].

How did this unfortunate regression come about? The author writes: "But solid food is for the mature, who by constant use have trained themselves to distinguish good from evil." (Heb 5:14 NIV). The recipients of the letter had not *trained in* or *practised* what had been entrusted to them, and as a result they had lost it.

Conflict in practice

At the beginning of my journey with Jesus I made the decision to pursue every word and impulse God gave me – "trial and error", just give it a try! As a safety belt, I determined that my listening exercises were not permitted to damage, injure or expose anyone. I learned a lot as a result of adopting this approach, however, I often experienced conflict on account of my inexperience.

For example, I didn't yet recognise that hearing and understanding God do not necessarily happen simultaneously. If I did not immediately understand what God was saying, I found it stressful and frustrating[400]. I also thought that every prompt from God required direct action. As a result, I regularly asked too much of myself and those around me. When I noticed that those around me often had problems following me, I began to rethink my approach[401]. It did not appear that I was hearing God incorrectly, however, my interpretation and relaying of His word were without wisdom.

I finally began to grasp that He spoke to me as an expression of relationship and not as means by which to continually issue commands. He speaks because friends talk to one another, to explain things to me so that I can pray in accordance with His will,

---

399   This reproach would be similar to if, after ten years of home group leadership, someone suggested that you attend an Alpha course.

400   Today, if ever I do not understand what He is saying, I ask: "What are you trying to say to me?" and I then await further clarification. However, sometimes this only comes days later. God has infinite time at His disposal and He is happy to make use of this advantage.

401   Our gifts should serve to build up those around us – if we lose this along the way then our service becomes meaningless (see 1 Cor 14:12).

to teach me, to calm me, to reveal Himself to me and because the Word[402] will not keep silent. I learned an important lesson: God's desire to talk *to* me is much greater than His desire to talk *through* me[403]!

TEAM TALK: "LACK OF PRACTICE" AS AN OBSTACLE TO HEARING GOD

1. What do you make of the concept of intentionally practising the art of hearing from God? Discuss among yourselves: What are the arguments for and against?

2. Have you already developed your own listening exercises? Share them with the group and tell of your experiences.

Lacking mindfulness as a practical obstacle

"Although God speaks again and again, no one pays attention to what he says."[404]

God is a God who speaks – we are aware of this fact from the Bible and based on our knowledge of Him. Everything we know of Him, *He* has made known. Our purpose in life is to come to fully know who He is[405] – this happens by way of relationship and communication.

Where possible, mindfulness is our greatest key to unlocking communication, as Job informs us: "Although God speaks again and again (…) no one *pays attention* to what he says".

All sorts of meditation seminars and hocus pocus courses are offered on posters around Hamburg under the heading of "mindfulness". When I say here that mindfulness is the key to hearing God, I do not mean the act of concentrating on one's own condition and experience, but rather God-focused spiritual presence or an intentional interest in encountering God.

---

402 "The Word became flesh and made his dwelling among us." (John 1:14 NIV).

403 A schoolboy error often made by beginners in the prophetic.

404 Job 33:14 GNT.

405 "Now this is eternal life: that they know you, the only true God, and Jesus Christ, whom you have sent (John 17:3 NIV).

Many followers of Jesus go into a church service or home group gathering with the expectation that they will meet with Jesus. Here, however, I am talking about approaching everyday life with this same energy, remaining continually attentive to him.

The gospels present Jesus to us as a model for an attentive, or mindful lifestyle – everywhere he goes he meets with his Father, for he is aware that his Father wants to meet with him everywhere.

The beginning of mindfulness is the recognition that our Father is always mindful of us – His interest in us is unimaginably great.

A mindful life is something we must practise. I will now share a brief exercise in mindfulness, which each individual can adjust to suit his or her needs.

Mindfulness training

We begin by regularly taking brief moments out during the day to focus our attention on Him, by stopping and asking: Dad[406], what are you saying to me now?

We pause to listen for a few seconds and to receive what comes our way with thanks[407]. If we hear "nothing", then we thank Him for His continual presence within us – even if we cannot discern it in this moment.

If we want to intensify the training we can set an alarm on our phones that reminds us to carry out the exercise every four hours. If we practise exercises such as this over a long period, we will notice how our thoughts become focussed and we will develop a much greater expectation that we will hear His voice. We thus begin to become aware of His prompting, without having asked Him.

If this happens it is not a sign that God is now talking to us *more*, but rather that we have achieved a greater level of mindfulness. "Although God speaks again and again! (...) — no-one pays attention to what he says." (Job 33:14 GNT).

---

406   Here you can insert the name by which you feel most comfortable addressing God.

407   While performing an exercise such as this as part of my daily routine I often only hear a hint of a word, or sense a brief internal or physical touch. Sometimes it is just a passing awareness that I am loved and seen. If I learn to recognise God in this "hint", then my level of mindfulness is high (See 1 Kings 19:11ff).

TEAM TALK: "LACKING MINDFULNESS" AS AN OBSTACLE TO HEARING GOD

Perform the *mindfulness training* within the group and then discuss. You can use the following template for the group exercise:

- Ask ("Dad, what are you saying to me now?"), listen and write down. *(5-10 minutes)*
- Internal thanks for what we have heard. *(5 minutes)*
- Discussion: What do you believe God said to you? What is the meaning of His prompting to you? Can you imagine yourself doing this exercise several times a day? How would it benefit you?

Lacking expectation as a practical obstacle

*"I **eagerly expect** and **hope** that (…) Christ will be exalted in my body, whether by life or by death."*[408]

True expectation is extremely valuable, for it is *condensed hope.* At the beginning of my relationship with Jesus I had the *vague hope* that I would hear from God now and then. This has since become my *daily expectation.* This came about primarily as a result of the understanding that my longing for Him is but a dull reflection of His longing for me.

Our expectation is like a magnifying glass, with which we can uncover Him speaking in our daily lives.

A divine "coincidence" and a "lucky" purchase

On the way to a difficult church leadership meeting I urgently asked God for encouragement. I felt empty and was afraid that the meeting might end in a row. In the stairwell I met one of the other leaders holding a bag of sweets, which was intended as comfort food – something to calm the nerves. He smiled at me and said: "Look what I have here, funny eh?" On saying this he held out the receipt for the sweets he had just bought in front of me: €7.77! I laughed out loud. This

---

408   Phil 1:20 NIV, emphasis KR.

was the encouragement I had been asking for[409]. When I explained to him that I had received a great deal of encouragement from this slip of paper, he was a little sheepish, and replied: "Hmm, I didn't even think about God – I just took it as a funny coincidence!" I looked at him and thought to myself: "With Jesus there are no coincidences!" God had planned this moment specifically for me, right down to the second decimal place.

Weeks later, as I was standing at the checkout in Aldi, the moderately amused cashier suddenly smiled at me and said: "€77.77 – that is a lucky purchase for you!" Upon hearing these words I was filled with the warm presence of God right there in the supermarket. I closed my eyes to keep from breaking down in tears in front of the cashier, and tried desperately to maintain my composure. This was the "hidden track"[410] – what a loving and humorous God we have!

A lack of expectation that God wants to say something relevant to you can be the result of a feeling of inferiority. The inner accuser taunts you saying, "You are not worthy that God would speak to you!" In the same way, a religious self-image can block our expectation. The inner accuser challenges you: "As a *good* child of God, you have to do things by yourself!"

In both cases the inner accuser is facilitated by a lack of understanding of God's love for us and of His longing for us.

Reigniting expectation

Expectancy towards God must be a significant component of our relationship with Him. If we realise that we are lacking in expectation that we will hear God, it is worthwhile asking ourselves for how long this has been the case. Was there a special event that robbed us of the hope or the expectation of hearing God's voice, or have apathy and everyday distraction gradually crept in?

If I can find out why my expectation has dwindled, then I am in the position to take counter-measures. By repenting and, if necessary, speaking out forgiveness, I establish conditions in which my expectation can be restored.

---

409   This combination of numbers has a personal significance for me.

410   A hidden song on an audio recording.

As another step on the road to the restoration of our expectation, it may be advisable to ask friends to intercede for you in this regard. Trying to pull yourself out of the pit of hopelessness and a lack of expectation without the help of others is extremely difficult when you have lost the firm ground beneath your feet.

TEAM TALK: "LACKING EXPECTATION" AS AN OBSTACLE TO HEARING GOD.

Discuss among yourselves: Have there been phases in your life during which you have had a greater or lesser expectation of hearing God's voice compared to now? What was different? What caused your expectation to drop/increase?

A lack of withdrawal and silence as a practical obstacle

A lack of withdrawal and silence prevents us from hearing God and is also a frequent cause of inner exhaustion and loss of vision. The more filled and active our daily life, the more important regular times of withdrawal will be for us.

Jesus' appearances were generally accompanied by huge gatherings of people. With the coming and going of all of these people, he occasionally lacks the time to speak with his disciples or even to eat[411]. Interestingly, however, the gospels also show us that Jesus regularly withdraws from the crowds, and sometimes even from his disciples. During times of mutual withdrawal with his friends he deepens his relationship with them[412] and explains his actions and his mission. If he withdraws to be alone, he seeks instructions for important decisions or simply loving closeness with his Father[413]. Although at various moments Jesus also receives supernatural[414] strengthening, he is aware of the importance of being mindful of his mental limits and those of his friends.

Jesus often feels compelled to withdraw in times of success, and this is something that those around him often find difficult to understand. The fact that Jesus is just as willing to

411   Mark 6:31.

412   Luke 9:18ff; Mark 14:32ff; Luke 9:28.

413   Mark 6:46; Mark 14:34; Luke 4:42; Luke 5:16; Luke 6:12; Matt 14:13.

414   John 4:31ff; Luke 22:43; Matt 4:11.

follow his Father[415] to places of withdrawal as he is to follow Him to the crowds makes it clear that the Father's will is more important to him than his "success".

So we can see that Jesus regularly withdraws with his friends or to be alone. It is sometimes the case that he initially withdraws to be with his friends, before then separating off even from them. By first leading them into a place of withdrawal, he presumably wants to ensure that they too take some time out. What happens in the times he spends alone with just his Father is generally not clearly recounted to us. We do, however, see that it is after these times that he often makes resolute decisions[416] and is strengthened[417].

His plans to withdraw, for both himself and his friends, do not always run smoothly, and sometimes even prove more difficult than walking on water!

Here is an example: in the Gospel of Mark[418] it is reported that Jesus sends out[419] and authorises his disciples to carry out his ministry. When they return and report to him of their successes[420], he instructs them: "Come with me by yourselves to a quiet place and get some rest." (Mark 6:31 NIV). The attempt to reach this *quiet* place by boat is unsuccessful, as the crowds simply follow them there – the disciple's break has to be pushed back for now.

When Jesus sees the people following him, he feels compassion and takes a great deal of time to teach them. Finally, he also takes care of their physical wellbeing and multiples a few loaves of bread and some fish, feeding more than 5,000 people. Jesus now remembers that he actually wanted to allow his friends the chance of a break, and he urges them into the boat to get going. We read: "After leaving them, he went up on a mountainside to pray." (Mark 6:46 NIV). Jesus now takes some time out for himself. Unfortunately the disciples don't fare so well during their break, as they are forced to struggle against extreme headwinds. They determine to proceed against the wind by their own "physical strength", rather than overcoming the threat by exercising their spiritual authority. Only

---

415   "Then Jesus was led by the Spirit into the wilderness (...)." (Matt 4:1 NIV). See also John 7:6.

416   Luke 6:12.

417   Luke 4:14.

418   Can be found in Mark 6:7-13; 6:30ff.

419   Mark 6:7ff.

420   Mark 6:30.

when Jesus – having walked on the water to reach them – climbs into the boat does the wind die down. An attempt to withdraw quickly turns into what is, to all extents and purposes, a fairly jam-packed day!

In the report we see the attempts made by Jesus and his disciples to withdraw hampered on several occasions. The three obstacles that present themselves are: 1) people who want to be close to Jesus and are even travelling around after him[421]. 2) Jesus' deep compassion, which moves him to teach the people for a long period of time and to feed them[422]. 3) The storm on the lake, which may have been of natural or demonic origin[423].

Obstacles preventing withdrawal are therefore not necessarily evil or demonic attacks, but may even be the result of compassion. Jesus intends to take a break, but an intense sense of the compassion of the Holy Spirit prompts him to change his plans – how exciting! The important thing is this: in spite of all the distractions, Jesus still eventually finds a window in which to be alone with his Father.

Withdrawal is not an add-on.

Based on this example from Jesus' life it is clear that phases of isolation and silence are part of a God-focussed lifestyle. They are also reflected in the commandment to observe Sabbath rest, which for Jesus generally means personal times of rest.

It is also clear that withdrawal brings with it a struggle, which can only be won with determination. The conflict can result from the needs of others, distractions or the voice of the inner accuser, who by no means wants to allow us to unburden ourselves of him.

If we want to grow in hearing God's voice, we must make withdrawal part of our everyday lives – as was the case with Jesus, what this withdrawal looks like very much depends on the person.

---

421   Mark 6:31-33.
422   Mark 6:34ff.
423   Mark 6:45ff.

Exercises in withdrawal

If we go through extreme, draining seasons in life (e.g. as a result of having small children, an exam period, moving house or starting a new job), we need to be a little creative if withdrawal is going to be possible. Here are a few simple ideas as to what withdrawal might look like in everyday life.

Walk

Try to walk to work, uni or to play sport rather than taking your bike, driving or using public transport. Allow a little more time, switch off your mobile and, if it helps you to withdraw, wear sunglasses and a hat. Be aware that your choice to forego getting there quickly is an act of prayer and fasting.

Moderate the speed of your steps so as to find a peaceful rhythm when walking. Experience the moment, do not think ahead or back – just focus on the present. If you feel prompted to talk to God, do so – if not, simply be aware of Him – give him some time and space.

> I got to know Jesus during my school years and experimented a lot as I tried to make my prayer times with Him effective. In order to get through the day, it seemed a good idea for me to pray before school. I tried this but was often much too tired to concentrate.
>
> I finally began walking to school with a view to spending some time with Jesus. On my bike it took about 15 minutes, compared to 30 minutes on foot. I used the 30 minutes in the morning for prayer and then again on the way back. This meant that on arriving home from school I had already spent a good hour with God.

Auto-isolation

For many of us, driving the car is the only time in our daily routine when we experience spatial separation from those around us. If we are aware of the value of this time, then the drive to work can become a "place of silence".

As we climb into our car we thank Jesus that he is travelling with us and ask him for an encounter. We set aside a little more time for the journey and switch our phone and the radio off. We drive in a relaxed manner, without rushing. We enjoy the silence and rest in the knowledge that we cannot be reached. If we so desire, we can begin saying things out loud to Jesus – he is travelling with us after all – that we wouldn't dare say in the presence of others. This may an emotional declaration of love, secret wishes or even expressions of our disappointment or sadness.

We end the journey by thanking Jesus for this space to withdraw and for being with us in the car.

Feed on the Word

Don't use your lunch break in the canteen or university refectory to browse through the daily newspaper, to play with your phone or gossip with work colleagues, but instead use it to engage with God's Word.

Sit by yourself and read the Bible as you eat. Read a few verses in the knowledge that God's Word is nourishment for your spirit; in just the same way as your food nourishes your body. If a verse really speaks to you, try to read it a few times and remember it for the rest of the day. The middle of the day is a great time to lay what has already happened and what is yet to come down before God.

Stocktaking

Just pause 2 or 3 times during the day[424] and attempt to "find yourself" and to be aware of your surroundings. Focus on the moment. Ask yourself: How are things going for me right now? Look inwardly and lay down both positive and negative feelings, giving thanks to God. This exercise is something you can do in less than 5 minutes. It helps you to be self-aware as you go about your day.

---

424   You can align these moments with your meal times or a visit to the loo.

TEAM TALK: "A LACK OF WITHDRAWAL AND SILENCE" AS AN OBSTACLE TO HEARING GOD.

1. Describe how you experience withdrawal and silence in your life. What are the challenges you encounter? What works well?

2. Which withdrawal exercises do you reckon would be possible for you and which would not? Explain why.

3. What is your greatest wish with regard to withdrawal and silence? Compile a list of these wishes and pray for one another, then bless one another.

Speaking as a practical obstacle

"My dear brothers and sisters, take note of this: Everyone should be quick to listen, slow to speak and slow to become angry (...)."[425]

"The fruit of silence is prayer (...)"[426]. *(Mother Teresa)*

Last but not least, I want to address the greatest obstacle to hearing – speaking.

The majority of us spend much more time talking to God than we do listening to Him. The question is, which causes more profound change in our lives – one hundred words that we say to Him, or one word that we hear from Him? The answer is clear.

If we want to hear God, we simply have to stop talking, but continue to be with Him. "In repentance and rest is your salvation, in quietness and trust is your strength, but you would have none of it." (Isaiah 30:15 NIV).

People have an enormous longing to be heard, but there are only a few who want to listen. When I asked God to teach me to love people, He revealed to me that listening is one of the greatest gifts of love that I can give someone. I thus began to intentionally allow time

---

425   James 1:19 NIV.

426   Source: www.beliefnet.com/quotes/christian/m/mother-teresa/the-fruit-of-silence-is-prayer-the-fruit-of-pray.aspx, accessed 09.05.2016.

in various relationships to listen to the stories of the other person, and I was astounded at the riches that I found in this.

I consider the act of listening to be a secret recipe for a happy marriage. But here too I first had to learn how to listen. During my work as a church leader I have developed the habit of thinking in an extremely solution-oriented manner. Some days I have found myself spending the entire day solving problems and putting out fires. I then also brought this pattern of thinking in to our marriage. If Kim ever shared a stressful situation with me, I would – often before she had even finished speaking – suggest three different possible solutions. Once she had made *very clear* to me on several occasions that I wasn't her pastor, but rather her husband, I began to handle such situations a little better. I took note: she didn't want solutions, she simply wanted to be listened to!

If we actually listen to people we will soon notice that tips and solutions are not at all what they are looking for. When I give someone the gift of being fully present with them for a few minutes, I show him that I am being attentive. The feeling of actually being listened to bestows honour and worth, and brings freedom from isolation.

In the same way as we learn to lend other people a sympathetic ear, we must also learn to lend an ear to God. The amount of time that we are willing to set aside for God is an indication as to how important He is to us.

TEAM TALK: "TALKING RATHER THAN LISTENING" AS AN OBSTACLE TO HEARING GOD.

(1) Discuss the quotation from Mother Teresa: "The fruit of silence is prayer (...)". What other images come to mind when you think about silence?

(2) Do you generally find it easier to talk or to listen? Describe your approach in this regard in everyday life. And what about in your relationship with God?

(3) Have you ever shown love to someone by listening to them? What happened? What impact did the act of listening have on you personally?

Summing up – Staying ready for action!

In this section we have considered emotional, external and practical obstacles to hearing from God. What I suggest to the reader is not that he or she should attempt to break through every obstacle as quickly as possible, but rather that they should develop an awareness of these obstacles first.

If I am aware that spiritual blockades, external distractions and questions as to how I lead my life affect my ability to hear from God, this leaves me best equipped to embark on a life of listening.

If I then continue to place my trust in God and am in a place to thank Him for continually working on the breaking down of all of these barriers, then these barriers shrink away, revealing their true size. I can then see for myself what the psalmist meant when he wrote: "(...) with my God I can scale a wall." (Ps 18:29 NIV).

Chapter 14

Learning to distinguish God's voice

"God alone is able to hear and understand Himself perfectly."

The need to tell God's voice apart

For most of the day we are, either consciously or sub-consciously, in the practice of evaluating the information we encounter with regard to its content, its message and its relevance to us. The need to check and distinguish what we are hearing in a world with a seemingly infinite number of voices is unavoidable. The fact that we sometimes find it difficult to filter God's voice out from all of the other voices is not something we should view as a threat and nor should it cause us to feel insecure or inadequate. If we continually find it to be a challenge to distinguish God's voice from others, this is often a sign that we are taking our pursuit of God seriously, rather than being a mark of inferiority.

Our ability to test God's voice depends on a host of factors. Some of these, such as mindfulness, the quality of our relationship with God and our knowledge of the Bible, are things that we can influence. Others, such as our knowledge of God, our level of spiritual experience, and the spiritual quality of our environment depend more on the length of time we have been following Jesus, or on the decisions of others.

God Himself encourages us to test[427] from which source we are hearing. On the one hand this shows that He is aware of our situation, and on the other hand, it serves as evidence that He "believes" in us. He trusts in our desire to make good decisions and to learn from Him.

The presence of a great many voices, paired with our ability to make an assessment is by all accounts an expression of our God-given dignity, and is certainly not an expression of our sinful nature[428]. If we were only able to hear God's voice, it would be impossible for us to choose for or against Him. To devote ourselves to Him and to love Him are only made possible through the existence of alternatives. God set things up in such a way that our continual devotion and love towards Him should define our discipleship. These values are expressed in countless everyday decisions. This is precisely what Jesus modelled to us[429].

Jesus, is that you?

"Jesus, is that you?" is often our first question when we have a thought, an impression or a feeling that we attribute to God. Anyone who regularly hears God will be well aware of this line of inquiry, which is generally conducted internally.

In my day-to-day life, I test prompts I feel from God using various quick-fire test questions. A quick-fire test like this is generally required when I get the feeling that I should respond to God's prompting within a short period of time. For instance, this may also mean passing on a thought God has given me to someone else.

---

427 "(...) do not believe every spirit, but test the spirits to see whether they are from God, because many false prophets have gone out into the world." (1 John 4:1 NIV). See also 1 Thes 5:20f.

428 We can observe that even before the Fall there existed alternative "voices" to God's, such as that of the snake or the enticing appearance of the forbidden fruit.

429 "(...) so that the world may learn that I love the Father and do exactly what my Father has commanded me." (John 14:31 NIV). "In fact, this is love for God: to keep his commands. And his commands are not burdensome." (1 John 5:3 NIV).

The answers that the quick-fire test produces are not always super specific, but they do tend to help me decide how I should move forward with the prompting. In the two stories that follow, I will present the four main quick-fire test questions I use, and demonstrate how I apply them[430]. I will then look at them in closer detail afterwards.

"Jesus, is that you?" (1)

In 1997 I attended a prayer meeting in our church. The evening was running along nicely, until a girl suddenly stood up – her face was as white as a sheet. With tears in her eyes, she said aloud: "God has revealed to me that persecution is going to break out in a big way in Hamburg this evening – the majority of us will not survive the evening!"

As you can imagine, a murmur spread around the room. Her unexpected declaration would normally have been assumed to be a joke within the group, and would not have been paid much attention. However, as she spoke, a "spirit of fear"[431] began to take hold within the room, and an eerie dread came over all those present. The fear was accompanied by spiritual blindness[432]. As I looked at the girl and continued to ponder her strange word, I suddenly noticed that everyone else was looking at me, and waiting to see how I, as a leader, would react.

Now I was unsettled (the spirit of fear in action!) and felt unable to say anything meaningful. In order to gather myself, I murmured, "let's ask God what He has to say!" I turned to the wall and began to go through my "Jesus, is that you? checklist in my head. At this point in time it consisted of four questions.

1. Bible: Is the idea in keeping with our understanding of the Bible? The answer in this case was actually 'yes'! The persecution of believers can be found right throughout the Bible and is even foretold by Jesus[433].

2. Family: What does my spiritual family say about this impression? In this case my spiritual family weren't any great help – they were speechless and uncertain.

---

430   I often spontaneously vary the order of the questions depending on the situation.

431   An impure spirit, whose task is to spread fear, terror, panic etc.

432   You suddenly feel stupid, clueless, and unable to weigh things up and make good decisions.

433   Matt 5:11 among others.

3. Logic: Is there any logic to this word from God? As I reflected on this point clarity began to return to me. I put together a chain of thought: this is 1997, we live in Hamburg, there is no persecution of Christianity in Hamburg – this word really makes no sense at all!

4. Confirmation: Jesus, is that you? Finally, in my head I asked: Is that you Jesus? My gaze settled on a picture on the wall. It showed Jesus at the last supper. The image was terribly kitsch, and for a laugh someone had written on it with a marker pen: Jesus was here! In this moment, as I looked at the picture and before my eyes the letters began to change: That's not me! Taken aback, I squinted at the picture and the text had returned to normal. It was now entirely clear to me. I turned around and said: "Sorry, but your word is not from Jesus. None of us will come to any harm today." All of a sudden the atmosphere in the room changed, as the spirit of fear withdrew[434]. We all survived that prayer meeting, and our respective journeys home.

"Jesus, is that you?" (2)

I was a guest at a meeting in the Ruhr area. After I had said my bit, the microphone was opened to the floor for the sharing of "prophetic words". Unfortunately the majority of the contributions had no power and nor were they particularly specific, interesting or even amusing[435]. I felt frustration building in me: Was that all? Did no-one there have an insightful word from God? As I was caught up in my thoughts, I suddenly sensed I was receiving a download from God, which was indeed both powerful and specific, but that left me shivering inside. I sensed this: there are two people in the room who have committed adultery. Both have decided that no-one should ever find out about it. God is asking both of them to confess their guilt and promises them blessing and support if they will repent.

My stomach was churning – under no circumstances did I want to share this word! I looked around the room in order to gather my thoughts.

---

434   Truth dispels lies like light dispels darkness.

435   If someone in church takes the microphone and what he or she says is neither spirit-led nor informative, it should at least be funny.

1. Was this impression biblical? Yes, definitely! On several occasions Jesus recognises people's thoughts and calls them to repentance[436].

2. Could I draw on someone I trusted for verification? I did have some friends present, but finding them amongst all the people would have taken too long.

3. Did the word make sense? I was unsure – there was no particular atmosphere of repentance – in actual fact my impression wasn't really in keeping with what was happening in the moment. Although what did speak in its favour was that I had just been complaining to Jesus about the lacking spiritual dynamic in the room.

4. Finally, I asked a few times internally: Is that you Jesus? No answer. I just thought to myself: "Aw, thanks so much Holy Spirit for your *great* help!" After a little weighing up, I arrived at the conviction that this was not the occasion to put myself out there in this way. With a view to making my decision clear to God, I turned around and just wanted to leave the room (quickly!). As I turned around my gaze fell upon a little[437] sticker on a rubbish bin. It read: Never back down! Oops! – That was His answer!

I felt the Holy Spirit lovingly grab me with a pair of tongs and slowly lead me onto the stage. I gave the word in as inviting and understated manner as possible and crept back to my seat. I don't think anyone wanted to share anything after that – they were probably all asking themselves: does he mean me[438]? As I sat down beside my friend Daniel, he looked at me with wide eyes, as if to say: it's not me by the way!

As we were leaving the event a little later, two people stopped me. The man looked completely distraught. He looked at me and mumbled, barely audibly: "We are the two people." To be honest I had very quickly consigned the word to the back of my mind, and I asked him relatively loudly: "Which two?" "The two adulterers", he murmured even more quietly. I was astonished: When I was giving the word I had thought it was about two people who didn't know each other – God had not revealed to me that it was adultery committed by two people together. We moved into a

---

436 Matt 9:4; Mark 2:8; Luke 5:22, and many more.

437 If insignificant objects, comments or thoughts suddenly become blatantly obvious, light up or become very apparent, God is generally using them as a medium through which to speak.

438 Matt 26:22.

side room and they shared their story with me. We considered together which steps they could take in order to experience healing and restoration with their spouses. As I told Daniel the rest of the story on the way home, we both shuddered at God's revelation that evening.

TEAM TALK: THE NEED TO TELL GOD'S VOICE APART.

"God alone is able to hear and understand Himself perfectly." Consider: do you agree with this statement? What advantages and disadvantages does this observation have for your relationship with God?

Which voices can we hear?

Alongside God's voice, the world is full of countless other voices, that are vying to be heard. If we are thinking about trying to distinguish between them, it makes sense that we first clarify which other "voices" we might be hearing. We can assign voices that do not belong to God into three rough categories. The voice of *one's inner self*, the voices of *other people*, the voices of *impure spirits*.

The Bible tells us that Jesus himself was confronted with each of these voices. However, he did not let them impress upon him or influence him. Below we will consider how Jesus handled such voices.

The voice of one's inner self in the life of Jesus

At various points in the gospels it becomes clear that Jesus had his own will. Jesus is thus familiar with the voice of his inner self.

In the Garden of Gethsemane he prays in the knowledge that great suffering lies ahead of him. "Father, if you are willing, take this cup from me; yet *not my will*, but yours be done." (Luke 22:42 NIV, emphasis KR).

Jesus doesn't want to have to suffer death on the cross. However, instead of listening to himself, he submits his will to that of his Father. The letter to the Hebrews comments of

Jesus' struggle in this regard as follows: "Son though he was, *he learned* obedience from what he suffered." (Heb 5:8 NIV, emphasis KR).

Jesus *learns* to be obedient by repeatedly submitting his will and his own thoughts to those of the Father[439]. Because Jesus is fully human, he is capable of forming his own thoughts and drawing his own conclusions. He has the same freedom to make decisions as God has given everyone. As a result, Jesus does not express devotion to God in robotic fashion, but this is something he grows in and that is an expression of love.

The voices of other people in the life of Jesus

Jesus spends the majority of his time around people. They come primarily to listen to him, however there are individuals or even groups who repeatedly attempt to impress their opinion on Jesus. In these moments, he is required to distinguish his Father's voice from these others. On several occasions even his own disciples attempt to influence Jesus. When people bring children to him seeking his blessing over them, the disciples seek to prevent this. Jesus sees that the Father has other plans and corrects the disciples with these words: "Let the little children come to me, and do not hinder them, for the kingdom of God belongs to such as these." (Luke 18:16 NIV).

When Mary anoints the feet of Jesus with extremely expensive oil, she is harshly criticised by some of those present. Here, too, Jesus adopts a heavenly perspective. He sees her love and the prophetic value of her actions, objecting to the criticism and praising Mary by saying: "Why are you bothering her? She has done a beautiful thing to me. (...) Truly I tell you, wherever the gospel is preached throughout the world, what she has done will also be told, in memory of her." (Mark 14:9; 6 NIV).

When Jesus openly shares with his friends for the first time that he will soon die a violent death, Peter vehemently attempts to dissuade him from continuing down the path he is on. Jesus can tell that this objection is not the will of the Father, and answers him: "Get behind me, Satan! You are a stumbling block to me; you do not have in mind the concerns of God, but merely human concerns." (Matt 16:23 NIV). Jesus exposes Peter's statement as being demonic and of human inspiration.

---

439   Learning takes place through repetition.

When Jesus heals a lame man on the Sabbath, the nearby Pharisees condemn him inwardly. Jesus can read their thoughts and confronts them. "Knowing their thoughts, Jesus said, "Why do you entertain evil thoughts in your hearts?" (Matt 9:4 NIV).

The voice of impure spirits in the life of Jesus

It is astonishing how many followers of Jesus are afraid of hearing demons or being led astray by their influence. Jesus does not allow himself to be particularly affected by the voice of the enemy, in spite of the fact that he does regularly hear his voice. The devil speaks directly to him in the wilderness[440], demons speak in his presence[441] or answer his questions[442]. He is also forced to experience Satan speaking to him first hand through one of his best friends[443].

Summing up – Which voices can we hear?

The manner in which Jesus handles the three categories of voices is one thing first and foremost – relaxed! Jesus is not afraid of being contaminated or influenced. Neither does he strive to distance himself from the voices of people and impure spirits. He does not attempt to silence his own inner voice through meditation or self-denial. Jesus recognises these voices as part of life in our world and does not attempt to flee from them. He hears them – but he does not listen to them! He is aware of them – but does not accept them!

Our rule of thumb is to listen to His voice

If we follow Jesus and live in relationship with him, we are laying the foundations on which to live a life in which we regularly hear and understand his voice. When Jesus says: "My sheep listen to my voice; I know them, and they follow me;" (John 10:27), he makes it clear that our calling - the norm and the basis of our discipleship – is to listen to him.

---

440   Matt 4:1ff.
441   Mark 1:34; Luke 4:41.
442   Luke 8:30.
443   Matt 16:23.

If we sense His prompting and internal voice or thoughts, or if we see logical connections or feel otherwise directed in life, it is generally God who is leading us.

Paul describes being directed by the Holy Spirit as the main feature of our status as sons and daughters of God. "(…) In order that the righteous requirement of the law might be fully met in us, who do not live according to the flesh but according to the Spirit." (Rom 8:4). "For those who are led by the Spirit of God are the children of God." (Rom 8:14). If we live in constant anxiety that we are being misled or infected by voices contrary to God's, this merely reveals that we have already listened to them. In any case, this type of anxiety never comes from God.

Longings

However, listening to God does become problematic when we have longings or desires[444] that become idols. These can be relationships, positions of leadership, life plans, material objects or something else altogether. If we allow things or people to capture our hearts in this way, there will be voices that justify our longing and encourage us to claim our "right".

In the story of the Fall, we see the snake acquire power over Eve by awakening Eve's longing for the forbidden fruit. "When the woman saw that the fruit of the tree was good for food and pleasing to the eye, and also desirable for gaining wisdom." (Gen 3:6 NIV). Eve first *hears* the words of the snake, and *then listens to them*, in that she follows them. In contrast, in the case of Jesus the enemy is not able to awaken a false longing. At no point does the devil have influence over the course of his life or the time of his death. Jesus explains the devil's powerlessness over him to his friends: "I will not say much more to you, for the prince of this world is coming. He has no hold over me, but he comes so that the world may learn that I love the Father and do exactly what my Father has commanded me." (John 14:30–31 NIV).

Satan does continuously try to awaken longings in Jesus, but he cannot offer him anything attractive – Jesus' longing was not for things of this world, but instead was directed towards his Father[445].

---

444   "Then, after desire has conceived, it gives birth to sin;" (James 1:15 NIV).

445   "Do not love the world or anything in the world. If anyone loves the world, love for the Father is not in them." (1 John 2:15 NIV).

Know my pitfalls

The spiritual world has an interesting dynamic: What we desire will be offered to us[446]– whether sin or God's blessing[447].

We reach a place of safety when faced with voices other than that of Jesus in that we become aware of our weaknesses and longings. If I know my weaknesses then they cannot surprise me and I can rule over them. If I am blind to my inner pitfalls, then I am sure to fall into them[448]. If we ask Him, God is more than happy to inform us of our "inner pitfalls". He doesn't do this to expose us, but rather so that we are able to conquer them.

We can see this in the story of Cain and Abel. Before Cain murders his brother Abel, God makes him aware of his anger problem and urgently advises him to take control over it. "So Cain was very angry, and his face was downcast. Then the Lord said to Cain, "Why are you angry? Why is your face downcast? ⁷If you do what is right, will you not be accepted? But if you do not do what is right, sin is crouching at your door; it desires to have you, but you must rule over it." (Gen 4:5–7 NIV).

I love David's prayer from Psalm 139 and like to pray it myself as a means of expressing my devotion towards God and to ask for His help and guidance. "Search me, God, and know my heart; test me and know my anxious thoughts. See if there is any offensive way in me, and lead me in the way everlasting." (Ps 139:23–24 NIV). If this prayer reflects our inner posture, then we need not worry about voices that are not from God.

TEAM TALK: WHICH VOICES CAN WE HEAR?

1. Have you ever confused the voice of your inner self, the voices of other people or demonic voices with the voice of God? Discuss amongst yourselves: What happened? What was the reason for your misjudgement? What were you able to learn?

---

446 "For everyone who asks receives; the one who seeks finds; and to the one who knocks, the door will be opened." (Luke 11:10 NIV).

447 This applies in particular to followers of Jesus. Paul writes to the Corinthians: "All things are yours: (...) the world or life or death or the present or the future—all are yours (...)" (1 Cor 3:21–22 NIV).

448 "The wise see danger ahead and avoid it, but fools keep going and get into trouble." (Prov 22:3 NCV).

2. Do you know your "inner pitfalls"? How could you become more aware of your "pitfalls"? To what extent does a healthy self-perception help you not to follow voices that are not of God?

Selective perception

In our world we are pelted with thousands of prompts, voices and impressions every single day. Everything we encounter has some form of message, wants to say something and attempts to claim our attention. We must continually decide which voices we are paying heed to, which impulses we will follow and which we will allow to pass us by. We often make this decision within a fraction of a second, guided by an internal system of experiences, values and habits.

Our specific situation also governs which impulses are "valuable" to us at a specific moment in time and which are "worthless". For example, if I *pass by* a street with traffic lights, the colour red has no effect on me. However, if I walk *across* a street with traffic lights, I immediately perceive the colour red as a warning. If I have just eaten then I will not classify the smell of delicious food as a valuable impulse. If I am hungry, on the other hand, then the opposite is true!

God's promptings are of the highest priority for us. Within the course of our discipleship we learn to **continually** classify them as "valuable" and to constantly pursue them.

This choice is an act of mindfulness. We are attentive towards that with which we fill our thoughtlife. We will be sensitive to receiving God to the same extent that we focus our thoughts on Him. Interestingly, this also applies to all other things: Our mindfulness is always geared towards the content of our thoughtlife. We notice the things that we are focussed on. If our thoughts are not directed towards the things of God, this doesn't mean that we will not hear Him – however, His prompting will not be classified as "valuable" by our internal data processing centre, and will therefore be "moved back" behind other events. So we hear it, but we do not take note of it.

If we keep our level of preoccupation with God high, we are like a goalkeeper following his team's play from a distance. Although the ball remains far away from him for a prolonged period of time, the goalie gives the course of play his full attention. He knows how quickly the play can switch to taking place in his third of the pitch. So when the counter-attack begins moving towards his goal, he can see this while it is still some way away. Due to his mindfulness, he is best equipped to keep the ball out of his net. If we allow our expectancy or mindfulness to drop off, we are living according to the motto, "I will hear God when it is important". This strategy is akin to the attitude of a poor goalkeeper, who doesn't follow the entire game and thinks to himself: Why should I take an interest in the game when the play is in the opponent's final third – when the ball comes close to me I will still be able to react. Anyone who knows even a little bit about football will know that at this point it is already much too late. The "impulse" will presumably pass the goalkeeper by (on its way into the net).

One of my life's goals is to read the Bible everyday. One reason for this is that I want to remain open to God's voice. Regularly occupying myself with his "written Word" positions me to recognise His voice in my everyday. In the same way, I like to take time to look upon His creation[449] and His deeds[450], to meditate on this and to talk about Him with other people[451]. This preoccupation with His works and deeds also increases my accessibility to Him.

Now that we have recognised our responsibility in the process of distinguishing His voice, we will now focus on the role of the Holy Spirit.

---

449   "Great are the works of the Lord; they are pondered by all who delight in them." (Ps 111:2NIV).

450   "Come and see what God has done, his awesome deeds for mankind!" (Ps 66:5 NIV).

451   "For where two or three gather in my name, there am I with them." (Matt 18:20 NIV).

The tester lives in us

While it is up to God to speak to us, it is up to us to filter out His voice from the 10,000 different stimuli we encounter on a daily basis. However, we are not on our own in this: His Spirit in us is a constant helper[452] in the process of distinguishing God's voice, revealing[453] the "truth"[454] to us.

This "Spirit of Truth" releases us from the burden of having to determine by our own initiative what is "good and evil[455]", in that he reveals God's work to us. He confirms God's truth to us by means of internal testimony. This takes place within our spirit – that is, on a level of control that goes beyond logic, emotion and experience. Paul describes the work of the Holy Spirit in relation to our position as children of God like this: "The Spirit himself testifies with our spirit that we are God's children." (Rom 8:16 NIV).

The Holy Spirit thus works in us like a form of lie/truth detector: If we come into contact with something that contradicts the truth, he kicks in. How this looks can vary: Bible verses springing to mind, sudden and opposing insight, an inner peace or even nausea or physical pain.

In the same way, the Spirit confirms himself as our signpost to truth. He knows the precise area in which we currently require truth and leads us to this truth through Bible verses, helpful books, encounters, thoughts or by other means. If we come into contact with the truth, he can testify to this through a sense of physical wellbeing, relaxation, inner peace or the like. Sometimes these symptoms are also referred to as being the effect of the gift of discernment of spirits[456].

---

452   "But the Advocate, the Holy Spirit, whom the Father will send in my name, will teach you all things and will remind you of everything I have said to you." (John 14:26 NIV).

453   "But when he, the Spirit of truth, comes, he will guide you into all the truth." (John 16:13 NIV).

454   When we talk about revelation of truth it is important to understand we are talking about a person – that is, Jesus. The Holy Spirit reveals to us the things that come from Jesus, that lead to him and that are in keeping with his character.

455   See Gen 3:5.

456   The discussion as to what the gift of "discernment of spirits" (1 Cor 12:10; 1 John 4:1ff) is, how it functions and how it should be used is a contentious one. To summarise, we can say that our physical reality exists under the influence of the spiritual reality. As followers of Jesus we must therefore be able to "distinguish" the origin and the requests of spirits as well as different callings on individuals

Paul also refers to this same work of the Spirit under a different name, stating that we have "the mind of Christ"[457]. Alternative translations for the word "mind[458]" are "thoughts" (NLV) or "wit" (WYC, in the sense of God's manner of thinking).

The help of the Holy Spirit and our sharing of the mind of Christ are our most effective tools with which to test what we hear. However, they are limited by the level of maturity of our relationship with God and the existence of our free will. These tools are not automatically effective, but are instead dependent on the quality of our discipleship.

For example, if we have decided – consciously or sub-consciously – to believe in a lie, we are limiting the gift of truth in ourselves. For God does not control us against our will.

When we believe in a lie it generally happens by means of a process, which begins with tiny doubts that we fail to shake off. Small untruths can often put us at ease and are thus gladly welcomed. If we discover grey areas such as this within us, there is the risk that we will justify them through self-righteous thoughts such as: "I do so much good in other areas – so this is okay", rather than simply repenting. Through this unholy alliance, we have actively decided to shut the Holy Spirit out of this area of our lives.

God doesn't do us any harm with the truth, and in His love, He generally doesn't let us recognise more truth[459] than we can bear. We can therefore expect that the Holy Spirit will lead us into the truth, but only to the extent that we *really want it* in that respective moment and to the degree that we can cope with.

The previously outlined 4-step process by which to distinguish God's voice thus, to a certain extent, offers the Holy Spirit a runway, by which to lead us to the truth. In order

---

or groups. We can differentiate between the spirit of a person, an impure spirit, an angel of God or the Holy Spirit. Like all gifts, and like our entire spiritual life, this gift must be practised.

457   " "Who has known the mind of the Lord so as to instruct him?" But we have the mind of Christ" (1 Cor 2:16 NIV).

458   Greek: "nous". "Nous" is a term with many possible translations, among them the English words spirit, mind, intellect, understanding, reason.

459   Truth is revealed to us within the context of love and not as a standalone value. If God were to reveal to us the entire extent of His holiness in a single moment, we would die. Therefore God only allows Moses to see Him from behind (Ex 33:20ff). In His love, he dispenses his revelation to us in small doses. Paul summarises the interplay between love and truth once again when he writes: "(…) speaking truth in love, we may grow up in all things into him, who is the head, Christ." (Eph 4:15 WEB).

to demonstrate *his involvement in my testing of words from God* in a manner that is a little easier to grasp, in the next section I will again address my four practical test steps in greater detail.

TEAM TALK: THE TESTER LIVES IN US.

1. Have you ever noticed the Holy Spirit leading you into a truth? Tell the group what you experienced. Did he guide you by means of a long process or within just a few short moments?

2. The gift of discernment of spirits: Have you ever experienced the Holy Spirit revealing to you that you are being confronted with a lie, through Bible verses springing to mind, a spontaneous feeling of discomfort, physical pain or another sensation? Share what happened with the group.

4 quick-fire test questions

As already mentioned, if I am ever unsure as to whether or not an impression I have comes from God, I have developed the habit of asking a few simple questions. They can help you to weigh things up in case of doubt. Below I explain the questions in detail

Jesus, is that you? – Ask the question and then wait for the answer

Jesus lives in me through the Holy Spirit[460]. If I am unclear as to the origin of an impression that I feel I am getting, then "Jesus, is that you?" is my first question. Oftentimes I receive clarity regarding the situation in that very same moment, in that I hear a short, internal 'yes' or 'no'.

Confirmation, whether positive or negative, can also be issued by means of an inner certainty, peace, a Bible passage, an encounter etc.

---

460   "(...) I do not live anymore - it is Christ who lives in me." (Gal 2:20 NCV).

Spontaneously hearing from the Holy Spirit is of course something that has to be practised. I would therefore encourage everyone to ask Jesus to speak into everyday matters. Looking for a car parking space, picking out a gift or finding lost keys are examples of such everyday activities. If we hear incorrectly in this setting, there is no harm done and we learn to distinguish His voice from others.

Asking questions is a dangerous business

After delivering a sermon, I had sold a few of my books and CDs on the stage and stuffed the money in my trouser pocket. It felt good to have earned a few quid, and aside from that I was actually in urgent need of the money. As I looked across the room, my gaze settled on one particular person and a quiet, internal prompting instructed me to give this person the contents of my trouser pocket. I tried to shake the notion off and asked the question: 'Jesus, is that you?' There was no answer, but the impression stubbornly persisted. I continued thinking over the notion of simply giving the money away and finally said: 'God, don't you know that I need this money myself?' It was then that I heard that quiet, internal voice: "Kristian, what has it got to do with you what I do with *my* money?" At that same moment, the subject of input, which I had just talked about, shot through my mind: Being a radical follower of Jesus. I had been disarmed – asking questions is a dangerous business!

Stilling myself and asking questions have been valuable tools for me in distinguishing God's voice. Like any good father, God doesn't just say things to us once; He keeps repeating it until we have understood.

The more faith His word requires of us, the more we can expect His repeated, clear instruction. The New Testament provides us with countless examples of God repeating Himself.

On his journey to Rome, Paul finds that the Holy Spirit "(...) warns [him] that prison and hardships are facing [him] (...)[461]" in every city through which he travels – so repeatedly.

---

461   Acts 20:23.

On several occasions Jesus speaks to his friends about his death and the Kingdom of God. Although his disciples hear this message in person, right out of Jesus' mouth, he deems it necessary to repeatedly remind them of it.

When "overwhelmed with sorrow"[462] in the Garden of Gethsemane, Jesus himself requires repeated confirmation regarding the task ahead of him. Luke tells us that God sends him an angel as confirmation, who strengthens him[463].

Peter repeats himself to his listeners and writes: "You already know about these things but I want to *keep telling you* about them. You are strong in the faith now. I think it is right as long as I am alive to *keep you thinking* about these things." (2 Pet 1:12-13 NLV, emphasis KR).

Paul also repeatedly speaks to churches about the same things[464] and encourages Timothy to do the same[465]. If certain statements are particularly important to him, he also repeats them directly: "Rejoice in the Lord always. *I will say it again*: Rejoice!!" (Phil 4:4 NIV, emphasis KR).

God is a god of repetition and confirmation. He reminds us again and again and again. He doesn't give up until His message has got through to us. He knows before He speaks how long it will take for us to understand, and calculates this into his planning. Our request for a confirmation of His word leads us deeper into relationship with Him– encouraging us is in keeping with His character.

---

462   Mark 14:34.

463   "An angel from heaven appeared to him and strengthened him." (Luke 22:43 NIV).

464   "Don't you remember that when I was with you I used to tell you these things." (2 Thes 2:5 NIV).

465   "Keep reminding God's people of these things." (2 Tim 2:14 NIV).

Does what I am hearing line up with the testimony and the spirit of the Bible?

In order to test impressions using the Bible, I must first get to know my Bible. Although reading the Bible admittedly has its challenges, unless we regularly get to grips with the Word, we can easily start to believe in a fantasy God. There are some really crazy notions about Jesus going around – even in Christian circles! One thing is clear: the Jesus of the Bible is the only Jesus there is! If we want to discover him as part of our everyday lives, it is worthwhile getting to know him in the Bible. This is the only way we can be clear what we should be looking for on a daily basis.

Furthermore, we can state that God does not contradict Himself. If we believe that the Bible is inspired by Him, then what we hear from him will not contradict its spirit and testimony. This principle can serve as a good rule of thumb by which to verify that it is God speaking to us.

However, if we are to test God's word in this way, it is not advisable that you take individual Bible verses out of the overall context of the text, but instead you should listen to the overall message of the Bible (and this is what I mean when I refer to the testimony and spirit of the Bible)[466]. Although God never contradicts himself, we do find varying statements on the same topic in the Bible – this is no coincidence. The best approach is to allow them to stand alongside one another and to be aware of the tension between them[467]. The reason for this is simple: the Bible contains reports from the lives of many different individuals, who were all in different places in terms of their relationship with God. The way God speaks to different people can therefore vary. The rule whereby "the sum of the Bible is truth[468]" can help us to maintain balance in our assessment.

---

466   We can successfully back up the most absurd statements by quoting individual verses out of context.

467   As a child I always wanted to lead a radical life – only since I began reading the Bible has it become clear to me that I am actually living in a radical tension.

468   "The sum of thy word is truth, (...)" (Ps 119:160 RSV).

What does my spiritual family say?

Following Jesus without the help of a spiritual family is extremely hard work. We all need spiritual mothers, fathers, aunts, uncles etc. They have greater experience and can help us to test God's word, thus serving as spiritual safety harnesses.

"Though one may be overpowered, two can defend themselves. A cord of three strands is not quickly broken." (Ecc 4:12 NIV). This means that it is essential that we move within an environment that allows for, welcomes and encourages our desire for profound growth. We must associate with people who have a deeper knowledge of God than we do and are prepared to live as models for us.

Paul describes the church as a body that has different parts, which each fulfil various tasks and are in desperate need of one another. This image is in no way treasured by followers of Jesus who like to emphasise their own independence and individuality. When it comes to the subject at hand, let's just say that it confirms that when carrying out the practice of testing – and in other aspects of the life of faith – we are all "reliant on others"[469].

The concept of mutually testing God's word was also known to the first followers of Jesus. Paul describes how he submits the message of the gospel for the gentiles, entrusted to him by means of a revelation, to the leaders of the church in Jerusalem for assessment. The reason he offers in so doing is this: "I wanted to be sure I was not running and had not been running my race in vain." (Gal 2:2 NIV).

Mutual testing and regular discussion of what God says to me are like fertiliser in my relationship with God and accelerate my spiritual growth. I regularly ask friends to help me explain my dreams or to show me ways that I could encourage God to speak in my life. I find that together we have a deeper understanding of what God is doing and of His will. Perhaps this is why Paul writes: "But *we* have the mind of Christ."[470]

469　"For just as each of us has one body with many members, and these members do not all have the same function, so in Christ we, though many, form one body, and each member belongs to all the others." (Rom 12:4–5 NIV).

470　1 Cor 2:16 (NIV).

What prevents us from testing what God says together?

Pride and insecurity often prove to be obstacles to joint testing. These two factors are all the more likely to stand in our way if we hear God often, in comparison to those closest to us. If we find ourselves worried that we will annoy those around us by continually asking them to help us test what we think we have heard, one option is to seek out a coach who will help us to grow in an intentional manner.

If we believe that we are hearing God on other people's behalf – e.g. for our church community – then mutual testing is extremely worthwhile[471]. Here it is important that, when we are sharing what we have heard, we make it clear that we do not necessarily think that our thoughts are 100% accurate[472]. When sharing a word from God we often underestimate God's desire to talk *to us* and overestimate His desire to talk *through us*. In church services at which "prophetic words" for the church or for individuals are publically shared, I regularly feel an urge to interject, saying: 'That was a good word – for yourself!'

Does what you have heard make sense?

*"Love the Lord your God with all your heart and with all your soul and with all **your mind**."*[473]

The extent to which God values our mind and our intellect is made clear in that He instructs us to love Him with our mind. We love God with our mind by applying our mind in a Christ-like manner, that is, in such a way that God is honoured.

Our intellect is a powerful gift from God to man. With its help we have created amazing things – unfortunately both good and evil. We use our minds to assess our life, to live out our individuality and to recognise that God created the universe.

---

471   It is really unpleasant when we publically stand up to speak on behalf of God and then later find out that we have misfired.

472   We can do this by leading with the following words when sharing a word: I think/I have the impression/the sense that God is saying... Speaking directly on God's behalf (Thus sayeth the Lord...) should be avoided!

473   Matt 22:37 NIV, emphasis KR.

Our understanding is fed by that which actually influences us. If we do not live in community with God, then we are generally[474] influenced by the thought patterns of this world, which are often inspired by demons, or at best by humans. One impact of a life lived separated from God is that we attribute too great a value to our own understanding. As a result we view ourselves as being almost on a par with God, as we think that we can accurately judge between good and evil ourselves[475].

If we live in relationship with God, then we should pay heed to Paul's call for us to learn "to think in a new way". Our understanding thus goes through a learning process, whereby we develop the ability to assess "whether something is God's will." "Do not conform to the pattern of this world, but be transformed by the renewing of your mind. Then you will be able to test and approve what God's will is - his good, pleasing and perfect will." (Rom 12:2 NIV).

By changing our habits, we are once again able to apply our understanding in a godly way: "But solid (spiritual) food is for the mature, who by constant use have trained themselves to distinguish good from evil." (Heb 5:14 NIV, addition KR)[476].

For those of us who are actively getting to know God and who are being transformed as a result of this, the question as to whether a word from God "makes sense" is definitely worth asking – it just makes sense. However, we must not forget that our understanding – as well as our entire being – is like a construction site. Therefore, to rely solely on our understanding as we walk with Jesus will not work. There is a reason why the testing of words from God using our understanding is listed as one element within a list of four questions. As such it should neither be overlooked not overemphasised.

If we favour testing words from God using our own understanding, we must also bear in mind the fact that some words from God appear meaningless, as we do not share His perspective – judgements made using our understanding are, after all, made on the basis

---

474 Even people who are not following Jesus can live according to God's will in individual areas of their lives, as they too hear Him and are inspired by His will.

475 "Furthermore, just as they did not think it worthwhile to retain the knowledge of God, so God gave them over to a depraved mind, so that they do what ought not to be done." (Rom 1:28 NIV).

476 However, if we read the entire section (Heb 5:11-14), it becomes clear that we can take steps backwards in the development of our "spiritual understanding" – even if we know God.

of a particular perspective. A word from God may only come to make sense with a time delay, some time after the message is delivered.

Recently, on the way to my usual supermarket, I suddenly had the impression that I should shop in another store. Initially this appeared to make no sense. However, I followed my internal guidance system, mainly out of curiosity, to find out whether this had indeed been God's voice[477]. Standing in the supermarket, I suddenly noticed a special whiskey on offer, the name of which had a personal meaning for me. This whiskey wasn't normally here! To find it there, in that moment, was of great comfort to me. Absolutely delighted, I lifted the bottle and felt moved by God's guidance and caring love.

TEAM TALK: 4 QUICK-FIRE TEST QUESTIONS.

1. What do you think? Do these test questions make sense based on your experience? Work through the four test questions and share your thoughts.

    - *Jesus, is that you? – Ask the question and then wait for the answer.*
      Have I ever used this test before? What happened? What was I able to learn?

    - *Does what I am hearing line up with the testimony and spirit of the Bible?*
      Have I ever used this test before? What happened? What was I able to learn?

    - *What does my spiritual family say about it?*
      Have I ever used this test before? What happened? What was I able to learn?

    - *Does what I've heard make sense?*
      Have I ever used this test before? What happened? What was I able to learn?

2. Put your heads together: What other quick-fire tests do you use to test what you've heard from God?

---

477   Learning to hear – just give it a try!

Summing up – Learning to distinguish God's voice

Because there are an endless number of different voices competing for our attention, we must learn to distinguish God's voice from the others. The Holy Spirit helps us in this – however, we do share some of the responsibility, in particular with regard to mindfulness, expectation and our desire for the truth.

God encourages us to test what we hear – however, at the same time, our checking should not develop into a never-ending story. Some people like to keep on checking until they reach complete clarity on what God is saying. They will in fact never reach this point, as we live from a place of faith. Thus, testing can also mean stepping into risk and trying things out. For me, adopting a posture whereby we listen, test and then act means remaining open to correction. Regardless of how clearly I hear God's voice, I remain aware of the fact that God alone is perfect in His ability to hear and understand Himself. If I act from a mindset whereby I am open to correction, I remain humble and reliant on Him. This is how I can take Him up on His invitation to be a disciple, i.e. someone who learns from Him.

Fadeout – Can God keep silent?

"In the beginning was the Word."[478]

"But Jesus remained silent."[479]

This book should be understood as a passionate plea, urging you to choose a life lived from a place of hearing God's voice. I hope that for anyone reading it that it has become clear that God is a God who speaks and that we, as His listeners and conversational partners, are highly valued and longed for.

Hearing and following His voice enables and directs our discipleship. His voice is our handrail on the path that is relationship with Him. It is God's idea to actively lead us, His children, through this life[480]. In order that this can happen, constant communication from Him is essential. In this light, our status as children of God is not just lifeless fact, but is actually something we experience on a continual basis. The father-child relationship between us and our heavenly Father only comes to life and takes on true meaning as a result of communication.

Having described in detail the fundamental dynamic of hearing God speak, I will now draw to a close by discussing the question as to whether or not God is actually capable of keeping silent. At this point this question may appear surprising, however, without it

---

478   John 1:1 NIV.

479   Matt 26:63 NIV.

480   "For those who are led by the Spirit of God are the children of God." (Rom 8:14 NIV).

I sense that my book would be incomplete. God's "silence"[481] is a subject that people have been forced to grapple with ever since the tragic events surround Adam, Eve and the forbidden fruit[482].

Can God's "silence" speak to us?

A superficial answer to the question "Can God keep silent?" could be provided by pointing to the omnipotence of God – "Yes, He can, for God can do anything that He wants".

This is an answer that one would generally expect to come from someone who does not really know God personally[483]. They aren't really considering the real question that is meant when we ask whether or not God can keep silent. For people such as this, His silence is likely the rule rather than the exception. As such, God's "silence" in the life of a person who does not know Him personally does not convey any discernable message.

But what meaning does His "silence" have to people who are used to hearing from Him and being guided by His voice? We have to ask ourselves whether His "silence" can be viewed as one of His channels of communication and actually contains a message for us. For within a relationship silence does not mean the absence of communication – it can in fact be an integral part of communication[484].

There are moments in a romantic relationship in which silence is a negative sign, while there are also moments of harmony in which words are not necessary and can even be distracting. In the latter case mutual silence is actually an expression of the closest intimacy.

Silence can also be an expression of our concentration or our enjoyment when looking at a work of art, an artistic performance or a natural spectacle.

---

481   The term "silence" will from this point on be stated in inverted commas, as it must be considered whether God's silence cannot actually be considered a form of communication. This question generally arises at times when we are aware that He is being silent.

482   Gen 3:6 ff.

483   That is, someone who only knows God as an idea, a concept, a culture or a non-personal force.

484   If Kim is unexpectedly silent towards me, this is an important signal to me. Kristian, rethink your behaviour or the last thing you said and apologise quickly!!!

When attending a lecture we can also observe how the speaker inserts a rhetorical pause before or after he or she says something important or initiates a change of tact. In this context, silence can thus serve as an indication that something meaningful is to come, that listeners should pay attention to what is being said[485] or that a new subject is to be addressed. God's "silence" can therefore have this and other meanings. It becomes clear: For those who know God and are aware of fundamental communication with Him, His silence really can speak volumes!

What does the silence of heaven mean?

"When he (the lamb) opened the seventh seal, there was silence in heaven for about half an hour." (Rev 8:1 NIV, explanatory note KR).

We find a number of reports in the Bible regarding times when the "silence" of God becomes discernible. The apostle John describes one such moment. For "about half an hour" (NIV) there was silence in heaven. The fact that this seemingly incidental event is given space among the other majorly significant cosmic events is a sign of its own significance. This is the only period of time of which we are told when there is a state of silence throughout the entire Kingdom of Heaven. God Himself is silent and the whole of heaven holds its breath.

Because John experiences this event in a vision and no further comment is made, it is difficult to provide a reliable theological interpretation. However, it seems to me that there is only one event in the history of the cosmos that could trigger the whole of heaven to pause – Jesus' death on the cross. The entire history of creation leads up to this moment. The first-born son of the creator God gives himself up to death and condemnation out of love for every individual person who has ever lived or ever will live – and in so doing conquers both death and condemnation[486]!

Jesus himself is aware of his Father's silence on a spiritual level and calls out amidst the agony of death: "My God, my God, why have you forsaken me?"[487] As the Father turns His

---

485 The word "Selah" in the psalms is understood to be an indication to the performer (musician), however, for us as readers it also serves as a valuable indication as to the dynamic with which the lines are to be read.

486 "Death has been swallowed up in victory!" (1 Cor 15:54 NIV).

487 Matt 27:46; Mark 15:34.

face away from his son and is silent towards him for the first and only time, the whole of heaven is silent in reverence. The silence of heaven may be an expression of the impact of the death of the righteous one on the spiritual world.

Is God a silent god?

God at the South Pole

I experience times in which God's voice is so tangible to me that I find it difficult to imagine that there was ever a time when I didn't know Him. But I do also experience times that are not like this. These are times when it feels like God has gone on holiday to the South Pole and the only form of communication I am getting is a crumpled postcard. These are uncomfortable seasons of waiting[488]. There are times I catch myself looking back towards "Egypt", full of frustration, and turning to the questionable security of former idols[489]. For those who have set out to live by His voice, times such as these are unavoidable and provide – as reluctant I am to admit it – fantastic opportunities for growth.

Such a season of God's "silence" began for me in 1991, in a rather "strange" way. I had only known God for a short period of time, I was often aware of His closeness and was thankfully beginning to notice that He was bringing peace to my many inner battlefields. My communication with Him was going well.

I was attending a workshop on prayer. On the final evening there was a ministry time during which we had the opportunity to join with the person sitting beside us in asking God to draw us deeper into prayer and hearing His voice. I remember how I assured my neighbour that I had no problem at all with *this particular* issue[490]. Still, as a safety precaution, I accepted her prayers. Over the following days, the unimaginable happened: God's wonderful, loving, healing voice became very, very,

---

488 "It is written: 'Man shall not live on bread alone, but on every word that comes from the mouth of God.' " (Matt 4:4 NIV).

489 Ex 16:3.

490 Probably the only area in which I wasn't experiencing problems during this particular period of time!

very quiet. God had taken one of the afore-mentioned trips to the South Pole and for some inconceivable reason had left me back in Hamburg! What followed were weeks of internal struggle, doubt and questioning. I no longer understood the world: how could it be that my request for "more of God" had been answered with "less of God"?

I am presuming that you as readers are well aware what had happened[491]! As for me, it took a number of weeks before that light bulb moment arrived. I slowly began to understand: God is a god who thinks in the long-term and who bestows lasting blessing upon us. He had heard my prayer for more of Him and was beginning to prepare me so as to be able to receive, apply and retain that '*more*'. As a good Father, He did not simply hear my wishes, but was preparing me to see them fulfilled.[492]

This is how God acts towards all of his children. He sees our longing and wants to fulfil it. At the same time, He is aware of the long-term consequences and begins to prepare us for the desired blessing.

God always wants to give us more than we can handle in the moment – however, He generally[493] waits until we can actually handle it. If we ask Him for a blessing that surpasses our current capacity, He opens a construction site in our life. He lays a foundation with a view to ultimately fulfilling our wish – so that our joy will be complete[494].

---

491   All you clever clogs who are already almost at the end of my book.

492   In the same way, our initial answer when our six-year-old son Leif asked for a penknife was that he would have to pass a penknife class offered at an adventure playground near us.

493   In the parable of the lost son we see an exception to the rule. The father gives the departing son his inheritance in advance, fully aware that the son will not use it wisely and will be led astray by the fleeting wealth. It is a dangerous game to ask God for blessings that are obviously contrary to His will. He can in some cases teach us a lesson in that He finally gives in to our request and we have to bear the painful consequences. "Because the Lord disciplines the one he loves, and he chastens everyone he accepts as his son." (Heb 12:6 NIV).

494   Complete joy comes through complete preparation for my request to be satisfied. "Until now you have not asked for anything in my name. Ask and you will receive, and your joy will be complete." (John 16:24 NIV).

What His silence can bring into effect

Looking back now at the first time I experienced God's "silence" in my life, I can identify some spiritual fruit that grew out of this period of time.

Hunger

The vacuum created by His "silence" in turn created within me a hunger for His voice that I had not previously encountered up to this point. Everything within me began striving for Him. I was like a flower that was willing to grow in any direction whatsoever in order to reach more sunlight.

Sympathy

I developed sympathy towards other seekers and came to the place where I could acknowledge their confusion, questions and fears as being part of their journey. I began to grasp the longing of the protagonist of Song of Songs[495] and I understood the thirst of the psalmists[496], for I experienced both.

The experience of God's voice increased in value for me. I recognised the valuable asset that I had to lose.

Willingness to change

During the period of silence, there were fewer and fewer taboo subjects between myself and God. Parts of my life that I had previously considered "private", I was suddenly placing in His hands. I even made Him offers and was willing to let go of everything to simply hear His voice once again.

Profound knowledge

As I was searching for His voice, I studied people in the Bible, read biographies of spiritual role models and asked friends whether or not they had experienced a similar thing.

---

495   "Daughters of Jerusalem, I charge you — if you find my beloved, what will you tell him? Tell him I am faint with love." (Song of Songs 5:8 NIV).

496   "My soul thirsts for God, for the living God." (Ps 42:2 NIV).

All three groups were familiar with such times in which God appeared "silent". I found out how they reacted and how they had finally rediscovered God's voice. Drawing on their example, I was able to draw conclusions regarding my own life and to acquire an understanding as to how God works in people's lives.

Team spirit

It became clear to me that I would not get through this adventure on my own. I needed people by my side who were strong when I was weak, who were happy when I was sad, full of faith and hope when I was in despair, and who heard God when I did not.

My friend Charles Bello later said to me: "We are on this road *together* – life with Jesus is a team sport! Even if we are playing in different positions, we are playing in the same team – we need one another!"

Humility

As this period of silence came to an end, it became clear to me that God alone can determine the path that we will journey together. Although He ascribes infinite value to me[497], I cannot be the centre of my own life – this position belongs to Him. My world should not revolve around myself, but around Jesus[498] – around his rule and reign. I became aware that it was His decision that I should be able to hear Him and live in relationship with Him. I didn't find Him – He found me.

Jesus and God's silence

In the life of Jesus we find few situations in which he is required to wait on the Father's voice. There are, of course, the examples of his temptation in the wilderness and during his death on the cross. These moments in Jesus' life represent his toughest battles and most severe temptation he was required to face. Both involve waiting on God's voice.

---

497   I am of the same value to Him as Jesus.

498   Astonishingly, I find that when I give up the right to make decisions myself, God continually involves me in His decision-making.

The wilderness – Jesus waiting on His voice

During his baptism, Jesus experiences one of the most formative moments of his earthly existence. He hears the voice of God speak loving words of acceptance and esteem, in an open, public setting, while the Holy Spirit physically fills him with these very attributes. What a wonderful moment – it couldn't get any better!

If this scene were the introduction to a book, you would assume that a glamorous life lay ahead of Jesus. Before all the world, God declared him to be His beloved heir[499] and filled him with His Spirit. However, this is followed by something unexpected: the Holy Spirit guides Jesus into the wilderness, only to then abruptly cut off active communication with him:

Sand and stone in place of the refreshing water of the Jordan, solitude in place of the support of his social environment. During the day it is extremely hot while at night it is very cold. There is no food other than "wild animals"[500]. And if this were not difficult enough, the devil then approaches him in person and begins to tempt Jesus. I wonder how many hours I would have been able to bear this assault on multiple fronts. Jesus endures forty days – without a single complaint[501].

It is worthwhile studying the devil's three temptations and drawing conclusions with regard to our own lives. But what is even more interesting is to look at Jesus' reaction when the devil suggests that he end his hunger himself. Jesus counters: the only thing that I really need now is *one word* from my Father. Jesus does not consider his crisis to lie in hunger, cold, loneliness or Satan's taunting, but instead it lies in the fact that he cannot hear his Father's voice. Once his temptation comes to an end, the longed for word of God comes in the form of angels, who tend to him[502], and in his being filled afresh by the Holy Spirit[503]. Only after this desert experience does Jesus' ministry unfold in full force. He begins bringing God's power to the people, in word and deed.

---

499   He receives the first part of the Father's inheritance, the Holy Spirit, immediately, whereas the second part, creation, he will win back through his life, death and resurrection.

500   Mark 1:13. "Wild" can also be translated as poisonous or dangerous. So we're not talking about friendly St. Bernards here, but rather snakes, scorpions and desert predators.

501   Matt 4:2; Mark 1:13; Luke 4:1.

502   Matt 4:11.

503   Luke 4:14.

Golgotha – God's silence in the life of Jesus

In the Garden of Gethsemane Jesus struggled and came to the decision that he would die for the guilt of man. The one who had been accompanied by his Father's voice throughout his entire life, would experience damnation – total, hopeless separation from God. This is the one moment in his life in which Jesus not only cannot hear any communication from his Father, but also has no hope of an end to this break in communication in the natural. As he dies on Golgotha he endures the profound, existential experience of being abandoned by God. "About three in the afternoon Jesus cried out in a loud voice, *"Eli, Eli, lema sabachthani?"* (which means "My God, my God, why have you forsaken me?")" (Matt 27:46 NIV). In this moment, Jesus takes the consequence of man's infidelity upon himself. This means complete separation from his Father's presence.

However, even when separated from the source that has nourished him throughout his entire life, he draws on a word from the psalms, which refers prophetically to this very moment[504]. Jesus recognises how David had foreseen his death on the cross. The High Priests and Sadducees attending his execution had previously abused him using words from the same psalm[505]. They had quoted the psalm without understanding that it was being fulfilled before their very eyes. A tragic example of people hearing God's voice but failing to understand.

---

504   Psalm 22:1ff.

505   Matt 27:43.

301

Questions that can help us when experiencing God's "silence"

Times when God is being "silent" trigger stress, anger, doubt and self-pity in us. We blame ourselves, our churches, the enemy or God Himself. The apportioning of blame or other negative reactions then becomes our greatest obstacle in our attempt to clarify the process. Below I would like to illustrate how we can react well to times of God's silence. I will propose a number of questions that can help us to find reasons for our experience and to find ways out[506].

Does God want to expand my framework for hearing Him?

If I sense that God is being silent, this can simply mean that He is no longer speaking to me in the usual way. This can happen because He wants to expand my listening repertoire. If I am used to hearing God when reading the Bible, it may be that He is saying: "Over the next period of time I want to speak to you primarily through people, go and be amongst people – you spend too much time on your own!" Equally, it may be that I am unable to receive Him on my usual frequency, on account of my life situation. For example, if I am used to meeting God in times of silence, but now have a newborn in the house, like it or not I will have to develop a new favourite way of hearing God – there isn't going to be much silence for the next while!

> I experienced such an expansion of my listening framework a few years ago. Prior to this I had for a long time experienced God through His tangible presence. As I was writing in my spiritual journal, God made a surprising announcement. I wrote down: "Kristian, you won't feel me for a period of time, but you will come to know my faithful love." I really wasn't impressed, but God wasn't going to change His mind. As a result, I actually began to feel God's presence less. This was to the considerable detriment of my relationship with Him. Because this season wasn't showing any sign of coming to a close, through various measures I finally learned to believe in His faithful love. The process was unpleasant, but I grew considerably in my relationship with Him.

---

506 If none of the proposed questions seem to help, you can ask God directly: "What is the right question in my situation?"

Am I asking the wrong question?

God's "silence" can be an expression of the fact that I am continually asking the wrong questions. If we urgently need an answer or have great passion for a topic, people tend not to talk about anything else with one another. Exam preparations, professional challenges, major sporting events, illnesses or the birth of a baby can result in this kind of thematic fixation.

A dynamic can develop in our dialogue with God that is akin to us "besieging" Him with a topic that He actually doesn't want to discuss in this particular moment[507]. In such times, if we call on Jesus' instruction to "pray and not give up[508]", this impatient probing of God is a sign of pride, not faith.

By changing the topic or adjusting our question, we start to make progress. This is exactly what botanist and inventor George Washington Carver[509] found when he asked of God: "Dear Creator, please tell me what the universe was made for" The answer he received was this: "You want to know too much for that little mind of yours. Ask something more your size." Carver then continued his questioning: "Dear Creator, tell me what a man was made for." God answered: "Little man, you still ask too much." Once more, Carver adjusted his question: "Please, Mr. Creator, will you tell me why the peanut was made?"[510]

This dialogue between Carver and God is famous and is much quoted – it is retold with many variations. What is fact is that over the course of his work, Carver discovered 300 different uses for peanuts. In reference to his discoveries, he repeatedly said: "The Lord has guided me" and "Without my Saviour, I am nothing"[511].

For me it is impressive that, within the conversation, Carver is capable of adjusting his question in such a way that it complies with God's request. Had he stuck to his original formulation, the conversation would have led to a dead end in his relationship with God.

---

507   At other points in this book I encourage us to speak with God about every topic that is important *to us* and determine: If it is important for us, then it is important for God, as we are important to Him. My inference here that God may "not want to say anything" should not be viewed as contradictory to this.

508   The parable of the widow and the persistent widow. Luke 18:1ff.

509   1864 – 1943.

510   The conversation between Carver and God has been told many times, with many differing details. The reason for this is presumably that he himself often told this story with slightly differing emphasis. As my source, I referred to the following: prayer-coach.com/2010/11/10/faith-the-size-of-a-peanut.

511   Source: http://www.cbn.com/cbnnews/us/2010/february/george-washington-carver-master-inventor-artist/?mobile=false

Should I repent?

Isaiah experiences a serious case of God's "silence" towards the people of Israel. "After all this, Lord, will you hold yourself back? Will you keep *silent* and punish us beyond measure?" (Is 64:12 NIV, emphasis KR). Isaiah identifies the continual disobedience of the people as the reason for God's "silence": "But when we continued to sin against them, you were angry." (Is 64:5 NIV).

Even when God has taken into account Jesus' sacrifice as our justification, and thereby accepts us, throughout the New Testament we can see that continual disobedience towards His manifest will has dire consequences. We distance ourselves from His protective presence and become vulnerable to the attacks of impure spirits[512]. Our behaviour begins to negatively influence our environment[513]. Wilful sin makes us spiritually dull[514] and causes our love for God to grow cold[515].

If I do not hear God's voice, as I am accustomed to doing, over a long period of time, I would therefore consider whether His "silence" means that He wants me to repent in a particular area of my life[516]. God's call to repentance is not a sign that we are not following Him, but is rather a sign of the presence of the Holy Spirit[517]. Having repented and turned to Christ for the first time, every disciple will still experience moments in which God asks them to change.

---

512 "Then Satan entered Judas, called Iscariot, one of the Twelve (...)." (Luke 22:3 NIV); "Among them are Hymenaeus and Alexander, whom I have handed over to Satan to be taught not to blaspheme." (1 Tim 1:20 NIV).

513 "Don't you know that a little yeast leavens the whole batch of dough? (...)." (1 Cor 5:6–7 NIV). Here, in using the term "a little yeast", Paul is referring to the sinful behaviour of individuals, while the "dough" is the church community as a whole.

514 "But anyone who hates a brother or sister is in the darkness and walks around in the darkness. They do not know where they are going, because the darkness has blinded them." (1 John 2:11 NIV); "For since the creation of the world God's invisible qualities—his eternal power and divine nature—have been clearly seen, being understood from what has been made, so that people are without excuse. For although they knew God, they neither glorified him as God nor gave thanks to him, but their thinking became futile and their foolish hearts were darkened." (Rom 1:20–21 NIV).

515 "Because of the increase of wickedness, the love of most will grow cold." (Matt 24:12 NIV).

516 When His previous attempts to talk to us have had no effect, He gives silence a try.

517 "When he comes, he will prove the world to be in the wrong about sin and righteousness and judgement." (John 16:8 NIV).

Repentance of resentment

Every follower of Jesus experiences the fact that things God asks of us, says to us or refuses us have the potential to be explosive. We get annoyed or even intentionally distance ourselves from Him[518]. Sometimes the fact that we are holding onto such a sense of injustice is not easily recognised. Even if we outwardly submit to Him, our heart can still be full of hidden accusations and resentment. As a result we make the problem worse: if we harbour unspoken resentment against someone, we intuitively close ourselves off in order to protect ourselves from this person. Internal resentment therefore often marks the beginning of a crisis within a relationship – this also applies in our relationship with God.

God, on the other hand, responds to our resentment calmly. It is interesting to see how Jesus responds when he is *accused* in the run-up to his sentencing before the High Council: with "silence". "Then the high priest stood up and said to Jesus, "Are you not going to answer? What is this testimony that these men are bringing against you?" *But Jesus remained silent.*" (Matt 26:62–63 NIV, emphasis KR).

Although Jesus would have been capable of defending himself with divine wisdom[519], he waives this right. We see the same situation occur when he stands before Pilate a short time later – once again Jesus responds with poised silence and does not defend himself[520]. The reason for this is that God does not have to defend or justify Himself in order to achieve His objectives – no accusation can threaten or move him. God does not react, He acts. To attempt to compel God to speak by levelling accusations against Him or asking Him to justify Himself will get you nowhere.

---

518   "Even his disciples said, "This is very hard to understand. Who can tell what he means?" Jesus knew within himself that his disciples were complaining (...)." (...) "At this point many of his disciples turned away and deserted him." (John 6:60-66 TLB).

519   "But when they arrest you, do not worry about what to say or how to say it. At that time you will be given what to say." (Matt 10:19 NIV).

520   "Do you refuse to speak to me?" Pilate said. "Don't you realise I have power either to free you or to crucify you?" Jesus answered, "You would have no power over me if it were not given to you from above." (John 19:10–11 NIV).

Is there something I need to learn?

The question as to whether or not God is teaching me something new is a useful one to ask each time an unexpected irregularity crops up in our relationship with Him. Growth spurts in our spiritual life are generally initiated as a result of prior routine no longer functioning and our suffering as a result of this. Rob Bell expresses this wonderfully when he asks: "Because without pain, we do not change, do we?"[521]

Again, asking God the right question can help us to rediscover a sense of what God is up to. To ask God: "Are you being silent because you are teaching me something new?" of course seems rather humorous. However, we must not forget that His silence towards us is also a form of communication. God's blessing and attention are continually directed towards us. Every instance of "silence" on His part should ultimately strengthen our relationship with Him. If we are aware of this, formulating a good question can help us to achieve a change in perspective and thus take a step in the right direction. Taking a look back over the past few months by reading over our spiritual journal or by asking friends is also useful. In this way we can, if this was indeed the case, identify that God had actually announced a season of spiritual renewal or learning in advance. God's interaction with us never happens spontaneously, but is in fact planned well in advance. It is prepared and/or announced by Him ahead of time. We can generally find hints in past dreams, events, encounters, thoughts or Bible verses that we found particularly moving[522]. If we are convinced that we find ourselves in a learning phase, we can then ask: "What are you teaching me just now?" As with our first question, a process of clarification then begins. If we become aware that there is something we are meant to learn, we can offer this area over to God and give Him permission to evoke change in us. This point often marks the beginning of the end of His "silence".

---

521   Rob Bell, Velvet Elvis: Repainting the Christian Faith, P. 101, Position 1378, 2005, HarperCollins, ebooks.

522   "It is the glory of God to conceal a matter; to search out a matter is the glory of kings." (Prov 25:2 NIV). "If you seek him, he will be found by you;" (1 Chr 28:9 NIV).

Am I in a special time of trial?

"In the third year of Cyrus king of Persia, a revelation was given to Daniel. (...) The understanding of the message came to him in a vision (...)." In order to reach this understanding, Daniel committed himself to fasting. He had to wait three weeks for God's answer. This was down neither to his inability to hear God, nor to God's desire to make Daniel wait, but was rather the result of a battle in the spiritual world. When an angel finally appeared to him with the longed for explanation of God's message, the angel states that the reason for his "delay" was a battle with another "prince".

"(...) Do not be afraid, Daniel. Since the first day that you set your mind to gain understanding and to humble yourself before your God, your words were heard, and I have come in response to them. [13] But the prince of the Persian kingdom resisted me twenty-one days. Then Michael, one of the chief princes, came to help me, because I was detained there with the king of Persia." (Dan 10:1; 11–13 NIV).

We can read the entire story in the book of Daniel[523]. It is thoroughly enlightening and provides us with exciting insight into the dynamic of the spiritual world. We can see how regional spiritual battles in which we find ourselves as result of our geographical presence or spiritual involvement can lead to communicative bottlenecks with God. However, it is not always the case that we will be aware of circumstances such as this in the same way as Daniel.

Every follower of Jesus will presumably already have experienced how impure spirits attempt to disrupt communication with God in a targeted manner. Sometimes this happens through unexplainable tiredness, sudden headaches, internal unrest or the like, when we are just about to begin praying[524]. A brief spiritual word of authority is generally all that is required to quickly remove these barriers – however, we must first recognise the spiritual nature of these disruptions.

---

523   From Chapter 10 onwards.

524   Or an incoming phone call, which we just want to take quickly before we pray.

Is God testing me?

For various reasons, the story of Job is not one of my favourite books in the Bible. One of the reasons is that the main theme of the story addresses how an upright man[525] experiences a prolonged period of God's "silence".

The story begins with God giving the devil an astonishing audience[526]. The accuser accuses Job of only loving God because he is blessed[527]. He challenges God to remove His protection from Job in order that he can torment him and thus unearth Job's true character[528]. God goes along with his suggestion.

As a result Job experiences severe misfortune and loses everything he loves. He enters a time of waiting and doubting God, during which various voices become audible - each making all kinds of suggestions as to how he should react.

In the end God finally speaks to Job Himself and ends this "time of trial". I love Job's famous statement that makes clear the gain that he has acquired off the back of this period of trial: "My ears had heard of you but now my eyes have seen you." (Job 42:5 GNB). The result of Job's perseverance during God's "silence" is true knowledge of God.

The story shows that "silence" on the part of God can also be part of His testing. The level of His testing is different for everyone. What is evident is that He never tests anyone beyond what they can cope with. "No temptation has overtaken you except what is common to mankind. And God is faithful; he will not let you be tempted beyond what you can bear. But when you are tempted, he will also provide a way out so that you can endure it." (1 Cor 10:13 NIV). The goal of His testing is that we get to know ourselves and Him more.

---

525   "Then the Lord said to Satan, "Have you considered my servant Job? There is no one on earth like him; he is blameless and upright, a man who fears God and shuns evil." (Job 1:8 NIV).

526   Job 1:6ff.

527   "Satan replied, "Would Job worship you if he got nothing out of it?" (Job 1:9 GNT).

528   It is actually the case that times of crisis bring out character traits in us that had previously been hidden.

What was the last thing God said to me?

A much-cited quotation from John Wimber goes like this: "God's last orders are your standing orders until you get new orders"[529]. This word was of great help to me as I was maturing as a 'listening' follower of Jesus. One tendency of a very relationally-oriented life with God can be that we constantly want to hear new things from Him; that He still loves us or that we are on the right path. However, this is not an expression of discipleship marked by hearing God's voice, but rather one that is marked by spiritual dependence! Wimber's assertion that "God's last orders are your standing orders" provides us with a healthy balance between being dependent on God's voice and taking responsibility for acting in faith. It helps me to keep a healthy distance from my emotions and to focus on what He has said. This is the only way that I really take His voice seriously: I allow the last thing God said to determine my direction, until I hear something else from Him.

What good things has God done in the past?

In 2006 I began keeping a spiritual journal. I developed the habit of beginning a new journal every January and always carrying this with me when possible throughout the year. The writing of my spiritual journal has really become the most significant engine for spiritual growth in my life, as it allows me to track and thus acknowledge God's work in my life. It is amazing how topics crop up again and again, when God repeatedly has to say the same things to me and then I finally experience breakthrough in areas about which He has repeatedly spoken. I am no longer ashamed when God has to say the same thing to me over and over again – I know that each time I hear His voice, His work in my life takes a step forwards.

If I go through times when hearing God's voice is a rare occurrence, I read over what He has said to me in recent months. I thus rediscover forgotten guidance and receive great comfort. Being mindful of His faithfulness in my past fills me with faith, thankfulness and hope. It leads me out of a posture of doubt and into a more receptive posture, thus opening up my spiritual senses to receive His voice.

---

529   Source: http://yp- newlifevineyard.blogspot.de/; "New Beginnings", 07.01.2007.

TEAM TALK: CAN GOD KEEP SILENT?

1. Are you aware of times of God's "silence" in your life? Share how you found them. What helped you through seasons such as this? What were you able to learn about God, yourself and life during these seasons?

2. Have you ever experienced God's "silence" speaking to you? Share what happened? How did you notice God communicating with you in the "silence"?

Closing thoughts

This chapter is intended to show that there are times during which God's voice speaking to us falls quiet. However, these should be the exception and not the rule. Our calling is to live by His voice. If we sense God falling "silent", His "silence" is always an invitation to search for Him – and to find Him[530]. If we believe that "Hearing God is the exception – not hearing God is the rule", we have removed ourselves from Jesus' model of what it is to be human, and are living from within our own capabilities/limitations.

Perhaps we should occasionally do things the way they do them in the Kingdom of Heaven[531] - when God is silent, we should be silent too. Can it be that He is simply waiting for a chance to get a word in? This is, after all, how polite people choose to conduct themselves!

---

530   "And so I say to you: Ask, and you will receive; *seek, and you will find*; knock, and the door will be opened to you." (Luke 11:9 NIV, emphasis KR).

531   See Rev 8:1.

Made in the USA
Charleston, SC
02 July 2016